# READY FOR A
# BRAND NEW BEAT

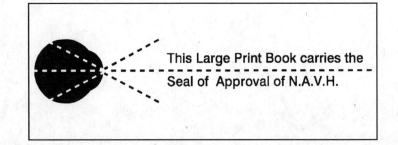

This Large Print Book carries the
Seal of Approval of N.A.V.H.

# READY FOR A BRAND NEW BEAT

## HOW "DANCING IN THE STREET" BECAME THE ANTHEM FOR A CHANGING AMERICA

# MARK KURLANSKY

**THORNDIKE PRESS**
*A part of Gale, Cengage Learning*

Detroit • New York • San Francisco • New Haven, Conn • Waterville, Maine • London

**GALE**
CENGAGE Learning®

**LIBRARY OF CONGRESS CATALOGING-IN-PUBLICATION DATA**

Kurlansky, Mark.
  Ready for a brand new beat : how "Dancing in the street" became the anthem for a changing America / Mark Kurlansky. — Large print edition.
    pages cm. — (Thorndike Press large print nonfiction)
  Originally published: New York : Riverhead Books, 2013.
  Includes bibliographical references.
  ISBN 978-1-4104-6195-7 (hardback) — ISBN 1-4104-6195-5 (hardcover) 1. Civil rights movements—United States—History—20th century. 2. African Americans—Civil rights—History—20th century. 3. Music—Social aspects—United States—History—20th century. 4. Vandellas (Musical group) Dancing in the street. I. Title.
  E185.615.K87 2013b
  323.1196'073—dc23                                    2013023965

Published in 2013 by arrangement with Riverhead Books, a division of Penguin Group (USA)

Then Creole stepped forward to remind them that what they were playing was the blues. He hit something in all of them, he hit something in me, myself, and the music tightened and deepened, apprehension began to beat the air. Creole began to tell us what the blues were all about. They were not about anything very new. He and his boys up there were keeping it new, at the risk of ruin, destruction, madness, and death, in order to find new ways to make us listen. For, while the tale of how we suffer, and how we are delighted, and how we may triumph is never new, it always must be heard. There isn't any other tale to tell, it's the only light we've got in all this darkness.

— JAMES BALDWIN, *"Sonny's Blues,"* *1948*

Perhaps in the swift change of American society in which the meanings of one's origins are so quickly lost, one of the chief values of living with music lies in its power to give us an orientation in time. In doing so, it gives significance to all those indefinable aspects of experience which nevertheless help to make us what we are. In the swift whirl of time music is a constant, reminding us of what we were and of that toward which we aspire.

— RALPH ELLISON, *Shadow & Act, 1964*

*To Talia, my girl,*
*in the hope that her life*
*is inspired by great music*

# CONTENTS

# INTRODUCTION: CALLING OUT AROUND THE WORLD

*Detroit, July 1964*

Summer's here and everything is about to change. Although the United States is not yet in full-scale combat in Vietnam, there are some troops there, and on May 27 President Lyndon Johnson said to his close friend Senator Richard Russell of Georgia, then chairman of the Senate Armed Services Committee, in a conversation that he secretly recorded, "We're in the quicksand up to our necks, and I just don't know what the hell to do about it."

Other invasions are in the works. The Student Nonviolent Coordinating Committee, a vanguard of the civil rights movement, had begun what they called "the Mississippi Summer Project," but it became famously known as "the Mississippi Freedom Summer." SNCC had gathered hundreds of volunteers, mostly college students, black and white, on a college campus in Oxford,

Ohio; trained them in the tactics of engaged nonviolence, which included such skills as how to act while someone is beating you; and were now sending them to penetrate the heart of segregation, rural Mississippi, and register black voters. In Mississippi villages, so-called klaverns of the White Knights of the Ku Klux Klan were reviving, and preparing to meet "the nigger-Communist invasion of Mississippi" with raw violence. Three volunteers for the Summer Project are missing, and President Johnson, under intense public pressure, has sent thousands of federal agents to Mississippi to look for their bodies. The grim hunt is occupying the front pages of most newspapers.

A group of academics, including Clark Kerr, president of the University of California at Berkeley, are off to travel to Russia, Poland, Czechoslovakia, and Yugoslavia for a series of discussions on the crumbling Soviet bloc. Kerr is not thinking about things crumbling at home as well, and in fact has said that the current college generation is "easy to handle." After the summer he would return to student demonstrations on his campus that would alter his assessment.

This is an election year, and this summer

there will be party conventions that will change the American political landscape. Even as the now almost-twenty-year-old nonviolent civil rights movement is having its most dramatic summer, another kind of black voice is emerging: At the same time that Martha Reeves is heading into her recording studio, in June 1964, in another week Malcolm X, a dissident voice with a growing following in Detroit and other cities, will declare, "We want freedom by any means necessary."

Another invasion, the British Invasion, is already under way. In February, four Liverpudlians rushed through America on a one-week, three-city tour. They appeared on Ed Sullivan's popular television variety show. It was the biggest coup for the tight-shouldered host in a suit since he had brought on Elvis Presley in September 1956. With songs such as "She Loves You" and "I Want to Hold Your Hand" — songs that seem adolescent when compared to the heart-wrenching rhythm & blues from Detroit — they seem to have won over huge numbers of teenagers. More and more teenage boys are showing up with dark, collarless sport jackets that make them look like waiters, their hair seemingly trimmed with a salad bowl over their head, in a style weirdly reminiscent of Moe from the Three Stooges.

The four were to return for a far bigger tour that summer, but before they landed in August, another group, the Rolling Stones, arrived for a tour in June. More and more British groups are coming, and a country that only a few years before had so few rock concerts that young people went to American rock 'n' roll movies instead is now starting to dominate American music.

Black-owned Motown, in Detroit, would be one of the few companies to withstand the Anglophile encroachment and produce top American hits. But Motown's success, with a bunch of untried black kids from inner-city Detroit, had been as improbable as that of the Beatles in Liverpool. Since the birth of rock 'n' roll in the 1950s, popular music has been a field that offers enormous stardom, and it is seemingly and excitingly unpredictable whom the young public will choose. A man in ringlets and mascara calling himself Little Richard; a wild-looking black man named Chuck Berry, who hopped around the stage madly; an even wilder Texas redneck named Jerry Lee Lewis, who could play the piano with his feet — who could say who the next star would be, or the next big hit?

■ ■ ■ ■

America is about to change, but for very different reasons, so is the life of Martha Reeves. Living with her mother and father and ten siblings in the two-story wooden Eastside house that her father had bought with earnings from his job with the city water company, Martha will soon turn twenty-three years old. It has been only three years since she gave up her job with a dry cleaner. She has now had three Top 40 hits with her group, the Vandellas. In fact, she is a famous R&B singer not only in the black world but on the white charts as well, reaching number 4. People who know popular music know who Martha Reeves is. She is one of the top recording stars of the now very hot Motown studios.

But to her this is still new and strange. Growing up, she knew that she was a good singer and a gifted musician. Her family told her so, and so did her teachers. But being famous was never something she had seen in her future. A few years later, black Detroit high school kids would dream of going to Motown and becoming famous, but when Martha was in high school, such things did not happen.

Now, despite her fame and her three hit records, she is taking the bus across Woodward Avenue to that warm family-like studio that felt like her second home, the little place that has made her famous.

As far as she knows, the studio has no new song lined up for her at the moment. She is between records, so she is going there to get instructions that will improve her act. On this particular day Martha is going to the studio to see Maxine Powell, a tiny woman who had a finishing school and advises Martha and other Motown singers on their public demeanor. She always respectfully calls her "Miss Powell." Sometimes she goes there for music instruction from Maurice King, an old pro from the big band days, whom she always calls "Mr. King." Even though her twenty-third birthday is in a few weeks, in some ways she is still a kid going to school.

She takes the westbound bus on Grand Boulevard. She is not thinking about Vietnam or Mississippi. The conflict she thinks about every time she takes the bus past the country houses and busy factories of Detroit is an ongoing gang war between the Eastside and the Westside. An Eastsider like herself could get beaten up just for crossing Woodward Avenue if she wasn't on the bus.

She gets off the bus deep in the enemy Westside territory and walks into a house about the size of her own, with a hand-painted blue wooden sign on the front that says Hitsville U.S.A. She is in Motown.

She hears that Marvin Gaye is in Studio A recording a song called "Dancing in the Street." She doesn't think much of the song, or at least the title.

But the song was written by Mickey Stevenson, the director of Artists and Repertory, the division responsible for developing talent. Stevenson had brought her into Motown as his secretary, and among his coauthors of the song is Marvin Gaye. Martha had begun her Motown career singing backup for Gaye and developed enormous admiration for him and always wanted to hear his recording sessions. Many people did. In fact, at twenty-two Martha still has what appears to be a teenage crush on Gaye. Gaye was a sexy, enigmatic man who crooned, played several instruments, wrote songs, and wandered the little Hitsville house wearing a hat and sunglasses and smoking a corncob pipe. Almost a half century later, in her seventies, she will still get misty-eyed speaking about him, and drives through Detroit listening to his recordings. "I followed him around,"

Martha confessed.

On this June day, Martha steps down into Studio A — a not very large room with white padded walls and a wooden floor, with a piano resting on one side of the room and four microphones hanging by their cables from the ceiling — and it is empty. The track has already been recorded, and Marvin is at the control console in the glass booth at one end of Studio A, listening to his take and singing over it. Martha immediately changes her view of the song when she hears the bouncy brass introduction. This song has a special sound. And she is hooked from the first line: "Calling out around the world." This is good. There is a sense of a call going out. Marvin is singing it in his romantic way. "When Marvin sang 'The Star-Spangled Banner,' it was romantic," Martha said many years later.

Mickey Stevenson, another tall, handsome man, is in the control room with Marvin and their small, quick-witted coauthor, Ivy Jo Hunter. Seated at the controls is Lawrence Horn, the sound engineer. According to Martha, and this is one of her most cherished memories, suddenly Gaye looks down in the studio and then turns to Mickey Stevenson, who is producing the record, and says, "Hey, man, try this on Martha."

Martha at this point has decided it is a good song but a song for a male voice, which in fact it never was intended to be. But she doesn't argue with Marvin Gaye. She puts on the headphones and stands in front of a hanging microphone as a music track unlike anything she has ever heard erupts into her ears. Normally a demo tape was made and taken home and studied for a week or two before the recording session. That was what Gaye was trying to make. But Martha just sings it, as she would later say, the way she felt it. It reminds her of summers in Detroit. Someone would put a record player on the porch and everyone would go out in the street and dance.

When she is done, Ivy Jo Hunter has bad news for her. The take is great but they have failed to put the recorder on, and she will have to redo it. And so for the second time she sings "Dancing in the Street." This time it is a bit edgier because she is irritated. She doesn't like to redo takes. Her mother always said, "Put your best foot forward so you don't have to do it again." And that is the way Martha likes to work.

But when she finishes the second take she looks up at the control booth window and the men are congratulating each other as though something special has just happened. It happened in less than ten minutes. The take, like many recordings in those days of 45 rpm single records, is only two minutes and thirty-six seconds because that is the length that radio stations like to play. There is no talk of revising or altering anything. Rosalind Ashford and Betty Kelly, the two other Vandellas, are called in to sing the backup. Ivy Jo Hunter sings along with them to show them how it should go.

In June 1964 the social, political, and cultural upheaval that would be known as "the sixties" was about to explode, and Martha Reeves, knowing little about such things, has just sung its anthem.

# CHAPTER ONE:
## ARE YOU READY?

For my generation rock was not a controversy, it was a fact.

My earliest memory of rock 'n' roll is Elvis Presley. For others it may be Bill Haley or Chuck Berry. For people born soon after World War II, rock 'n' roll was a part of childhood. The rockers, especially Elvis, are remembered as controversies. But there was no controversy among the kids. They loved the songs, their sense of mischief and especially the driving beat. The controversy came from adults. Only adults attacked Elvis or rock 'n' roll. The controversy was only in their minds — on their lips. It was the beginning of what came to be known as "the generation gap," a phrase coined by Columbia University president Grayson Kirk in April 1968, shortly before students seized control of his campus.

There has never been an American generation that so identified with its music, regarded it as its own, the way the Americans who grew up in the 1950s and 1960s did. The music that started as a subversive movement took over the culture and became a huge, commercially dominant industry. The greatest of the many seismic shifts in the music industry is that young people became the target audience. In no previous generation had the main thrust of popular music been an attempt to appeal to people in their teens.

Since this music was an expression of the changing times, it is not surprising that it was profoundly about racial integration. When it started, blacks and whites lived in two completely different worlds within America. It was not only that they lived in separate places and sent their children to different schools. They had separate cultures, listened to completely different music on separate radio stations, had different jokes, different professional baseball leagues, different Boy Scout troops, and a totally different perspective of America and the world.

White people knew very little about, and most gave little thought to, the people they politely referred to as "Negroes." *Negro,* a Spanish word, descended, like the people it labeled, from the slave trade. Whites were called "white" because it was good to be white, but to call black people "black," to remind them of their blackness, was to insult them. In slave times the words *nigger* and *black* were used almost interchangeably, often as a label. If Joe was black, he would be called "Black Joe" or "Nigger Joe," so as not to be confused with a white man named Joe.

The language reversed itself in the great social shift of the 1960s. The first well-known figure to promote the term *black* was black nationalist Malcolm X, who almost always used it, and when he used *Negroes,* he would say "so-called Negroes." His point was that blackness should be a source of pride. He also attempted to turn the tables by making *white* a pejorative as in the frequent "white devils." Martin Luther King, on the other hand, rarely used the term *black* and almost always said "Negro." So the shift in language represented not only a shift in white thinking but an important cultural and political schism among blacks, even those who were politically active. By the end of the 1960s, both King and Malcolm had been murdered, and the word *black* had completely overtaken the word *Negro,* proving that the more militant Malcolm X's point of view had a greater impact than is commonly recognized. *Negro* has become a pejorative for a black who lacked pride. This shift in language showed that there were enormous upheavals and changes in thinking taking place. Music, like languages, also showed these shifts, and only a few songs, such as "Dancing in the Street," were able to stand solidly on both sides of the social fissures.

What became popular music in the 1950s was a fusion of many influences, some of them white and some black, but it all began with a black form known as "the blues."

The blues came out of African music by way of slavery, but no one has been able to date its exact origin. Among the many rhythms and traditions of African music that went into the blues and other African American music was the West African tradition of call-and-response, in which a chorus responds, often repeatedly, to the song line of the leader, and the leader reprises the chorus. In the blues, often performed by a single singer, the singer responds to him- or herself. This call-and-response form was central not only to blues but also to its later offshoot, rhythm & blues, and eventually Motown. "Dancing in the Street" would be only one of many examples. Jazz also bears traces of call-and-response. In the West African version, as in jazz, the chorus could improvise, going into long or short riffs as the moment moved them.

Another African characteristic found among blues singers and black vocalists who followed is a style of vocal distortions that has come to be thought of as "the black style of singing." It is why most black vocalists of the 1960s or earlier, including Martha Reeves, even unseen on the radio, would never be mistaken for white. These distortions include a variety of raspy shouts, growls, and, in the case of gospel singers such as Reeves, the stretching of one note into several tones.

Amiri Baraka, born in Newark, New Jersey, in 1934, originally named LeRoi Jones, a leading Beat poet, playwright, and commentator on black culture and especially music, wrote in his 1963 book on jazz, *Blues People:*

Melodic diversity in African music came not only in the actual arrangements of notes (in terms of Western transcription) but in the singer's vocal interpretation. The "tense slightly hoarse-sounding vocal techniques" of the work songs and the blues stem directly from West African musical tradition. (This kind of singing voice is also common to much other non-Western music.) In African languages the meaning of a word can be changed simply by altering the *pitch* of the word, or changing its stress. . . . Philologists call this "significant tone," the "combination of pitch and timbre" used to produce changes of meanings in words.

Highly improvisational jazz is said to have begun around the turn of the twentieth century, although it is difficult to define a beginning, since this music is rooted in blues, which is rooted in earlier forms of music. Big blues bands with blaring brass sections developed in the 1920s, particularly in western towns, most notably Kansas City, which was known for its casinos and night-clubs. These led to a style known as the "shouting blues," owing to the singers' efforts to make themselves heard, because the bands were so loud. The influence was not only on singers but on jazz musicians such as Ornette Coleman, Charlie Parker, and John Coltrane, whose instruments flew off into a kind of shout. While blues had been essentially a rural music for an essentially rural population, a growing urban black population developed an urban blues sound from these big bands, and this was the origin of a new black music called rhythm & blues. It was music purely for black people, and this, according to Amiri Baraka, spared it from the "sterility" that might have "resulted from total immersion."

Most historians credit a singer and sax player named Louis Jordan as the critical early step in the development of rhythm & blues and by extension one of the early roots of rock 'n' roll. He was in fact one of the first to use the word *rock* in his music, and recorded a number of pieces in the 1940s that may be considered among the first experiments in rap. He performed with six- to eight-player bands and took the important step of including the guitar. His music was aimed at newly urbanized blacks so that seemingly rural songs such as "Beans and Cornbread" turned out to be about actual urban life. He had several recordings in the 1940s that sold more than a million copies, including "Is You Is or Is You Ain't (Ma' Baby)" and "Caldonia." His appeal was partly musical innovation and partly humor, in both his songs and his constant asides.

R&B music was always regarded as an exclusively black form — in the music business, the definition of rhythm & blues was often simply "music for black people" — but Jordan also found popularity with whites. So this phenomenon known in music as "crossover" — blacks that could appeal to whites — was at the very beginning of rhythm & blues.

After World War II black bands occasionally became popular with white listeners, with the help of such musicians as vibes master Lionel Hampton and trumpeter Erskine Hawkins. Hampton, raised in Alabama and then in Chicago, was a natural for crossover. A percussionist, he took up and became the master of the vibraphone, which was thought of as a white instrument, developed in the 1920s for vaudeville orchestras. It was Hampton who brought it to jazz. Trumpeter Erskine Hawkins seemed destined for crossover as well. He was named after Erskine Ramsay, a wealthy Alabama-based Scottish industrialist who gave a bank account to any child named after him. As a musician, composer, and band leader, Hawkins became associated with many famous big bands of the World War II era. White bands such as the Glenn Miller Orchestra played his music. Nat King Cole, a gifted jazz pianist, abandoned his superb trio to croon songs such as Irving Gordon's "Unforgettable" in 1951 and

Victor Young and Edward Heyman's "When I Fall in Love" in 1957. Although Cole sang white songs in a white style for white audiences, he still held on to black fans.

A few of the R&B bands, especially Jordan's, were able to record for big national record companies such as Capitol, Decca, and Victor. One of the reasons for this crossover phenomena was swing, big band dance music with an up tempo and strong rhythm that became extremely popular during World War II. Many historians believe it began as black music in Harlem in the 1920s but never took off in the black community because the huge nightclubs and big payrolls required for the enormous size of the bands made it too expensive. It became associated with white musicians such as Benny Goodman. Benny Goodman even had a handful of black musicians. That was how Lionel Hampton became crossover. But swing's audience was white. Amiri Baraka wrote, "Swing music was the result of arranged big band jazz, as it developed to a music that had almost nothing to do with blues, had very little to do with black America, though that is certainly where it had come from." When jazz trumpeter Louis Armstrong was asked about swing he said, "Ah, swing, well, we used to call it syncopation — then they called it ragtime, then blues — then jazz. Now it's swing. White folks, yo'all sho is a mess."

Whites and blacks had taken black music in two different directions. Blacks had R&B and whites had swing. But after the war, swing was found too expensive even for white people, and though it fostered individual artists who were enormous stars, such as Frank Sinatra, and a legacy of enduring songs, swing itself began to falter and white audiences were looking for something new. Ironically, once they got something new, the new singers frequently sang swing songs. Rock 'n' rollers Fats Domino, Elvis Presley, and Jerry Lee Lewis all sang a few swing songs, such as Presley's 1960 "Are You Lonesome Tonight?," which was written in 1927 by vaudeville greats Lou Handman and Roy Turk.

In the early 1950s the white music industry seemed to be struggling to find a name for the new black music. All black music was called "race music." The pejorative attitude was unmistakable. *Race* at the time was a word like *black,* implying a second-rate status. Though there was a Caucasian race, race music would not mean white music because *race* almost never meant "white." Only blacks were *race.* "Race music" was immediately understood. Bruce Morrow, the popular white 1960s rhythm & blues disc jockey known to most of New York City as Cousin Brucie, said in a recent interview, "It is still upsetting to me that in my life I lived through something being called race music."

While the name persisted for more than a decade longer, in the late 1940s Decca started talking about "sepia music" while MGM used the term "ebony." *Billboard,* the magazine whose weekly sales charts define hits, in 1949 stopped calling its chart of black music "race" and it became the "rhythm & blues chart." It was not difficult for *Billboard* to distinguish between sales to black people and sales to white people, since each had their own radio stations and their own record stores.

R&B, like all black music, came from the blues. It had influences of gospel, which came from traditional spirituals and in the 1930s became the music of the black church. But it was also influenced by big bands and, most important, had a driving rhythm. It was distinctly urban, with the electric throb of the city characterized by the use of electric rather than acoustic guitars and the thump of a new instrument, the electric bass.

Jerry Wexler, the future record producer who is often credited with inventing the term "rhythm & blues," when writing for *Billboard,* said that he later regretted not calling it "rhythm & gospel." In fact, much of it was gospel singers such as Martha Reeves singing to a beat hardened by the throb of electric guitars and electric bass. Wexler, the son of a Czech-Galician Talmudic scholar turned New York window washer, would become one of the leading producers of R&B at Atlantic Records.

Amiri Baraka was interviewed at his home in a modest middle-class neighborhood of Newark. Given his résumé, it was reasonable to wonder who would come to the door. Would it be LeRoi Jones, the beatnik poet who displayed his verse in Greenwich Village with illustrations of erect penises, the innovative writer whose plays and poetry have earned him a place in the American Academy of Arts and Letters, the brilliant critic of black popular music, the wild radical renaming himself Amiri Baraka who was arrested with a gun in the 1967 Newark riots, the poet laureate of New Jersey whom the state tried to remove because of a verse in his poem that implicated Israel in the World Trade Center bombing? Governor James E. McGreevey demanded his resignation, and when Baraka refused to resign, McGreevey discovered that he did not have the right to fire him, whereupon the state legislature eliminated the post, which was how most people discovered that New Jersey had a poet laureate. Who would this man be, who has alternately been accused of sexism, homophobia, racism, and anti-Semitism, that angry voice who at times appeared to advocate violence and even rape?

The answer was none of the above. The small, slightly built man in a cardigan sweater with glasses and a white beard looked like a professor, a scholar, and teacher. And he was those things, too. A warm and gracious man, he ushered me past a room of African art, framed drawings, and mementos of a life in African American art into the kitchen, where we could sit at a table, sip orange juice, and talk music, a subject for which he has endless knowledge and enthusiasm. He defined R&B as "a blues deviation with a more modern rhythmic base — an emphatic rhythm." He dates it to Jordan and other bands of the 1930s and 1940s who mixed it with jazz. "The old big bands could do everything — switch back and forth. That was the delight of them. It was the more commercial division such as on radio stations that need to put things into categories." He said that bands led by Cab Calloway, Count Basie, and Duke Ellington occasionally did R&B. He remembered when he was growing up in Newark huge clubs where big bands performed to spacious but crowded dance floors. "They played jazz with a stronger rhythm for dancing," he recalled. "That's what made it popular." He had particularly fond memories of Lucky Millinder. Born in Alabama, Lucius Millinder earned his reputation in Chicago as a dancer and a master of ceremonies. Although he could not read music or play an instrument and rarely even sang, he became a popular African American bandleader and was featured at the Savoy Ballroom in Manhattan. His biggest World War II hit was "When the Lights Go On Again (All Over the World)," which, like much of his music at the time, was swing. After the war, he toured a great deal, and Baraka as a young man heard him playing R&B in Newark dance halls. His band's style went increasingly toward R&B and was one of the forerunners of 1950s rock 'n' roll.

Most African American music, including church music, true to its African roots, was about dance or at least movement. Body movement was often considered essential, even to singing gospel. The great gospel singer Mahalia Jackson used to say her hands and feet were essential and that she wanted "my whole body to say all that is in me."

Most of the new music of the 1940s and early 1950s was recorded by small independent record labels specializing in R&B destined for black audiences and popularized through black radio stations. These independent black record companies sprang up throughout the country from the early 1940s to the early 1950s in many of the black urban centers such as New York, Newark, Chicago, and especially Los Angeles, where many blacks had migrated during and after World War II. At the same time, black radio stations with black disc jockeys playing R&B for black listeners proliferated wherever there were concentrations of the black population. It is significant for the purposes of this story to note that by the 1940s Detroit was the rare important black urban center where there was no independent black label.

But few of the recording studios or radio stations were black owned. Black radio was largely white staffed, including not only producers and directors but also some of the leading deejays who adapted a black radio style.

World War II created social changes. Black GIs were unwilling to return quietly to the repression they had left. Some of those who returned to the Deep South began local grassroots organizing. At the same time war resisters who had protested against World War II turned their organizing skills to the issue of civil rights.

In the study of history, beginnings and endings are usually artificial, but if you had to find a beginning for the civil rights movement, it might be the draft resister of World War II. Of course they had been influenced by a pacifist movement that had begun with Mohandas Gandhi's celebrated nonviolent struggle against the British. These American war resisters included James Farmer, a large man with an even larger voice who had recently studied Gandhi at Howard University, where he had earned his doctorate, and Bayard Rustin, a black Quaker. Rustin, a tall, handsome man, had such a good voice that he had recorded a song with blues great Josh White. The song "Chain Gang" was on a subject about which he would learn much more in 1947, when he served thirty days on a North Carolina chain gang for organizing a so-called Freedom Ride. It was his second. In 1942 Rustin, acting on his own, carried out the first of what would become known as Freedom Rides. By himself he rode a bus from Louisville to Nashville and refused to sit in the "colored section." He was removed from the bus and taken to a local police station, where he was severely beaten. Rustin gave no physical resistance but kept trying to reason with the men who were beating him until the police chief ordered them to stop, saying, "I believe the nigger's crazy."

These men were brought together in the late 1930s by a radical organizer named A. J. Muste, whom *Time* magazine had labeled "America's number one pacifist." In 1942 they formed their own organization, Congress of Racial Equality (CORE), which also involved white war resisters such as George Houser.

CORE had as an adviser an Indian disciple of Gandhi, Krishnalal Shridharani. In 1943 they used sit-ins to force the integration of an all-white cafeteria in Detroit and movie theaters in Denver. Many of these men were sent to prison for refusing to serve in the war, including Farmer, Rustin, Houser, and David Dellinger, who later became a key organizer in the resistance to the Vietnam

War. Rustin could have been exempt from the draft as a Quaker but refused to apply, believing that going to prison made a stronger statement. The draft resisters were sent to two minimum-security prisons, one in Danbury, Connecticut, and one in Lewisburg, Pennsylvania. There they organized hunger strikes to force the integration of the prisons. Once released from prison, they continued their work, which included recruiting Martin Luther King Jr.

The war had another huge impact, because it pushed the rapid expansion of technology. Both the technology and the early civil rights movement had a profound influence on music. There probably would have been no Motown or at least it would have been something very different and less memorable, without these changes, and popular music would have taken some very different turns. The greatest technological change in music was the development of tiny transistors to replace large tubes. The transistor was the beginning of the semiconductor revolution that has led to the microchip computer world. It was a way of making communications devices smaller and began with the needs of radar technology in World War II.

Until the transistor, conduction of electronic impulses had been accomplished with gaseous materials contained in tubes. These large tubes, essential to radios, among other devices, did not work well for the military purposes of radar, and so solid conduction was developed. Numerous suitable materials, most notably silicon, were found to transmit electronic impulses. Such conductors, including the transistor used in radios, were far smaller than tubes. The radio transistor was less than a half inch long and turned the radio from a piece of living room furniture into something that could be carried in a pocket. It also made radios far less expensive. Small and portable became highly commercial ideas in the 1950s, and led to the shrinking of other products that didn't use transistors, such as record players. Up until then, young people had never had their own music, because they could listen to records and radio only when seated with the family in the living room. But now they could take their music with them.

Records themselves changed. In 1948 Columbia records introduced the long-playing record. Up until then music had been recorded in shellac with wide grooves. It was played at 78 revolutions per minute. During the war there was a shortage of shellac, because it was needed for military purposes and record producers were forced to look for a new material. Vinyl allowed a much smaller groove and a slower playing time, 33 1/3 rpm, and therefore allowed far more music on a record. The record album, a compilation of songs, was invented. Vinyl also led to the replacement of the 78 rpm shellac single with the 45 rpm vinyl single, although this did not become entrenched until ten years later, at about the time Motown was created.

The cheaper 45 rpm single records became the disc of the more marginal, while the album was for the more established, the Frank Sinatras. Black music from independent studios and most R&B was recorded on 45s. The singles charts generally featured artists very different from those on the album charts. So now black people and soon young people had their own radios, their own record players, and their own record. In 1952, for the first time, records outsold sheet music in America.

New technology, of course, not only creates new ideas but undoes old ones. Live performances disappeared from radio, and radio became entirely focused on records. Jazz was one of the great victims. Long improvisation fit only on LP albums. Because it did not fit on 45s, it was seldom heard on radio. Without radio and 45s it lost its traditional black market. It became music for white people, and an elite form at that.

The technology also changed other black music. It stifled the time-honored tradition of improvisation because that made songs too long. R&B became the first musical genre to exist principally through getting radio stations to play their records, and so an R&B song had to be short and hard-hitting.

Cousin Brucie recalled the challenge of his times. "So there was a new technology. Now we needed some new music."

The postwar establishment, General Dwight D. Eisenhower as president, upholding the official order with a famous smile and conventional steadiness, the Cold War dividing the world between only two countries, each prepared to annihilate the planet with nuclear weapons, the persecution and silencing of anyone who deviated from the norm on the grounds that they might be "Communist," expanding middle-class affluence and dull middle-class values reflected in the growth of uniform suburbs, the literal and metaphoric spread of new plastics — all of these things that were

1950s America made it a repressed nation ripe for rebellion. Because of that rebellion, the 1950s were much more interesting than they were supposed to be.

In art and literature there were the Beats, with poets such as Allen Ginsberg, Kenneth Rexroth, and LeRoi Jones redefining poetry and Jack Kerouac and William Burroughs redefining fiction. Abstract Expressionist painting splashed colors and forms that refused to be shaped by anything in the physical world. Hollywood churned out great mountains of pablum while the baby food industry literally did. Packaged baby food was needed for the new largest generation in history and an increasingly industrial food industry produced equally bland products for adults. But amid all the films promoting establishment, praising war and law enforcement and sexless romance, the image of the rebel emerged especially in the performances of Marlon Brando and James Dean. In Stanley Kramer's 1953 film *The Wild One,* directed by Laslo Benedek, Marlon Brando in the role of Johnny, the leader of a motorcycle gang that attempts to take over a small dull California town, established the image of the 1950s rebel. When a town girl asks him, "Hey, Johnny, what are you rebelling against?" he answers,

"What do you got?"

In Nicholas Ray's 1955 *Rebel Without a Cause,* parents, police, the established community are perplexed by James Dean, a troubled young man named Jim Stark, who says, "I don't know what to do anymore. Except maybe die."

Viewed today, these films are somewhat unsatisfying. They seem to be struggling to understand a social phenomenon that they never completely grasp. According to historical orthodoxy, the 1950s is the decade of conformism and the 1960s is the decade of rebellion. But the rebelliousness began in the 1950s, even the late 1940s. The restlessness of southern black soldiers who returned to Jim Crow racism are only one particularly poignant example. Many soldiers coming home from the war could not adjust to repressed American life.

Nineteen fifties rebels, like Johnny the wild one, expressed an aimless rejection of what the established order expected from them. Often, especially in the South, this rebellion was expressed by embracing the culture of the most marginalized people — black people. Working-class white youths could go to the wrong side of town and listen to R&B music on jukeboxes or they could just tune in to black radio stations.

For a black to cross the racial divide was literally to invite death, but whites could cross over to the black part of town — perhaps the origin of the music term *crossover* — with complete impunity while at the same time feeling the pleasure of breaking the rules. It is often suggested that what made Elvis Presley unusual was his love of black music but in fact this was not at all unusual for a Southerner of his age and economic class. Soon white people all over the country and from all economic classes were taking an interest in black music.

By 1954 black R&B recordings were garnering enough sales to occasionally slip onto the white pop charts, and by 1955 R&B music had gone from a backwater subculture of popular music aimed at ghettos and southern villages to a $25-million-a-year industry. The established record industry noticed this but generally dismissed it as a passing trend. Blacks making inroads on white music charts were no more welcome than blacks moving in on any other established white turf. It was when whites started taking prominent positions on the charts with what seemed to be black music, even sung and performed in a somewhat black way, that the record industry started to react. This happened in 1955, when

44

Decca released a white group, Bill Haley and the Comets, singing "Rock Around the Clock," and again in 1956 when RCA scored a phenomenal commercial success with Elvis Presley. This was music that appeared to have equal appeal to blacks and whites, a new phenomenon in the music industry that suggested both money (good) and social change (bad).

The record industry seemed eager to find an alternative.

The most promising was Latin music, which led to the mambo craze. Mambo was anything but white, having its origins among Haitian immigrants in Cuba. From Cuba the music traveled to New York, primarily to the Palladium Ballroom on Fifty-Third Street and Broadway. Most of the biggest Latin stars were black, including Beny Moré, Celia Cruz, Tito Puente, Arsenio Rodriguez, and Machito. The music had strong African roots. Arsenio Rodriguez often sang about Central African religions, a belief system known in Cuba as Palo Monte. But in the same way some dark Latinos were allowed to play major league baseball when black Americans weren't, this music was considered Latin, not black. Even the white performers such as Desi Arnaz, a wealthy Cuban who was a popular bandleader before marrying a white actress, Lucille Ball, and becoming the television version of the white Latino, sang black music. How many Americans understood that the conga line dance that he popularized in American clubs was African or that his signature song was to Babalu, a Yoruba religious spirit from Nigeria? But these foreigners would not threaten the American social order.

By the mid-1950s, Latin music had spread from the Palladium across the United States, and mambo led to other dance crazes such as the cha-cha, which was a step and three steps. But despite the many so-called mamboniks, it never really competed with the rapid growth of R&B, and the craze only lasted about ten years. Most historians believe that while Americans loved the music, few had the dance skills for these relatively difficult steps. With black music, people could simply feel the driving beat and move to it in any way they felt. RCA Records, a leading record company, became an important producer of Latin music in the early 1950s, leaving the new R&B to small independent companies. But in 1955, seeing how tastes were developing, they purchased Elvis Presley's contract from Sun Records for what was then an astonishingly high price of $35,000, making them a leading rock 'n' roll company overnight. They opened a studio in Nashville for Presley, but, being in Nashville, it became a leading country-and-western studio, where many of the biggest country stars would record.

The big promoters of R&B tried to play down its black roots, just as promoters of mambo did. Alan Freed started playing R&B on his Cleveland WJW program in 1951 and later when he moved to WINS in New York. But he stopped calling it R&B and named it rock 'n' roll to give it a name that was not specifically black. This may have deceived white people, but to black people, *rock 'n' roll* was a black term usually referring to sexual intercourse.

Unquestionably, rock 'n' roll was born from rhythm & blues, but there were also Latin influences and pronounced country and western influences, which, when most noticeable, gave rise to a style labeled "rockabilly."

Because of this evolution, it is not really clear what was the first rock 'n' roll song. "Sh-Boom," released by the Chords, is often suggested. This recording by a black group from the Bronx is based on an old jailhouse song and released on Cat, an Atlantic Records subsidiary created for such music.

What distinguishes it is its crossover history. Released in March 1954, by the first week of July it had reached number 8 on *Billboard*'s black rhythm & blues chart, at which point it also made the white pop music chart.

It was a crossover season, some music historians argue. On May 17 the Supreme Court ruled in *Brown vs. the Board of Education of Topeka* that segregated schools were "inherently" unequal. The decision, which rejected the school system and by extension much of the way of life of the entire South, gave new militancy to both southern racism and a civil rights movement that had been smoldering since World War II. It is not a coincidence that the age of civil rights and the age of crossover in music unfolded simultaneously.

"Gee" by the Crows, released the year before "Sh-Boom," is often cited as the first. And there are earlier contenders, including Ike Turner's 1951 "Rocket 88" performed by the now-forgotten Jackie Brenston. Also in 1954 Big Joe Turner recorded the original version of "Shake, Rattle and Roll." Bill Haley is often remembered as the first rock 'n' roller for his 1952 "Rock the Joint" and especially for his 1953 hit "Crazy Man, Crazy," which sold more than a million records. Haley demonstrated the commercial potential of white rock 'n' roll. A white artist could get exposure on radio stations and in venues not open to black artists.

How Bill Haley of Michigan, neither southern nor black, became the leading performer of this new music was a sign of the times. Haley liked guitars that were suggestive of cowboy music. After the commercial success of "Crazy Man, Crazy," Decca, a top popular music label, signed him and his group, the Comets. Their producer, Milt Gabler, reworked the group. Gabler had started in music by turning his father's shop into New York's leading retailer of jazz recordings. In the late 1930s he produced Billie Holiday recordings, including "Strange Fruit," the bitter condemnation of lynching and southern racism that became one of the classics of black protest music. He also produced Louis Jordan, and when Bill Haley and His Comets went to Decca, he tried to shape them into a sound that resembled Jordan's famous group, the Tympany Five. The result was white R&B, otherwise known as rock 'n' roll. To ensure access to white radio, Haley, or Gabler, cleaned up black music, which traditionally had raunchy lyrics full of humorous sexual innuendos. When Bill Haley redid, or covered, to use the musical term, Turner's "Shake, Rattle and Roll" it was cleaned, whitened by slightly altering lyrics to eliminate any hidden sexual references. The original began in the bedroom — "Get out of that bed and wash your face and hands" — which Haley changed to "Get out in the kitchen and rattle those pots and pans," because a bedroom was too suggestive. A line about the sun shining through dresses was changed to a line about "hair done up so nice."

The record did reasonably well but Haley's next recording, "Rock Around the Clock," made history. When first released, the recording did not appear destined for notable success, but then it was used dramatically in Richard Brooks's 1955 film *Blackboard Jungle.* This was not a small independent counterculture film. It was a Metro-Goldwyn-Mayer release starring Glenn Ford, Anne Francis, Richard Kiley, and a very young Sidney Poitier. It was another 1950s film attempting to understand rebellious youth, in this case in an inner-city school. Rock 'n' roll was widely believed to lead to juvenile delinquency, the very problem the film was addressing. Some theaters muted out the song in the opening credits. But it also played in the opening scene, mid-film, and at the end and these parts could not be easily expunged.

The film made the recording a huge hit. *Blackboard Jungle* is credited with establishing the social position of rock 'n' roll, though it probably would have happened without the film. It became the music of those young fifties rebels that the establishment could not understand — even though it was led by a balding Bill Haley who was about to turn thirty.

It also debuted a disturbing social phenomenon known as rock 'n' roll "riots." *Riot* is a curious word that took on increasing use and significance in the 1960s, but the term first became widespread in the 1950s in connection with "rock 'n' roll rioting." The problem with the word is that it has a whiff of the pejorative, a kind of dismissal, because the sense is that this is an uprising with no rationale behind it. In reality the absence of reason may often be attributed to a journalist or observer not being able to grasp it.

Certainly the reasons behind the uprisings at movie theaters where *Blackboard Jungle* played were difficult to understand. It seemed related to the sound track. The music would play and young people would begin tearing up the movie theater. This happened especially with the rebellious young, long-haired toughs of urban England known as teddy boys. Most of the British had never before heard rock, and British journalists, clergy, educators, and politicians were at a loss to explain the troubling violent response. But it seemed certain to them as it did to their American counterparts that this new music was dangerous.

Much of the "rioting" caused by rock 'n' roll was a generational misunderstanding. Young people would be inspired to movement because the driving beat of the new music made it unnatural to sit still. You cannot sit still and listen to Chuck Berry. No one had ever heard such a driving beat, and young listeners had to move. So they would stand up at concerts and start moving to music, singing, shouting, and screaming. This would not have been surprising in a black venue, but was something new and alarming in the white world. Audiences shouting in theaters had vanished in the white world in the eighteenth century, though it remains common to this day in black theater. The response was to have large numbers of police to keep the young audience in line. This led to conflicts in which the police tried to force the youths to remain in their seats and the young audience would delight in taunting the police. This back-and-forth became known as a riot. In Britain in the 1950s, before there were rock concerts, young people instead had to riot at movie theaters showing American rock music. When young people lingered outside a 1956 London screening of *Rock Around the Clock,* singing rock songs, the police considered it disorderly behavior and moved in to make arrests. The revelers were charged with "insulting behavior." At another screening, one hundred young audience members were forcibly removed by police. There were similar events in Manchester. Some theaters refused to show the film.

In March 1956, Bill Marlowe, a local deejay on WCOP, hosted a concert at Massachusetts Institute of Technology in Cambridge. The three thousand mostly young people who had paid ninety-nine cents each were irritated from the outset because they thought they had paid for a dance, and the concert was far too crowded for dancing. Instead, the crowd gathered ever closer to the stage, which worried the seven police officers patrolling the event, who panicked and ordered the concert stopped. The angered crowd began smashing chairs, tables, anything they could find, and it took police an hour and a half to subdue the violent crowd.

The authorities identified two culprits — the music and the deejay. At the urging of Mayor Edward J. Sullivan, the city council banned concerts hosted by deejays. Marlowe responded by turning against rock music, refusing to play it and regularly explaining on the air that he played "m-u-s-i-c, not n-o-i-s-e."

The Boston City Council called for a list to be drawn up of acceptable deejays. An incident at a San Jose, California, concert led neighboring Santa Cruz to bar rock concerts from civic buildings. Jersey City canceled a Bill Haley concert because it feared riots. Around the country, concerts were stopped in civic auditoriums for fear of riots. The belief was often stated that the music drew a "bad crowd" and sometimes just that the music itself caused violence. When a fight broke out during a Fats Domino concert in an enlisted men's club at a Newport, Rhode Island, naval station, the commanding rear admiral Ralph D. Earle insisted that the commonplace custom of brawls between enlisted sailors and marines had nothing to do with the disturbance but rather the fault was, as reported in *The New York Times* on September 20, 1956, "the excitement accompanying the fever-pitched rock 'n' roll." The press frequently made reference to "the three Rs" — rock, rolls, and riot.

In 1956, when the Columbia film *Rock Around the Clock,* an almost plotless showcase for rock 'n' roll starring Bill Haley and His Comets and Alan Freed, was released, a *New York Times* review attacked it not for its obvious lack of cinematic quality but for the music itself — "this raucous rhythmic commodity that is so far from the jazz with which it is sometimes unfortunately confused." The reviewer did not seem to understand that the young fans liked rhythmic raucousness exactly because it was a rejection of jazz.

In *Blackboard Jungle* a teacher brings to class his lovingly collected jazz records. He thought he would show his students their beauty and, through that, he could somehow reach them. Instead the students smash the entire collection. Seventy-eight rpm shellac records were brittle and could easily be broken. The young rockers had no use for jazz. Less remembered but more realistic was a scene from Richard Thorpe's 1957 *Jailhouse Rock.* This film was a true product of the 1950s, not only because it starred Elvis Presley in his third movie and was about rock 'n' roll music, but because MGM released the film with less than the usual publicity because it was based on a story by Nedrick Young, a World War II veteran, who had been blacklisted, banned from work, since 1953 because he refused to cooperate in the House Un-American Activities Committee's persecution of alleged Communists. The year after *Jailhouse Rock,* Young, under the pseudonym Nathan E. Douglas, won an Academy Award for *The Defiant Ones,* an exploration of racism.

In *Jailhouse Rock,* Judy Tyler, an actress known to every kid who grew up in the early 1950s as Princess Summerfall Winterspring on *Howdy Doody* — she died in a car accident before the Presley film was released — finds the young Elvis Presley playing a character named Vince Everett recently released from a prison term for manslaughter. He learned to play music from his cellmate, and Tyler, a music promoter and, of course, in love with Presley, tries to promote his rock 'n' roll career. She brings Presley home to meet her parents, who are white liberals not particularly fazed by their daughter coming home with this ex-con. They and their friends want to talk music with him and eagerly try out theories about modern jazz. But when one of them tries to include Presley in the conversation, he gives them his curled-lip sneer and mumbles, "Lady, I don't know what the hell you're talking about."

In his song "Rock & Roll Music," Chuck Berry explains why he does not like modern jazz — because it ends up sounding like a symphony.

In a Darwin-like manner, R&B and rock 'n' roll ate up the niche in the food chain that had been held by jazz. Jazz, which had been essentially music for the black working class with notable crossovers for white audiences, had been replaced. At the same time, and not by coincidence, vocals were replacing instrumentals. It seemed everyone wanted to be a Frank Sinatra. Even Marvin Gaye, growing up on the black side of segregated Washington, DC, the son of a preacher, dreamed of being a black Sinatra. Nat King Cole had achieved it, abandoning a brilliant jazz career to croon popular songs and become one of the great black crossover stars, along with Johnny Mathis and Sammy Davis Jr. All three were carefully marketed as "not too black." Mathis had the ultimate triumph, the only black to be featured in a 1958 *Life* magazine feature on rock 'n' roll.

The article, part of a special issue on

"U.S. entertainment," prominently featured the clean-cut Dick Clark, a model-acceptable deejay whose show tried to make rock 'n' roll "decent" and white for television, along with Pat Boone, famous for his antiseptic white covers of black music, and Elvis Presley in Army fatigues, successfully neutered by the U.S. military. There was also Ricky Nelson from the squeaky-clean and swell television family, innocent teen idol Frankie Avalon and slightly edgier Sal Mineo, and the Everly Brothers, a stirring and musically innovative duet. For their wilder side of rock 'n' roll, the article had a four-frame photo sequence of rockabilly singer Tony Conn's gyrations in a leopard-skin jacket with the caption "Like Wow." And in their midst was Johnny Mathis, in his white cardigan and his straightened hair, in Boston singing "Sleigh Ride." No one had to know he was black or, for that matter, that he didn't sing rock 'n' roll.

Jazz became a more elite form, performed in concert halls. Something good happens to an art form when it gives up attempting to garner popular appeal, and it led to a kind of golden age of jazz. Much of this jazz was called *bebop,* a term of uncertain origin that may go back as far as the 1920s. In the 1940s, this music took on new sophistication with the harmonic innovations of such musicians as horn player Dizzy Gillespie. By the 1950s it had become a profoundly sophisticated music, known for its riffs and lengthy improvisations, often with not always apparent political implications. Musicians such as Charlie Parker, Sonny Rollins, Art Blakey, Red Garland, Herbie Hancock, Thad Jones, Thelonious Monk, Max Roach, and John Coltrane became stars to a smaller black and white fan base. Some jazz musicians attempted and occasionally succeeded in reaching out to a wider audience, such as Ramsey Lewis, Cannonball Adderley, and Miles Davis. But after the explosion of R&B and rock 'n' roll it was an uphill struggle to attract huge sales from an all-instrumental recording.

One of the most followed of black deejays in the 1950s and 1960s, Nathaniel Montague, who called himself Magnificent Montague, later said in his autobiography, "For my time on the radio was indeed a time of fire. It was a time when music and society and race and technology all exploded like a bomb." It exploded in the early 1950s and kept exploding for almost twenty years.

The new music of the 1950s featured blacks who were idolized by white youth and whites who acted black and were embraced by black audiences. It was all part of that very dangerous idea of the times — integration. A white singer with sex appeal like Elvis Presley was more threatening than a black singer without it. But in a world where white teenage girls swooned, a sexy black man such as Chuck Berry was the most threatening figure. Antoine Domino, Fats Domino, from New Orleans, a great piano player, was acceptable because he was roly-poly and not in the least sexy. Richard Wayne Penniman, who called himself Little Richard and was a pivotal figure in carrying R&B to rock 'n' roll, exhibited calculated sexual ambiguity in sequined outfits, makeup, and false eyelashes, his hair puffed high on his head. Later in life he openly admitted that he had created this persona so that he would be perceived as sufficiently non-threatening to be allowed to play white clubs and break into white radio. Little Richard had an irresistible hard beat and played the piano standing up as though too energized by his music to sit, which may have been true.

Little Richard's producer H. B. Barnum, Hidle Brown Barnum — though when asked, he always insists his initials stand for "Handsome Boy" — said of the early age of rock 'n' roll, "Jackie Wilson, Fats Domino, Chuck Berry — all of them had huge numbers of white fans. Many times we would cross Chuck on the road and he was playing all white audiences with white groups. Bo Diddley, too."

Elvis Presley was white, but not in the least reassuring. His hair was long and he was impossibly beautiful and sexy; his body movements, which won him the nickname "Elvis the Pelvis," and his music were all about black culture. His hair was even shaped with pomade, a black product for straightened hair. Music historian Nelson George has pointed out that this hairstyle was always said by blacks to be an attempt to look more white. So Presley was a white who tried to look like a black trying to look white. Even his flashy, iridescent tight-pegged clothes were a black style. He was a bridge that helped bring black music to white teenagers. He sang both black and white music, but sang it all with the beat of R&B and with the gimmicks and flair of blues and R&B, such as "the freeze," where he would halt all movement for a half beat, and then burst forth again. And yet an Elvis recording never sounded like anyone else. Although rooted in traditions, he was at the beginning of his career an iconoclastic innovator, a rebel in the mold of James Dean and Marlon Brando.

Presley first gained widespread notice with his 1954 cover of Bill Monroe's 1947 bluegrass hit "Blue Moon of Kentucky." Suddenly this beloved waltz, which was becoming almost an anthem of white Kentucky, sounded black. Presley was recording a session for "That's All Right," a cover of a song by black Delta blues singer Arthur "Big Boy" Crudup. According to legend, his trio was taking a break and he was playing around with his bass man, Bill Black. They started parodying Monroe's redneck hit as a joke. It ended up as the B side.

They picked up the tempo and turned the waltz, a song that ironically constantly repeats the word *blue,* into the blues, but with a hard beat. It was rhythm & blues. To listen to the slow and sentimental waltz in 3/4 time and then hear it souped up to an upbeat 4/4 with an insistent beat is the quickest way to understand what rock 'n' roll was all about. In fact, for years, rock hits were created by switching an existing piece to four-beat measures with an upbeat tempo. In 1965, the Toys got to number 2 on the charts covering Bach with "A Lover's Concerto," in which songwriters Sandy Linzer and Denny Randell set words to Bach's

G major minuet and switched it from 3/4 to 4/4 time.

Crossover became a growing idea and not only in music. In 1950 Ralph Bunche won the Nobel Peace Prize, the first black to win a Nobel Prize. Also in 1950 Gwendolyn Brooks became the first black to win the Pulitzer Prize for Poetry for *Annie Allen.* James Baldwin, starting with his 1953 novel *Go Tell It on the Mountain,* became a literary star frequently published in mainstream white magazines such as *Esquire.* Sidney Poitier became Hollywood's first black leading man and also starred in Lorraine Hansberry's 1959 *Raisin in the Sun,* the first Broadway play by a black woman and the first Broadway play to be directed by a black, Lloyd Richards.

And yet blacks were producing little of black music. Independent studios for R&B music, most of which were not black-owned, were dying off with crossover. In the early 1950s there were about a hundred, only about a quarter of the number in the 1940s. In any event, a black musician could choose between being exploited at a major studio in which a musician would be paid five dollars for a finished side, or an independent, where songwriters gave up their rights to a work for two dollars. This stirred a New Orleans black musician named Harold Battiste. In the mid-1950s Battiste was moved by the teachings of Elijah Muhammad, leader of a growing black group called Nation of Islam. Among those ideas was the belief that the way for blacks to obtain their rights was to seize economic power, to become players in the economy with black-run businesses. "We sing and dance. We ought to own that," said Battiste. And so in 1959 he organized All For One Records and At Last Publishing. This idea of separate tandem record and publishing companies would later prove essential to the economic success of Motown. But Battiste was not a success. The cost of producing a record, including studio rental, musicians, record pressing was at most $1,000. The independents had been built on underpaying. It was hard to compete while paying artists fairly. Battiste went on to be a successful musical director for black singers such as Sam Cooke and white singers such as Sonny and Cher.

There were a handful of successful black record producers. Don Robey, a big, burly, light-skinned black man, started Peacock Records in 1949. He then acquired Memphis-based Duke Records and between the two became a leading producer of both

R&B and gospel. He helped to popularize gospel as secular music by hardening the beat, and was one of the first producers to get a gospel recording placed in a jukebox, "Our Father" by the Five Blind Boys of Mississippi. Robey had a reputation for ruthlessness, and he became wealthy from his records. According to an unproven legend, when Little Richard complained to Robey that he had not received all the money due him, Robey hit him so hard, he knocked him down.

In 1952, Vivian and James Bracken, a black couple in industrial Gary, Indiana, were selling the new 45 R&B records in a small store where aspiring young black singers gathered. Vivian was also a Chicago deejay. They created Vee-Jay Records in Chicago, which, until Motown, was the model of a successful black company. Starting with "For Your Precious Love," written by Jerry Butler, Arthur Brooks, and Richard Brooks and sung by the Impressions, they had a more than ten-year string of hits such as Betty Everett singing Rudy Clark's "Shoop Shoop Song (It's in His Kiss)" and Gene Chandler's "Duke of Earl." They also recorded white musicians such as Frankie Valli and the Four Seasons, who specialized in the black device of singing in falsetto. They were even the first American company to release a Beatles song, "She Loves You," but this British gold mine was quickly taken over by Capitol. To everyone's surprise, by 1965 Vee-Jay was bankrupt, allegedly due to mismanagement.

For those who denounced the three Rs, physical movement itself became the crime. The widely believed myth that *The Ed Sullivan Show* refused to film Elvis Presley below the waist seemed plausible because Presley was so often attacked for his movement. It was more serious when black people moved. When Bo Diddley appeared on national television in 1958, his contract stipulated that he was not to move. When he did, he was denied his entire fee.

A January 1958 *New York Times Sunday Magazine* article tried to understand the curious effect rock 'n' roll was having on teenagers. The article begins:

> "Rocking" the song as though in a life and death struggle with an invisible antagonist was a tall, thin, flaccid youth who pulled his stringy blond hair over his eyes and down to his chin. He shook his torso about as the beat of the band seemingly goaded him on. Screams from thousands of young

throats billowed toward him. In the pande-
monium, youngsters flailed the air with
their arms, jumped from their seats, beck-
oned madly, lovingly, to the tortured figure
onstage.

The song could scarcely be heard over
the footlights. No matter. The kids knew
the words. They shrilled them with the
singer — and kept up their approving,
uninhibited screams. . . .

What is this thing called rock 'n' roll?
What is it that makes teen-agers — mostly
children between the ages of 12 and 16
— throw off their inhibitions as though at a
revivalist meeting? What — who — is
responsible for these sorties? And is this
generation of teen-agers going to hell?

This article, which at one point began
sounding like the lyrics to "Dancing in the
Street" as it listed the cities where the
phenomenon was occurring, contained
interviews with remarkably cogent and
articulate teenagers. One identified as
"brown-haired Vivian" said "The main thing
about this music is that it's lively — it's not
dead. It makes you want to dance."

Another girl named Jerilyn said of Elvis
Presley, "My girl friend says he sends chills
up her spine. But I think the majority of the

girls just like the beat. It's new."

The music industry itself attacked the new music in the mid-1950s. Deejays denounced the music on the radio. Peter Potter of KLAC-Hollywood was particularly influential because he hosted a popular television show, *Juke Box Jury,* which broadcasted from 1956 to 1959. The program invited celebrity guests to vote "hit" or "miss" on the latest records. Many artists and fans in the R&B and rock 'n' roll world may have been bemused by the dubious relevance of having their music judged by the likes of aging crooner Dean Martin, the blond celebrity Zsa Zsa Gabor, or the folksy character actor Walter Brennan. But the show had a following. Potter seemed almost on a mission to attack rock 'n' roll, which he claimed was "lewd" and "not fit for radio broadcasts." He later said that such music was "as bad for kids as dope."

Even *Billboard,* whose bread and butter was the charts on which the new music was prominently featured, ran editorials denouncing it and urging the industry to suppress particularly tasteless recordings. They advised radio stations that there were records on their own Top 10 that might be inappropriate for broadcast. The chart, they explained, is merely a reflection of record sales and not a recommendation. *Variety* said that rock 'n' roll was about sex, and that such lewdness was all right in "special places" but was not suitable for "general consumption." This language is not difficult to decipher. This is black music suitable for black venues but not appropriate for white kids. Pamphlets circulated, warning white parents to keep this music away from their children.

Some radio stations, including six in Boston, set up their own boards of review to censor inappropriate rock 'n' roll. "Wake Up Little Susie" by the Everly Brothers was a frequent target. In this song a couple innocently falls asleep in a dull movie and accidentally sleeps through the night. The song makes clear that they really were innocent and had just fallen asleep. There is no other hidden meaning. Fats Waller, Cole Porter, and others had used far more overt sexual innuendos without such ire. Hoagy Carmichael even sang about a couple spending the night together because they were too much in love to say good night. But teenage girls were not dancing to that music, and it didn't have a hard beat. Then, too, the whole point of the Everly Brothers song, which may have irritated the guardians of morality, was that innocent teenagers could so easily be falsely accused by adult society.

A major shift was happening in the music world and there would be winners and losers. The older Italian crooners saw it as a shift away from northern Italians to southern whites and blacks. This was not exactly true. Frankie Valli, Bobby Darin, Frankie Avalon, Sal Mineo, and Dion DiMucci, generally known as just Dion, were all Italian rockers born in the Northeast, just as Frank Sinatra and Tony Bennett had been. But maybe this was even worse news for the Sinatras — younger New York and New Jersey Italians were trying to replace them and their music. The established white media — print, radio, and television — all treated the Italian rockers better than other rock singers because they were used to Italian singers. And in time, some such as Bobby Darin easily morphed into nightclub crooners in the Sinatra mold.

Sinatra was viciously opposed to the new music and seemed never to miss an occasion to attack it. This was particularly striking because Sinatra had a reputation as something of a liberal, supportive of progressive Democrats and civil rights. He also had an image of being hip, but now in his forties, he was aging. In a visible cultural midlife crisis, Sinatra told a congressional investigating committee that rock 'n' roll was "the most brutal, ugly, desperate, vicious form of expression it has been my misfortune to hear." He further stated, "Rock and roll smells phony and false. It is sung, played, and written for the most part by cretinous goons, and by means of its almost imbecilic reiteration, and sly, lewd, in plain fact, dirty lyrics . . . it manages to be martial music of every side burned delinquent on the face of the earth."

Sinatra had many allies in his celebrity anti-rock crusade. Bandleader and television host Mitch Miller said that rock music caused teenagers to wear sloppy clothes and was "one step away from fascism." He called it "the comic books of music." Composer Meredith Wilson, who became a star when his musical *The Music Man* opened on Broadway in 1957, said in 1958, "The people of this country do not have any conception of the evil being done by rock 'n' roll; it is a plague as far reaching as any plague we have ever had."

Though there is strong evidence that racism was a factor in virulent anti-rock, Sammy Davis Jr. also hated rock 'n' roll and told Mitch Miller that he would consider suicide if he thought that the music would not soon vanish. Nor can it be assumed that all of rock's opponents were threatened by it. Pablo Casals, the Catalan master of cello, was anti-rock. Perhaps the greatest classical cellist of all time, Casals was probably not worried about being replaced by Elvis Presley and Bo Diddley. But Casals said rock 'n' roll was "poison put to music." A movement of classical musicians against rock 'n' roll manifested itself in buttons spoofing the "I Like Elvis" buttons that thousands of teenagers wore. "I Like Ludwig" buttons were also worn by thousands, including Casals, violinist Isaac Stern, and conductor Eugene Ormandy. More disturbing was the observation in *The Times* of London in 1956 by BBC Symphony Orchestra conductor Sir Malcolm Sargent that young people were wrong to think of rock 'n' roll as new since it "has been played in the jungle for centuries."

Enough, said singer Tony Bennett, who also hated the music. His fear was that rock 'n' roll, which would have been a passing trend, was being kept alive by all this colorful and oft-quoted criticism. If everyone would stop talking about it, Bennett told the press, kids would in time grow up and "slow down and require less noise."

Religious leaders, captains of finance and industry, educators, politicians, and members of law enforcement all weighed in on the harmful effects of rock 'n' roll. It was a social conflict, but probably nothing fueled the fight more than the increased competition between two music industry organizations, ASCAP and BMI. The American Society of Composers, Authors and Publishers was founded in 1914 to register and license popular music and protect its creators. It completely ignored country music and R&B. In 1940 Broadcast Music Incorporated was established to break ASCAP's monopoly. But for the most part, it was only able to register the marginal music in which ASCAP had no interest.

By the late 1950s ASCAP had a real rival in BMI, which had most of the R&B and rock 'n' roll titles. ASCAP attacked its new competitor by attacking its music in the press, before Congress, in the courts. Many of the celebrities of Broadway, the record establishment, and Hollywood had strong ties to ASCAP.

But there was an even darker side to the opposition to rock 'n' roll. In April 1956 Nat King Cole was giving a concert in Birmingham, Alabama, to an all-white audience of 3,500, which was not unusual for Cole. He was about to start his third song, "Little Girl." Ted Heath's largely British and white band, modeled after Glen Miller, started the introduction. Three men charged up one aisle and two up the other. According to the following week's account in *Newsweek,* "The audience watched curiously as the figures raced into the light, vaulted onto the stage. Cole sprawled backwards under a welter of bodies."

According to *Newsweek* and other accounts, the audience was angered by the attack and people shouted, "Bring Cole back" and "Sorry it happened." Heath was so infuriated, he wanted to cancel the tour, but Cole convinced him to continue. The assailants were thugs with records of mindless assault, but what was disturbing was that four of the five were members of a group called the North Alabama Citizens Council, whose stated goal was to oppose integration. Asa Carter, who headed the group, said that he was not disturbed by the incident, explaining, "I've swung on niggers myself." Carter explained that rock 'n' roll music "is the basic heavy beat music of negroes. It appeals to the base in man, brings out animalism and vulgarity." He believed that rock music was part of an

"NAACP plot to mongrelize America" and that such Negro music was an attempt to impose "Negro culture" on the South.

According to the police investigation, the attack had been planned in a gas station four days earlier, and 150 people were involved. The target of Nat King Cole and the Ted Heath Band is odd, because no one involved seemed to notice that neither Cole nor Ted Heath's band played "the heavy beat music of Negroes" and that in fact the only thing to qualify this concert for their attack was the color of Cole's skin.

Throughout the South racist segregationist groups published literature warning white parents of the influence Negroes were having on their children through rock 'n' roll. Southern segregationists, on the defensive since the Supreme Court decision on schools, regarded rock 'n' roll as just one more attempt to unravel their way of life.

A month after the Cole attack, the Platters, Bo Diddley, and Bill Haley appeared at the same Birmingham, Alabama, concert hall, and despite the apparent sympathy of the April audience to Cole, this May concert was greeted with signs saying Jungle Music Promotes Integration. Similar demonstrations were seen at many rock 'n' roll concerts in the South, and at some in the North as well.

Of course, the music, designed to appeal to both races, did promote integration. Some civil rights activists also saw the biracial popularity of rock 'n' roll as an important force for integration in the South. Alabama-born Shelley Stewart, a popular black rock 'n' roll radio personality in the South, openly mixed civil rights and rock 'n' roll in his Alabama and Mississippi radio broadcasts. In July 1960 he hosted a white record hop outside of Birmingham. Some eighty Klansmen arrived, with the intention of breaking up the event. But the white audience of about eight hundred teenagers, furious, attacked the Klan.

Despite all the angry opposition, black music continued to cross over to white, principally young, audiences more than ever before in history. In 1957 Norman Mailer published an essay, "The White Negro," about the new white rebel, a "philosophical psychopath" and "hipster" who embraced black culture as a protest against white society and its ignorant fear of integration.

The record establishment tried to whiten the music. After all, if these marginal performers could attract significant record sales, think what a cover by a clean-cut white could sell. And so the Crew Cuts covered "Sh-Boom," the McGuire Sisters covered the Moonglows hit "Sincerely." The king of white covers was Pat Boone, a twentyish singer who seemed to try to embody the notion of white with his carefully combed blond hair and trademark white buck shoes. He could sing black R&B and rock 'n' roll and make it as reassuring, harmless, and white as Patti Page's 1953 number 1 hit "Doggie in the Window." The heart of Boone's repertoire was covers of Fats Domino and Little Richard. Fifty Boone recordings made the charts and thirty-eight were in the Top 40. In the late 1950s and early 1960s, the only performer to have more hits than Pat Boone was Elvis Presley.

But Boone was not a hit with black people, whereas Presley from the mid-1950s until the chart was temporarily dropped in 1963 had twenty-four hits on *Billboard*'s black R&B chart. No other white singer so penetrated the black market, though the Everly Brothers had eight R&B hits, as did the Newark Italian Connie Francis. Rick Nelson had nine, Frankie Avalon had five, and even Andy Williams, who crooned in cardigan sweaters, had three. The days of separate black and white music were showing signs of coming to an end.

But the pioneers paid a price. One of the first victims was Alan Freed, the white deejay who gave rock 'n' roll its name and through his radio programs, the concerts he hosted, and films, was the single greatest promoter of this new music. His childhood dream was to be a bandleader. Working his way up from smaller stations, in 1951 he began working for WJW Cleveland. There he met Leo Mintz, a record store owner who told him that he was selling an increasing number of records by black artists, R&B, to white teenagers and convinced him that there should be a radio show for this music. Freed began imitating black deejays, using black expressions, black vocal styles, and the personality-driven format of the deejays on black radio. He created a black radio program that played black music for a white audience on the kind of powerful white radio station to which blacks rarely had access. He seemed to genuinely love the music. He always claimed that he played only the records that he loved.

As early as 1952 Freed became a target of law enforcement and anti-rockers. That year one of the first rock riots broke out when a show he sponsored at the Cleveland Arena was oversold and angry ticket holders were denied entry. The crowd at the Cleveland Arena had been an equal blend of black and white, something troubling to a lot of citizens of Cleveland, a city where races had always been separate. Freed was blamed for the riot, though charges were later dropped.

Freed continued to be a controversial figure and a target of legal actions, ostensibly for his promotion of rock 'n' roll, but really for his racial integration, and he seemed to be able to attract equal numbers of both races. Racists found it particularly infuriating that he tended to ignore white covers such as those by Pat Boone, preferring to play the black original.

In 1954 he moved to WINS in New York, where he had the most popular show, which gave him the power to host more concerts and to break into television and movies. It was disillusioning when teenagers got to actually see Freed, because he was the ultimate dorky white guy who couldn't dance. But he wore bright-colored, outrageous clothing, often plaid.

In 1957, at the height of his popularity, Freed had his own rock 'n' roll television show on ABC. But on one episode he let Frankie Lymon, a rising black star who would later influence the music of such Motown greats as Smokey Robinson and the Jackson Five, dance with a white girl. There were angry protests, especially from southern ABC affiliates, and Freed's show was canceled.

He was not a completely innocent figure. He often did not treat artists on his shows well, was accused of stealing song credits, and very much underpaid the talents who created the music he loved. But in 1958 his life began to unravel in ways he did not deserve. On May 3 one of the worst rock 'n' roll riots took place at an event he hosted at the Boston Arena. A sailor was stabbed and others were punched, beaten, or robbed by an unidentified gang in satin jackets. Freed was charged with inciting violence. The charges were later dropped, but Freed was ruined financially after WINS would not renew his contract. He landed a job on WABC radio and also a dance show, *Big Beat,* on WNEW, a local New York channel.

The Boston incident increased pressure not only on Freed but on all of rock 'n' roll. Many towns simply refused to allow Freed to hold events. ASCAP had been intensifying its war against rock 'n' roll, which was really a war against BMI, by pressuring leading politicians. The junior senator from Massachusetts, John F. Kennedy, representing Boston, which had always been a very anti-rock town, stood with archconservative Barry Goldwater in the Senate, opposing rock 'n' roll. Kennedy had a *Newsday* article attacking the music read into the congressional record. A segregationist Florida senator, George Smathers, was supported by Kennedy in his call to investigate rock 'n' roll.

It was then, in 1959, that ASCAP opened a new front in its war on rock. They discovered that certain deejays, the ones who played BMI music, of course, were receiving money from record producers to play their records. The investigation went to the U.S. Congress. A number of deejays were found to be receiving "payola." In reality, the practice was fairly widespread but with different levels of payoffs. In a recent interview, Cousin Brucie Morrow laughed about it. "I took payola once. The manager of a local New York group had a mother who owned a bakery. I was told that if I played their record I would get two cherry pies. I played the record and took the pies. Everyone else was getting money, cars, and televisions. I got two cherry pies."

But in 1959 no one was laughing, and the deejay the investigation chose to go after was Alan Freed. He was the only deejay subpoenaed. Freed admitted to taking money but said that it was legitimate consulting fees. He was prosecuted and convicted on twenty-nine counts of commercial bribery and given a six-month suspended sentence and fined $300. But he was fired from WABC, though the station would give no reason for the dismissal. His six-day-a-week television show was canceled. Freed, a ruined, impoverished man, lived quietly. But he remained a target, charged in 1964 with income tax evasion on unreported income from 1957 to 1959. On January 20, 1965, he died of kidney failure at the age of forty-three. Alan Freed simply disappeared, but to the frustration of his enemies, rock 'n' roll didn't.

Bill Haley's attempts to avoid trouble by cleaning up his lyrics did not spare him criticism, but sat poorly with his fans, who started to see him as too old. Chuck Berry, a restlessly innovative rocker who combined the hard beat and body antics of rock 'n' roll with the ribald sense of humor of old-time Louis Jordan–style R&B, was always targeted by rock haters.

On August 28, 1959, after a concert in Meridian, Mississippi, a twenty-year-old white woman and her boyfriend approached Berry and asked for his autograph. For reasons that were never clear, he was arrested for attempting to date a white girl and was immediately jailed. He was released the next day. The same year he was arrested under the Mann Act for "transporting a minor across a state line for immoral purposes." The Mann Act, passed in 1910, supposedly to prevent white slavery, had loose enough wording to be regularly used against blacks involved with white women. Jack Johnson, the first black heavyweight champion, was arrested under the Mann Act twice, in 1912 and 1913. In Chuck Berry's case, he met a Mexican Indian woman in Juarez, Mexico, named Janice Escalanti and hired her for his St. Louis nightclub. They quarreled and she went to the police. It turned out that she was only fourteen years old. It is not clear if Berry had known her true age. It didn't matter. Law enforcement finally had him. In the indictment they accused him of luring her "to give herself up for debauchery," despite the fact that the girl was known to have worked as a prostitute before meeting the rock star.

The first trial and conviction were thrown out because of the appearance of racism of the judge, Gilbert Moore, who repeatedly brought up race. Berry was then immediately charged again for a 1958 relationship with a singer. But, like the earlier case against Jack Johnson, this one fell apart because the alleged victim had great affection for the accused and rose to his defense. No matter. They could still get him. They retried the Escalanti case, and this time the conviction was upheld. Berry served almost two years in prison, and after he got out, though he toured in rock 'n' roll revival concerts, he was never able to restart his career as a music star.

Even Little Richard, who tried to be harmlessly weird, was arrested in 1956 in El Paso, Texas, for shaking onstage. Many aspects of his career had been troubling Little Richard. He did not like the feeling that racist white society was using him. He tried to record songs ever faster in the hopes that Pat Boone could not keep up with the tempo. He also had deep religious convictions and was disturbed by the church's view that his music was immoral or even on the side of the devil. Little Richard believed in the devil. Suddenly in 1957 he gave up music and announced that he was becoming a minister. He said that he could not live with God and play rock 'n' roll because "God doesn't like it." He enrolled in Bible college but didn't graduate, and a few years later returned to music but, like Chuck

Berry, could not regain his status as a star.

Another rocker who deeply felt the conflict with religion was Jerry Lee Lewis. Lewis was first noticed at age fifteen in 1950 on Ted Mack's *Original Amateur Hour,* a popular radio and later television show where numerous stars, including Pat Boone, were first heard. Mack liked to keep the music tame and white, and Lewis, after a successful round of auditions, agreed to do "Goodnight, Irene." Although it was a folk song turned blues, and popularized by the great blues singer Lead Belly, in 1950, the folk group the Weavers had a hit with an easy version, with sanitized lyrics. Now it was an established song. Frank Sinatra sang it that year. But young Jerry Lee Lewis didn't. Instead, he sang a wild rock version of "When the Saints Go Marching In." Mack was furious but Lewis won the ten-dollar audience favorite prize. Then he went off to Bible school, where he was expelled for playing rock versions of hymns. It seems that Lewis just couldn't help rocking. In 1957 he became a star with a cover of "Whole Lot of Shakin' Going On," an R&B song by a number of black artists whose lyrics had inescapably sexual innuendo. Numerous radio stations refused to air it, and while it made Lewis a star, it also made him the leading target of Christian clergy, for a moment even eclipsing the denunciations of Elvis Presley. Not Elvis, not even Chuck Berry, had the wild physical antics of Jerry Lee Lewis, who kicked away his stool and pounded the piano standing, sometimes playing with his feet or even with his head, flapping his long blond hair. Between songs he would take out a comb and sensually rearrange his hair.

But he was never comfortable with himself. Just before the Sun Records 1957 recording session for "Great Balls of Fire," Lewis announced that he couldn't record it because it was the devil's music. Sam Phillips, the founder of Sun, who had launched Lewis's career along with those of Elvis Presley and other important rockers, sat down with him for hours and persuaded him to do the recording, which became his biggest hit.

Ed Sullivan, who still had not recovered from the Elvis appearances, refused to have Lewis on the show. He had refused to have Elvis on until the rocker appeared opposite him on *The Steve Allen Show,* and Allen stole away his audience that night. He then had him on three times. The first time, neither of them was there. Elvis was shot from Hollywood, and Sullivan, injured in a car accident, was replaced by actor Charles Laughton in New York. All three appearances — legs, pelvis, and all — were wildly popular and cemented Presley's stardom, though he was burned in effigy by angry mobs in Nashville and St. Louis. At the end of the third show, Sullivan gave him an endorsement that was a huge boost to the controversial singer, calling him "a real decent, fine boy." He apparently was surprised to discover that, despite his offensive music, Elvis had fine southern manners.

By 1958 Elvis Presley was in the Army and Lewis was momentarily the king of rock 'n' roll and the primary target of rock's enemies. Lewis was easy to go after. He had married his thirteen-year-old cousin, and after further investigation, it turned out that he had been married twice before and it appeared that he had not had divorces. So the evil rock 'n' roller was also an incestuous pedophile and a bigamist. At first he could still get concert bookings but the audiences shouted him down. Soon he could get hardly any bookings at all, and his career was largely over.

Meanwhile, Elvis was denounced for everything he did. Even his 1957 Christmas album was attacked for the sacrilege of having Elvis the Pelvis crooning Christmas carol standards. He was a famous person admired by kids and he was not promoting "wholesome," i.e., conventional, values. In 1956 the *New York Times* critic Jack Gould wrote a scathing review of Presley's television appearances with the headline "Elvis Presley: Lack of Responsibility Is Shown by TV in Exploiting Teen-Agers." Gould, trying to understand the inexplicable popularity of Presley, wrote:

Quite possibly Presley just happened to move in where society has failed the teenager. Certainly, modern youngsters have been subjected to a great deal of censure and perhaps too little understanding. Greater in their numbers than ever before, they may have found in Presley a rallying point, a nationally prominent figure who seems to be on their side. And just as surely, there are limitless teen-agers who cannot put up with the boy either vocally or calisthenically.

The article was a call to ban Elvis Presley from television. Such cries were relentless. Curiously, critics like Gould could not grasp that Presley was vocally and calisthenically, not to mention musically, brilliant. A large segment of society wanted Presley silenced as Berry, Lewis, and Little Richard had been. Urged by his manager, Colonel Tom Parker, Presley was trying to retreat from being a 1950s rebel to being Ed Sullivan's "fine boy." Those allegedly bland 1950s were turning out to be dangerous. Screenplay writers were being blacklisted for political convictions, rockers and deejays were destroyed for their music, even poet Lawrence Ferlinghetti would be put on trial for obscenity because he published a poem, Allen Ginsberg's *Howl,* which is now widely recognized as one of the great works of twentieth-century literature. Ferlinghetti, in his mid-thirties, the son of Italian immigrants and orphaned at an early age, had made his San Francisco bookstore, City Lights, the first all-paperback bookstore in America, and its publishing wing the center of the new upstart Beat poetry, the literary equivalent of rock 'n' roll. He expected trouble when he published *Howl* and had it printed in England. The bookstore manager was arrested for selling the book to undercover San Francisco policemen. Ginsberg could barely control his glee at being treated like a rock star, and in the end the court ruled that it was not obscene, leaving thirty-one-year-old Ginsberg a new counterculture literary star. But if you wanted to be a counterculture star in the 1950s you had to face a legal assault.

No one forgot how Freed, Berry, and Lewis were destroyed, or how Ferlinghetti and Ginsberg were almost destroyed. The only difference between the attackers of rock 'n' roll and the attackers of Beat poetry was that Beat's enemies tended to be better read. If you rebelled against the established norms, if you dared to be different, the forces of the Establishment would try to destroy you. Ginsberg was even more of a target, because he was openly homosexual and his poem referred to homosexual sex acts. This could be even worse than being a pedophile, bigamist, or integrationist. The civil rights movement kept their most brilliant activist, Bayard Rustin, in the background because he was homosexual.

In 1957 Presley was drafted and received a deferment so that he could complete the movie he was shooting, *King Creole.* He was inducted in 1958 into the Army's Second Armored Division's "Hell on Wheels" unit that had been famous in World War II under General George Patton.

The press had a great moment with the regulation haircut. A good-humored Presley quipped, "Hair today, gone tomorrow." But there was a significant metaphor taking place in the odd sight of Presley's being diminished, Samson-like, to a white-walled G.I. cut. The Elvis who emerged from the Army two years later was not the same. Colonel Parker steered him clear of further controversy.

Parker also steered himself that way. He was a Dutchman who entered the U.S. illegally and pretended for most of his life to be an American. Tom Parker was born in Breda, and was originally named Andreas Cornelis van Kuijk. Nor was he a colonel. He did serve in the Army, but deserted and was prosecuted and eventually discharged for mental illness. While most managers at the time were taking 10 percent of earnings, the Colonel sometimes took as much as 50 percent. But it was Parker who moved Elvis from Sun to RCA for a handsome fee and a bigger company. Presley was confident that Parker saved him and his career by steering him away from the controversy that had ruined others. Surely they would have gotten him sooner or later.

It was Parker who insisted that Presley serve as a regular soldier, a jeep driver, rather than as an entertainer in Special Services because this would be important to his new image. It was Parker who arranged to have the media witness the cutting of Elvis's hair. Presley grew his hair back but was much more clean-cut in appearance. The rebel look was gone.

Parker, a heavy man with a high voice and a fake southern twang to his accent, remembered how Jerry Lee Lewis had been ruined, and urged Presley to marry Priscilla Wagner, his girlfriend who was ten years younger, fourteen, when they had met. The Colonel argued that if they married, they would seem more respectable.

Elvis did not make a concert appearance again until 1967, and this prevented the unseemly scene of screaming teenage girls. He did appear regularly on television. His first appearance was in 1960 with Frank Sinatra, for which Parker got Presley $125,000 for two songs, which was more than Sinatra was making for the special. This was a complete reversal for both of them. It is often seen as Sinatra relenting on rock, and now that he was in his mid-forties, he seemed somehow hip again. But in reality it was the new Elvis, no longer one of Sinatra's "cretinous goons," looking "normal" and joining the Establishment. He recorded mostly ballads, and appeared in a series of films, mostly harmless romantic comedies. Elvis the rebel was replaced by a Hollywood crooner. In the 1960s, a uniquely volatile decade for which he was one of the early harbingers, Elvis was largely irrelevant, a fact that Presley was aware of and about which he often complained to his manager. But his manager wanted to keep him out of trouble.

When the great popular crooner Bing Crosby predicted that rock 'n' roll would soon vanish, he was asked what would take its place. He said, "Slow, pretty ballads." If rock 'n' roll had been nothing but Elvis Presley, he would have been right.

In 1960 rock 'n' roll entered into a brief period in which, avoiding controversy, very little interesting music was produced. Had it continued, there might have been a complete British takeover of American music, because the British were just beginning to find their rock 'n' roll voices. Cousin Brucie said about that time, "We had nothing to play. We had British stuff. I played the Beatles before they came over."

Nothing to play was, of course, an exaggeration. The excitement of the 1950s rock 'n' roll era was gone, but there was still some very good music, mostly black. For one thing, there was the emergence of an important 1960s phenomenon known as "the girl groups": the Shirelles, the

Ronettes, the Crystals. A few of their songs are memorable classics, such as the Shirelles' 1960 "Will You Love Me Tomorrow," a number 1 hit on the white pop chart and number 2 on the black R&B, and the Ronettes' 1963 number 2 hit, "Be My Baby." Others were less memorable, such as the Crystals' 1962 song "He Hit Me (It Felt Like a Kiss)." Both the Crystals and the Ronettes were produced by Phil Spector, who was a pioneer in girl groups. His Philles label produced music with a large, carefully orchestrated band, which he called "the Wall of Sound," aimed at small radios and jukeboxes. The songs had prominent hooks with staying power and throbbing drum bridges that made people move. The girl groups were tightly choreographed. Most of the girls were from New York. You could tell that the Ronettes were New Yorkers because they were able to rhyme "Since the day I saw you" and "I have been waiting for you." Not as enduring or as productive as Motown artists, they still had twenty-five Top 40 hits in the early 1960s, a huge presence on the charts at a time when Gordy was trying to figure out the Motown way. Spector was a somewhat forgotten but huge influence on Motown.

Another influence on Motown was gospel,

and though they were far from the church music, Motown records were to have an unmistakable gospel tinge. Popularized gospel, "rhythm & gospel" as Wexler said, was at a high point in the early 1960s. Gospel had always been there. It was a huge influence on Elvis Presley, who enjoyed listening to it and could impress gospel singers with his knowledge of their music. But in the early 1960s, a few R&B singers who had come out of gospel were singing the church music with a very hard beat and secular lyrics, so that it was really pop music in gospel form. Two enormous pop stars of gospel emerged, Ray Charles and Sam Cooke. Ray Charles, who had been born with sight but lost it by the age of seven, had a background in classical music but loved jazz, gospel, and blues, and somehow put them all together, so that, defying all labels it was all those things at once and appealed to lovers of all forms of black music. He developed a huge black following in the 1950s, but as white ears grew more accustomed to black music, he started acquiring a huge white audience in the early 1960s.

Sam Cooke was a gospel singer, and though he switched to rock, even the rather inane version of rock in the early 1960s, he always went back to gospel, recording it and singing it in churches. Cooke always had the emotional and vocal power of a gospel singer and a flawless lyric voice so that he became a star with such lightweight songs as the 1957 "You Send Me" or the 1962 "Twistin' the Night Away." He also continued to sing with gospel groups and even made gospel recordings with his own money. R&B deejay Montague said, "It was Sam, in the early sixties, who showed us how to lift the rising, majestic feeling that swirls within the Negro church and apply it to rhythm & blues."

In Detroit, the Motor City, an important black center that had still not made its mark on the new music — a city where great music was performed in both churches and nightclubs — a huge change was quietly taking place.

# CHAPTER TWO:
# A BRAND NEW BEAT

Among the great and often overlooked immigrant stories of America is the twentieth-century migration of southern blacks to Detroit. They came, as most immigrants did, not for riches but for a somewhat better deal, an escape from poverty and persecution for the opportunities, no matter how much of a long shot, of a better life. Immigrants are people who dare to dream.

From the beginning of the twentieth century until the 1960s, there was an enormous transformation in the African American population of the United States. It dispersed from its largely southern concentration to the rest of the country, and went from rural roots to urban settings. At the beginning of the century the African American population of the United States was almost entirely southern. In 1930 the state populations of both Mississippi and North Carolina, where few blacks were able to vote, had black majorities. But by 1960 only a little over half still lived there. They had moved to northern cities because jobs there were far better than those the rural south could offer. By the 1960s, 95.3 percent of blacks outside of the South lived in cities, which meant that northern cities were much blacker than they had ever been. Chicago went from 14 percent black to 28 percent. Newark, New Jersey, went from 17 percent to 47 percent, and Detroit went from 16 percent to 30 percent. In such cities as Detroit and Newark, if trends continued, blacks would soon represent the majority of the population, as in fact they did in Detroit by the mid-1970s.

Detroit, a French trapper settlement on the straits — *détroit* — of a river that would divide the United States from Canada, opened its first important chapter in African American history before the Civil War, when it became one of the critical last stops on the Underground Railroad. From there, escaped slaves had only a short boat ride across the river to Canada and freedom.

Detroit gradually became a city. In 1825 it was the vital link between the Great Lakes, which were connected to New York City through the Erie Canal, and the exploration and settlement of the Pacific North-west. In 1884 Detroit became more of a center when a railroad link to Chicago was completed.

But Detroit got its big boost in 1909, when Henry Ford began producing Model T Fords. Ford offered no real technical innovations but rather a game-changing marketing concept. Automobiles up until then had been toys for the rich. But it was Ford's idea to use the existing technique of assembly-line production to make an affordable car that would make everyone want to drive. The original price was $825. By 1915 he had produced a million Model T cars and by 1927 the Ford Motor Company had turned out 15 million of them — a single car design for everyone. To do this required a huge workforce, far more laborers than Detroit could supply. And so Ford offered a very high wage for labor and attracted workers from around the world, changing the face of the city.

Ford drew workers from eastern Europe and as far away as Palestine. But he drew mostly southern blacks trying to escape a life of endless humiliation and hopeless poverty. By 1927 Ford had competition from other carmakers who had newer ideas, and stopped making Model Ts. Meanwhile, Detroit had become the car center of

America, had earned the nickname Motor City, and was home to the highest-paid blue-collar workers in America.

Not only was Ford offering unheard-of salaries — in 1914 he offered five dollars a day and a profit-sharing plan — but he was offering white jobs to black people. They were not just hired to be cleanup crews but to work side by side with white workers on the assembly line. Factory work appealed to southern blacks raised on agricultural labor because factory work had no association with slavery.

None of this is to say that Detroit was a haven from racism and poverty. Many jobs and much housing were for whites only. High wages in the Detroit economy went only slightly farther than the low wages in the economy of the rural South.

Still, for many rural southern blacks this northern city was the Promised Land, just for the possibilities, the chances that were offered. In the South, blues songs were written about going north to work for Ford.

I'm goin' to get me a job, up there in Mr.
   Ford's place
Stop these eatless days from starin' me in
   the face.

Later in Detroit, blues songs were written about the hardship of working on the assembly line. But as with the Jews of eastern Europe, there was no question of going home if things did not go well. Conditions were even worse at home, and as Amiri Baraka pointed out, the South would always be "the scene of the crime."

So rural was the immigrant population of Detroit that even today, with the exception of downtown, Detroit is largely a city of country houses, many of them in the design of farmhouses. Detroit-born Ivy Jo Hunter, one of the coauthors of "Dancing in the Street," said of his hometown, "This is the largest country town in the world." Though housing projects were built later, many of the new people from the South lived like Martha Reeves's family, in wooden shingled houses with porches and yards surrounded by chain-link fencing and a gate. Though humble, small two-story homes, usually too small for the size of the family, they were often a step up from the shacks and log cabins the families came from.

And so Detroit became a city of blacks who would strive to succeed in endeavors typical of immigrants, primarily the assembly line. Those who dreamed larger, like other immigrants before them — the Irish,

the Italians, the Jews — saw their two greatest possibilities for success in sports and
entertainment. Gordy and singer-songwriter
Smokey Robinson were first-generation Detroiters. Martha Reeves, the original three
Supremes, and Wilson Pickett were all born
in the South and, like boxers Joe Louis and
Sugar Ray Robinson, were childhood immigrants to Detroit. Detroit was a city of
immigrants aspiring to be athletes and
entertainers. Detroit-born Berry Gordy, the
classic first-generation son of immigrants,
tried both.

As with all great American immigrant
stories, the Gordys worked hard and with
determination and advanced in each generation. For the Gordys this was a process that
had begun long before they immigrated.
Berry Gordy Jr.'s great-grandmother, Esther Johnson, a major influence on the early
life of his father, was a slave, impregnated
by her owner, a white man named Jim
Gordy. In the 1960s, when such prominent
black people as the boxer Cassius Clay and
the writer LeRoi Jones changed their names,
stating that they would not carry slave
names, it was undoubtedly true. The Gordy
family name was an example of what had
happened. But the Gordys made the name

their own and took great pride in it.

When Berry Sr., the music producer's father, known in Detroit as Pop Gordy, was a child, Jim Gordy, his white grandfather, was still alive but Berry never met him. Pop Gordy's father was also named Berry Gordy, and both he and his wife were born a few years before emancipation. So Berry Gordy Jr.'s father, Pop Gordy, was the first generation not born into slavery. Pop Gordy was one of their twenty-three children, of which only nine survived to adulthood. They grew up in a log house in rural Oconee County, Georgia. Pop recalled lying in bed in the early morning, watching the sunrise through the cracks between the logs.

Their father, Berry, taught himself how to read and write and make arithmetical calculations. He worked for ten years on a plantation, but from that work he scraped together enough money to buy 168 acres of land while his children were still young, and to produce and sell cotton, peanuts, sugar-cane, and various food crops. Most of his neighbors were sharecroppers who worked a white man's land and earned very little. Berry Gordy was respected by blacks and whites in the county as a successful black man.

The Gordys were strongly influenced by

Booker T. Washington, a man of the first Berry's generation. Washington, too, was born a slave but he became a successful educator. Washington taught that black people should work hard, get educated, and strive for financial success. Their rights, in time, would come. He had a huge following among both blacks and whites, though many other black leaders, most notably W. E. B. Du Bois, one of the founders of the NAACP, strongly disagreed. Du Bois and others believed that blacks could obtain their rights only by fighting for them through political activism. In the 1960s, when Berry Gordy Jr.'s Motown was an exemplary black-owned enterprise, this nineteenth-century debate between Washington and Du Bois was still a central conflict.

The first Berry's son, Pop Gordy, was an unusual child. When his siblings went off to play, he was staying close to his father, learning the business. When Pop was only ten, he went with his father to market and took on the job of calculating the value of the cotton they were selling. Pop attended school and also his father gave him books, including a law book, to study while the father's holdings were ever expanding — another one hundred acres, a blacksmith shop, a big white house, a grocery store, and a sugar mill for their cane. Berry let his son operate the sugar mill. The Gordys were, in the local parlance, "big dogs."

In 1913 the father was suddenly struck dead by a bolt of lightning. White people immediately approached the family, offering their services as business advisers. This had been common practice in the South, to have white people manage black holdings. But, distrustful of the white offer, the family decided to name twenty-five-year-old Pop as the administrator. Whites constantly approached Pop with schemes to swindle him out of the holdings, but, consulting the law book his father had given him, he saw through all of the traps.

Toward the end of World War I, Pop was drafted into the Army. Pop's concern was that the family holdings would somehow be stolen while he was away, " 'Cause I know the white people'd take that property." His legs went bad, then his eyesight. He pretended to be illiterate. He played the racist stereotype and he was discharged after three months. Back home at age thirty, he married a smart and ambitious nineteen-year-old schoolteacher named Bertha.

In 1922 Pop sold a load of timber stumps from the Gordy land for $2,600. This was more money than a black man was supposed to make in Oconee County, and the whites immediately plotted to get that money. Local whites had been annoyed and frustrated that they could not get the Berry holdings, but now this was too much. Pop understood that this was the game that was played. Often blacks would let themselves be swindled because it was too dangerous to frustrate whites. Black people could be murdered with impunity. Between 1882 and 1922, according to a research project by the University of Missouri–Kansas City Law School, 4,433 black people were lynched, mostly in the South. The rate had somewhat slowed but was still staggering. In 1921 there were sixty-four lynchings, whereas in the 1890s there were more than one hundred every year. Not infrequently, lynchings involved not only hanging but burning, dismemberment, and other forms of torture. Huge, festive crowds would turn out to watch. Most of these lynchings were of men accused of murder or rape, usually unproven, but almost a quarter, according to a famous study by the Tuskegee Institute, were for vague reasons, including a perceived insult to white people, peeping in a window, attempting to register to vote, or testifying against a white man. This meant that if a black person had any kind of dispute with a white person, the white had only to stir up an angry crowd and have his adversary hanged. Most of the charges had nothing to support them but one or two unverified accusations from white people. A black man's word was never taken over any white man's. All of the studies show that whatever the charges, in many cases the real motivation was that the black man had gained some economic advantage, which was resented. As W. E. B. Du Bois put it, "The white South feared more than Negro dishonesty, ignorance and incompetency, Negro honesty, knowledge, and efficiency." Poor white people saw a black man with a check for $2,600 as a threat, unless they could somehow relieve him of that money.

One of Pop Gordy's brothers had already taken a train north to Detroit, and Bertha convinced Pop that it was time to follow him. The Gordys were a rare example of a black family moving north because they had made too much money.

Berry Gordy Jr.'s own description of his family arriving in Detroit demonstrates how much in common their story had with those of American immigrants:

Like so many other black people who migrated from the South in the twenties, Pop was filled with hope and dreams. He was thrilled to bring his family to this new world, leaving bigotry and hatred behind. There was a real competitive spirit among the people in Detroit, a determination that came from the need just to survive.

But the typical life of a black immigrant in Detroit, renting a home and working on an automobile assembly line, was not acceptable to Pop. He had to own his own home and run his own business. This was the path to success advocated by Booker T. Washington. He started by selling whatever he could — ice, Christmas trees, car parts, fruit. A careful research of 1920s Detroit led him to choose a Westside neighborhood of home-owning, hardworking, churchgoing black people, most of whom were also from the rural South.

On Thanksgiving Day 1929, a month after the stock market crash that launched the Great Depression, Berry Gordy Jr., the Gordys' seventh child, was born. A year and a half later, the Gordys had their eighth and last child. In these difficult times Pop lost their house, the family went on welfare, and fixed up a small shack in the same neighborhood. Eight children slept in three beds. Late at night, young Berry would watch his father fight large rats in the kitchen, crushing them under his feet.

The promised land, like all promised lands, was not all it was supposed to be.

Racism was everywhere in Detroit, from Hudson's, the leading downtown department store, owned by an automobile manufacturing family, which refused to have black sales personnel, to the Checker Cab company, which would not hire black drivers. Many downtown bars and restaurants would not serve black people. Even Henry Ford was a notorious racist, though he himself didn't think so, using his own weekly newspaper, *The Dearborn Independent,* to publicize his racist theories about blacks and Jews. Detroit was also home in the 1930s to the pro-Nazi National Workers League.

Yet years later, a wealthy success, Berry Gordy Jr. credited the "good fortune" of spending his first six years in Detroit's Westside with its family-oriented community. "It was the place that gave me a sense of right and wrong, a sense of safety in the family, a sense of love and kinship in the community, where being good was actually a good thing to be." Gordy said that up until the age of five, the only white person in the world he knew of was Santa Claus.

According to Gordy, the two things every home had, no matter how poor, were a radio and an upright piano. Gordy learned to play theirs by ear, copying tunes he heard on the radio, although he never learned to read music well.

With money he made from a job as an apprentice plasterer, which he eventually developed into his own plastering business, Pop started a small grocery store and named it after Booker T. Washington. They moved to the Eastside, where he bought a commercial building, and the family moved into the top two floors. Gordy said, "Coming to the Eastside was like moving from the country to the city." Suddenly Gordy was no longer in a quiet community of houses and churchgoers but in a world of prostitutes and gambling and nightclubs wailing the blues. But the Booker T. Washington Grocery Store was a place where people in the neighborhood could spend time socializing, talking about business opportunities — a commercial place but also a warm and welcoming place and the center for the large Gordy family.

Racial tensions grew during World War II, because while black migration continued, many of the wartime jobs were not open to them. About a quarter of the 185 defense-related factories in Detroit would not hire any blacks, and famously in 1943, when Packard, converted to a wartime defense plant, promoted three black workers to the aircraft assembly line, twenty-six thousand Packard plant workers walked off the job. Packard had had a policy of using blacks only for menial jobs.

In the summer of 1943 fighting broke out between whites, mostly Polish and Appalachians on the Westside, and blacks, mostly immigrants from the South, living on the Eastside. Much of the violence consisted of whites attacking blacks. It continued for days until six thousand Federal troops were called in. Of the thirty-four people killed in the incident, twenty-five were black, and, according to a subsequent investigation, seventeen of the black deaths had been caused by the police.

Yet the Gordys prospered in those years. While Pop pursued his business interests, including the Booker T. Washington Grocery Store, Bertha advanced her education and engaged in a variety of often socially minded businesses, such as the Friendship Mutual Insurance Company, which helped advance black enterprise in Detroit, and the Friends

Club, founded in 1959, to raise money for the NAACP and even more radical civil rights groups such as CORE in its organizing efforts in Mississippi.

The Gordys were role models, and not only for their children. In 1949 *Color* magazine ran an article with the headline "America's Most Amazing Family: The Famous Gordys of Detroit Have What It Takes." The article wrote of not only their business accomplishments but their various leisure activities, such as bowling and horseback riding and music. The children emulated their parents. George and Fuller worked in their father's plastering business, while Esther started a printing company.

But Berry wanted more. He wanted to be special. His earliest hero was Joe Louis, who when Gordy was seven years old, had knocked out James J. Braddock in the eighth round to become heavyweight champion of the world. At the time, the heavyweight champion was the most celebrated athlete in the world. Joe Louis was only the second black man to win that title, and the first to gain wide acceptance in the white world. His background was similar to the Gordys': born in Alabama, he grew up in Detroit — and he became a hero not only in Detroit, not only in the black world, but in the broader world of blacks and whites, and this made an enormous impression on young Berry. He described it in his autobiography as "a burning desire to be special, to win, to be somebody." Other childhood heroes were middleweight Sugar Ray Robinson and singer Nat King Cole. It is significant that these were all black men who had become popular in both the black and white world — crossover successes.

Gordy started with boxing. In his junior year of high school, impatient to make his mark, he dropped out of school to become a professional boxer. As a result, he never read or wrote well. He was a small, square man, burly for his weight classes — bantamweight and featherweight, which are below 130 pounds. As a boxer, he was fairly successful. The high point of his career was a Friday-night fight on November 21, 1948, days before his nineteenth birthday, when he appeared on a card with Joe Louis as the main event. They both won their bouts.

It is difficult to get attention and therefore big money in the smaller weight classes. Most people want to see heavyweights or middleweights. Gordy told this story about a hot August day in 1950, sitting in the gym, looking at two posters on pillars:

The top poster announced a Battle of the Bands between Stan Kenton and Duke Ellington for the same night. The one below was advertising a bout between two young fighters scheduled for the following Friday night. There it was again. Boxing versus music. This time it was visual.

I stared at both posters for some time, realizing fighters could fight once and maybe not fight again for three or four weeks, or months, or never. The bands were doing it every night, city after city, and not getting hurt. I then noticed the fighters were about twenty-three and looked fifty; the bandleaders about fifty and looked twenty-three.

The genius of Barry Gordy Jr. — and *genius* seems the correct word for it — was rooted in the fact that he understood the unique value of his hometown. These newly urbanized immigrants were redefining black culture, which, in musical terms, meant abandoning blues and developing R&B. Motown could not have been built anywhere but Detroit. It was based on what the city had to offer that had not yet been fully tapped. It could have been done in Chicago or New York or LA, but in those cities the music industry was already well organized.

Detroit was a city of raw talent. Talent could be found literally on street corners and schoolyards. Kids learned music in school, sang it on the street, and famously sang in black churches and local clubs that sponsored amateur nights. Even with all this, Detroit had not developed independent record companies for young black artists.

It was clear in Gordy's mind. To escape the ordinary world and be a special person there were only two possible routes, and music was clearly the better one. He wrote songs that he never sold, and dreamed of being his other hero, Nat King Cole, except that he had what he termed "a voice problem." He described his voice as sounding like a mixture of Cole, Billy Eckstine, and Donald Duck. He would try out his new songs on his siblings Fuller, Esther, and George, who would try to avoid the ceaseless performances by being very busy. Finally they produced Berry Gordy's first song, "Let Gordy Be Your Printer Too." The Gordys arranged for Berry to record it at a basement studio and air it on WJLB with Berry singing in an imitation Nat King Cole.

Then he was drafted. His Army stint in wartime Korea, partly served as a noncombatant, he described as "a total disruption to my focus and goals." He did, however, earn his high school diploma. In 1953, discharged from the Army, he returned to Detroit and his goals. In his parents' view, he was the one child who was not accomplishing anything, and Pop hoped that on his return he would settle into the family plastering business. Instead, he borrowed money from Pop and got an investment from his brother George, who partnered with him in a record store. The records were to be jazz, because jazz was the music Berry loved. It was to remain a major influence on his career. Like many young blacks of his generation, he was contemptuous of blues, the old-time back-country music. But he loved the new bebop jazz of the 1950s: Charlie Parker, Dizzy Gillespie, Miles Davis, and Erroll Garner. Gordy called jazz "the only pure art form."

It seems strange, given what later could plainly be seen as a commercial bent in the Gordys going back to Pops and the teachings of Booker T. Washington, that he would stake his business on something as noncommercial as jazz. But it had once been commercial, and Gordy had failed to recognize the large shift to R&B and rock 'n' roll that had occurred while he was in the Army.

Detroit was a jazz town, and Gordy spent

his evenings in clubs such as the Minor Key, Baker's Keyboard Lounge, the West Inn, and especially Club Twenty-one. In these clubs he would hear such greats as Elvin Jones, Charlie Parker, and John Coltrane.

But at his store, these records were not selling. In his autobiography, Gordy recalled, "People started coming in and asking for things like Fats Domino. Pretty soon I was asking, 'Who is this Fats Domino? What is this rhythm-and-blues stuff?' I listened and ordered a few records by these people and sold them."

But he didn't sell enough of them, because his capital was invested in jazz records that he couldn't sell, and soon the store was bankrupt. Gordy, his wings burned, resorted to what was always available in Detroit at the time. He worked on an assembly line at the Ford Motor Company's Wayne Assembly Plant, earning $86.40 a week as an upholstery trimmer on Lincoln-Mercury sedans. This was exactly what Gordy did not want to do with his life, but from his tedious work he picked up valuable ideas.

What is most telling about Gordy from his 1994 autobiography, *To Be Loved,* aside from the way he doesn't acknowledge a ghost writer, though he begins by confessing that he had never written a book before and hasn't even read that many, is the way every success and every failure along the way were seen as lessons from which something valuable could be derived for the future. "A smart man profits from his mistakes," his father had always told him.

Gordy was on the assembly line in 1955, and the cars that were made in Detroit in those years were admired around the world and are still remembered as a high point in the auto industry. Their engineering and bold panache made them products that gave worldwide prestige to the town called Motor City. Evidence of the central role of Detroit cars in American culture from the mid-1950s to the early 1960s is the fact that in 1963 Alfred P. Sloan Jr.'s account of running General Motors, *My Years with General Motors,* was a major *New York Times* best seller. The jacket refers to General Motors as "the largest industrial complex in the world." General Motor's innovation was to offer a variety of cars in different prices. They started in 1908 with Buick and Olds, and then brought in Oakland and Cadillac, named after the Frenchman who in 1701 built a fort that was the beginning of Detroit. They started manufacturing their own car parts and components — an idea that led to the upholstery section of an assembly line where Gordy worked. In 1916 they acquired the low-end Chevrolet, which was designed to compete with Ford.

In the 1930s GM embraced the idea of changing every car every year, a policy that other car companies adopted, so that, by the 1950s there was great excitement every year to see what the new cars would be like. New models took two years to develop, so the car companies were always working on the future. By 1955 the car industry was offering 272 models a year. Automatic transmissions, which made it easy for anyone to learn to drive, became standard equipment by the 1950s. The cars were ever larger, with little competition from small foreign models built for fuel efficiency. Detroit's cars were huge and imposing, with fins and other design flairs suggestive of space travel, with tremendously powerful engines that were capable of greater speeds than the still undeveloped highway system allowed. In 1955, the year Gordy worked on a different assembly line, Chevrolet produced the Bel Air, with a "small," newly designed eight-cylinder engine, the V8, a gas-slurper that produced 162 horsepower. But for an additional $59, a modified version was available with a bigger carburetor and a different manifold, an air cleaner, duo-exhausts, and a 180-horsepower engine. It has become one of the most collectible vintage cars.

In the 1920s the DuPont laboratories had discovered a chemical reaction that led to nitrocellulose lacquer. This led to a lacquer-based paint that held more pigment in suspension, which resulted in brighter colors, and to an extremely durable and bright paint called Duco. By the 1950s, all of the defects of Duco, such as poor adhesion to metal and slow application, had been worked out, and the painting was just another swift process on the assembly line. Throughout the 1950s GM worked with resin manufacturers, and in 1958 came out with an acrylic resin that allowed even bolder colors. The powerful, big-finned machines were turquoise and pink and sky blue and red and emerald green — often two colors, all accented with slashes of sparkling chrome. They were beautiful, and the durability of both the cars and the paint has been proven in Havana, Cuba. The Cuban moneyed class imported these cars, and after the Revolution the new government saw that they didn't leave with their owners. Even with replacement parts embargoed they have kept them running and beautiful for more than half a century.

The popular appeal, the variety of products, the rapid output of quality cars, the constant planning and adjustments for changing trends and popular taste, the efficiency of assembly lines, and the benefit of a quality-control board were all valuable lessons to Gordy.

How does an assembly-line worker keep his mind occupied while confronted with the tedium of a highly repetitious task? In the case of Berry Gordy, he made up songs — to the point where he decided that what he really wanted to do was be a songwriter. The idea had always been there. As a teenager he had won honorable mention in a talent show for his song "Berry's Boogie." His sisters Anna and Gwen were also interested in the music business, and once they decided to help their brother, they were an irresistible force. Attractive and savvy, they had many contacts in the music world through their cigarette and photography business at the Flame Show Bar.

The Flame was opened in 1950 by Morris Wasserman, an experienced Detroit club owner, a block east of Woodward Avenue on John R Street, known for its black clubs. Wasserman brought in Maurice King, a big band veteran, who played alto sax and wrote, arranged, and led. King, another immigrant from the Deep South, the Mississippi Delta, had spent most of the 1940s as music director of a national touring all-girl band, the International Sweethearts of Rhythm. It was the first girl band in which musicians were picked for their musicianship, not their looks or race. At a time when there were no mixed-race bands, except Benny Goodman's, King's Sweethearts were black, white, and Asian. Always a courtly gentleman, King never got romantically involved with his musicians.

Wasserman wanted to bring in national musicians, and commissioned King to build a big band to play with them. King's band made the Flame the premier club in Detroit for black musicians. Among the young talent he brought to his band was baritone sax player Thomas "Bean" Bowles, and trumpeter Johnny Trudell, both of whom, along with King himself, Gordy would one day hire for Motown.

The Flame had a stage built into the bar. Detroit local Della Reese performed there, and years later said that the Flame Show Bar "was named correctly because it was hot." So did Dinah Washington. Gordy recalled in his autobiography, "She'd walk the bar, shakin' her behind, working it from

end to end (both the bar and her behind)."
He also saw Sarah Vaughan and Billie
Holiday, about whom he wrote, "My fascination with her was total." At the Flame,
Gordy learned great respect for female
vocalists, something he would have in common with King.

Gordy's sisters were beautiful and glamor-
ous. The Flame was usually packed with
record producers, singers, all kinds of
people from the music industry, and the
men among them all wanted to chat with
the Gordy sisters, who made their way
through the club selling cigarettes and taking photographs, which were developed in a
back room by two of their brothers. And
they talked about their brother the songwriter.

They connected Berry with Jackie Wilson's handlers. Jackie Wilson, according to
Gordy, was "Mr. Excitement." Wearing
heavy makeup onstage and off, unbuttoned
shimmering shirts, diamond rings, and gold
chains, Wilson dazzled. Gordy said with a
sigh, "If only I could be Jackie, just for a
night."

Gordy began writing songs for Wilson. His
first hit for Wilson was "Reet Petite." It is
surprising that Berry Gordy, who would
become deeply connected to crossover com-

mercialism, got his first hit from a song in "bop talk." Bop talk was a coded language of jazz musicians in the 1940s that used rhyming phrases and sometimes African expressions. A "hip cat" comes from Wolof, the language of Senegal, in which a *hepicat* is someone whose eyes are open. Lionel Hampton's "Hey! Ba-Ba-Re-Bop," an R&B hit in 1946, was a huge influence on Jerry Lee Lewis in the 1950s. Bop talk had gone from 1940s black jazz into 1950s rock 'n' roll, especially with Elvis Presley. Little Richard's 1956 hit "Tutti Frutti," containing such lines as

Tutti frutti, oh Rudy
A whop bop-a-lu a whop bam boo

Or Clyde McPhatter and the Drifters' 1953 hit "Money Honey" and Larry Williams's 1957 "Bony Moronie," later more famously covered by John Lennon, are all examples of bop talk.

Bop talk was already an old-fashioned thing by the time of "Reet Petite" in 1957, and in fact the phrase was borrowed from Louis Jordan's 1947 "Reet Petite and Gone." Gordy's "Reet Petite" was coauthored by his sister Gwen and her boyfriend Billy Davis, who later did numerous hits for the Chess label. Wilson had recently left the Dominoes, and "Reet Petite" was his first hit as a solo performer. It made it to number 62 on the *Billboard* 100 chart. It even made it to number 6 on the UK singles chart.

Berry Gordy was now a hit songwriter for the biggest black entertainer in Detroit. He continued to write songs with Gwen and Davis, and they produced several other hits for Jackie Wilson, including "To Be Loved" and "Lonely Teardrops." But royalties were not huge and he found himself in a similar position to the one he had been in as a boxer, winning fights but getting neither rich nor famous.

In 1957 an act called the Matadors was auditioning for Jackie Wilson's managers, who were not impressed. But when the young singing group was sent away, Gordy followed them outside. He liked the fact that they did original material, most of it written by their lead singer, William "Smokey" Robinson. He offered to manage them, renamed them the Miracles, and worked on Robinson's song-writing. Gordy impressed on him that "the hook," the phrase by which people would remember the song, must never be buried. It must be repeated over and over, what Frank Sinatra had called "imbecilic reiteration." It became a credo of Motown. Recently Mickey Stevenson, one of the key creative figures of Motown and a coauthor of "Dancing in the Street," was asked in an interview in Los Angeles, where he now lives, what the key was to a good song. Without hesitation he replied, "A good hook — the part that grabs you."

Together Gordy and Smokey Robinson sold several successful songs, for which Gordy earned about three dollars. It was increasingly clear to him that he had to produce his own records.

In the spring of 1958, a singer named Raynoma Mayberry Liles won a talent show at the 20 Grand, one of the premier clubs of downtown Detroit. It had a bowling alley, a separate jazz club, and a number of lounges, of which the most famous was the Driftwood Lounge, which got top acts from around the country. There was also an amateur night and a large dance floor. There was even a 20 Grand Motel next door under different ownership where out-of-town artists could stay.

Raynoma was advised to see Gordy, who was earning a reputation for developing young talent. Gordy was more impressed with her songwriting than her singing; the two formed a company. Soon Gordy divorced his first wife, Thelma Coleman, who had also advanced his career and with whom he had three children, and married Raynoma, the second of the numerous marriages and liaisons with which he would produce eight children.

The Rayber Music Company, the name coming from Raynoma and Berry, was established with an $800 loan from the Gordy family to produce their first record. The money came from a fund to which each family member contributed two dollars every week. The primary purpose was to buy real estate. Raynoma ended up in charge of a publishing division that he called "Jobete" from the names of his first three children: Hazel Joy, Berry IV, and Terry James. Gordy always loved to make up acronymic names.

Rayber produced "Come to Me," which Gordy cowrote with the performer Marv Johnson, a local Detroit kid who had cut two records without great success. But Gordy, who always had a remarkable eye for raw talent, saw a future for this singer. Even though they did not have funding for distribution and sold it to United Artists for $3,000, this was really the first Motown record. It reached number 30 on the *Billboard* Hot 100 chart.

Tellingly, Gordy named his first label Tamla. His intentions were clear. Though he was recording black R&B music from Detroit street talent, he named his label after "Tammy," a 1957 saccharine hit ballad by Debbie Reynolds. That was about as white as music gets. He wanted to call the label "Tammy" to cash in on the popularity of the Reynolds recording, but that name had already been registered.

The home of the Tamla label was a typical Detroit building — a two-family house on Gladstone Street on the Westside. A closet was converted into a sound booth, and the bathroom made an effective echo chamber.

This first recording already had some of the fundamentals of what would become "the Motown sound." To begin with, he used Thomas "Bean" Bowles for the session and would continue using him. One of the backup singers, Brian Holland, would later join his brother Eddie and Lamont Dozier to make one of the most important songwriting teams of the 1960s, penning hit after hit for Martha and the Vandellas and for the Supremes.

But Gordy never lost his admiration of jazz, and scoured Detroit jazz clubs for musicians. One of his first acquisitions became central to that sound — James Jamerson, who was to become one of the most influential bass players in R&B history.

He was from Edisto Island, one of South Carolina's Sea Islands famous for slave plantations that produced Sea Island cotton. The island was so isolated that the African American population there spoke their own African-English hybrid language, Gullah. When he was a teenager, his family moved to Detroit, and he learned to play bass at Northwestern High School, which, like most Detroit schools at the time, had a solid music program that produced many future musicians. They were competitive and spurred one another on. Some of Jamerson's classmates also had successful careers, such as Richard "Popcorn" Wylie, who later wrote hit songs for the Platters, and Clifford Mack, a future drummer with Ramsey Lewis. Jamerson began performing in local jazz clubs while still in high school. Underaged, he had to get a special permit from the Detroit police to perform in clubs where alcohol was served. Even after he started playing for Gordy, he continued to play jazz in the clubs at night, as did most of Motown's musicians.

Jamerson started at Tamla with the same German upright double bass he had played in high school. But around 1962 he switched to an electric bass — a 1962 Fender Precision. This instrument, first available in 1951, was part of the new electric sound of rock 'n' roll. Partly because of Jamerson, it became the bass of R&B. Paul Riser, the arranger for "Dancing in the Street" and many other Motown hits, said, "Why would you use an upright bass on an R&B song? You couldn't get the feel of it."

Jamerson played upright on many of the early Motown hits, including those of Martha and the Vandellas, such as "Heat Wave." Before Jamerson, there was not a great deal of invention to the bass line in R&B songs — a simple two-beat pattern. What made Jamerson unique and influential was the importance he gave the bass line. It was often so melodic that it seemed to be a secondary theme to the song. The jazz influence was unmistakable. He liked to swing eighth notes, shave a little off so that they seemed to hop into the quarter note next to them. He was very syncopated — that is, he shifted accents off of what would logically have been the strong notes — and his playing had an improvisational feel. Riser said, "Jamerson did mostly his own bass line. I would have a lot of parts written out but the rhythm instruments were left to do things for themselves." Jamerson said of himself and the rhythm section, "We didn't need sheet music. We could feel the groove together."

Other bass players often cite Jamerson as their primary influence, including Bernard Odum, who played for James Brown; the Band's Rick Danko; Led Zeppelin's John Paul Jones; and Paul McCartney. Stevie Wonder, blind from childhood, said, "Jamerson's bass playing made a certain fabric of my life visual." Marion Hayden, who plays upright bass in jazz clubs around Detroit today, said that in her classes, she teaches Jamerson. "Although I never heard him play and although I am a jazz player, I study his bass lines, even on a Fender."

The original band also included baritone saxophonist Thomas Bowles, from King's band at the Flame. Guitarists Eddie Willis and Joe Messina, who played on this first record, became mainstays of the Motown band for many years. Messina played a top backbeat and Willis a bottom. Later Robert White was added for the bottom, and Willis played a middle with soft riffs. Willis was born in Mississippi. He started out at age nine as a blues player. Later he got interested in rock 'n' roll. Living back in Mississippi, he said in a recent interview, "Everything happened when I got to Detroit."

The band labeled the guitar section the Oreo cookie, because Messina was the rare white player. He was from an Eastside Detroit Italian neighborhood. His father, who could not read music, played guitar at Italian weddings. Messina, born in 1928, and one of the older Motown artists, had played with the ABC studio band in the late 1950s with such notable jazz players as Charlie Parker and Stan Getz. He also played with Miles Davis. Gordy heard him in clubs in Detroit and hired him for his first recording. An inventive musician, Messina created his own modified Fender with six small bridges — an instrument later produced in Japan and sold as "the Messina Funk Machine." Recalling his years at Motown from his suburban home north of Detroit, Messina said, "Sometimes a track could take nine hours to make. But on the way home I listened to jazz on the radio."

Calling themselves the Funk Brothers, they seemed to love playing together. At night, if the session was over, they would go to the Chit Chat Lounge, a small club on Twelfth Street, a rapidly deteriorating black neighborhood. There, in the heart of the ghetto, they would improvise jazz, jamming with Smokey Robinson or whoever was free, playing extraordinary music for anyone willing to go to Twelfth Street in the middle of the night. According to Jack Ashford, whose tambourine smashes may be heard throughout the "Dancing in the Street" track, many improvised ideas in the Motown sessions were never written but came from the session the night before at the Chit Chat Lounge. Ashford said that they would be handed music for a session and start playing and someone would recall something he had done the night before at the Chit Chat and, as Ashford put it, "Bam!! It would fit like a glove and sound like the parts were written out on the charts."

Six months after settling into the new Tamla studio, Gordy concluded that they needed a better space, and his new wife, Raynoma, found another house at 2648 West Grand Boulevard. This house also was far from an ideal studio. Joe Messina remembered originally recording in the garage, "with a dirt floor and old carpeting on the walls." In his autobiography Gordy recalled the two-story house as "always under construction."

One of the first improvements was "studio A," a small room with a wooden floor where hit after hit was recorded. Today the floor in the control room still bears the splintered hole worn through by foot tapping. They cut a hole in the wall of a bathroom to use as an echo chamber. "Don't flush while they're recording," Martha Reeves recalled was a constant reminder. Four microphones hung from the ceiling. They had only four tracks, which meant limited mixing possibilities and a great deal of overdubbing from separate recording sessions. The sound was constantly being improvised. Although Ivy Jo Hunter refutes the often-repeated legend that he beat a crowbar in "Dancing in the Street," they did do things like that. Holland, Dozier, and Holland in particular invented percussion. They placed two-by-fours in studio A and covered them with plywood, and would recruit the first four people they found with leather-sole shoes — they did not want rubber soles — to stomp rhythmically during a recording session. Reeves remembers that during the track session for her hit "Nowhere to Run," a Holland-Dozier-Holland song, one of the Holland brothers beat a chain with a hammer, and by the end of the session his hand was bleeding.

Gordy placed a hand-painted sign, blue on white, that read "Hitsville U.S.A." on the front of the building. "There was no way our purpose was vague," Gordy said. He always maintained that confidence was a key to success, which interestingly was what General Motors' Alfred Sloan always said as well. Gordy made it clear that he expected hits. He encouraged competition. The studio also had a family atmosphere; it was a place where people met and talked, like in the Gordy family's grocery store. But there were also intense expectations.

Gordy and his lieutenants would go to amateur nights in local clubs and find talent to bring to Hitsville. Amateur night at the Warfield Theater on Saturdays was one of their scouting grounds. The Warfield, only about a dozen blocks from Hitsville, was a small 1914 theater later redone with a flashy Art Deco façade, seating fewer than four hundred people. Later torn down to build I-94, it was never one of Detroit's premier halls or clubs, but Gordy found undiscovered talent there. Ivy Jo Hunter said, "That was the genius of Berry Gordy. He invested in raw talent. It was the only place you could learn as you earned from your craft."

The studio was always open. Martha Reeves recalled, "We worked without a time clock. The studio was open twenty-four hours. You could schedule a two a.m. session."

Hunter added that the two a.m. sessions

were "when you got the big drinkers." But Reeves reminded him that they drank outside in their cars because Gordy did not allow drinking in the studio. A few musicians, chiefly Jamerson and drummer Bennie Benjamin, had serious alcohol problems. But a two a.m. session was also a way of getting string players from the Detroit Symphony, who were recorded in a small trapezoidal room.

Gordy would grab talent anywhere in his city that he could find it. Unlike today, it was rare in those days for classical musicians to play on popular recordings. They grudgingly wore "I Like Ludwig" buttons. But Gordy wanted their abilities, even though the communication was often a struggle. The classical musicians would tell Gordy that what he wanted could not be done because it was against the fundamental rules of music. Gordy would tell them, "I don't care about the rules because I don't know what they are."

One of the primary talent hunters was William "Mickey" Stevenson, a handsome man with magnetic charm and a wide range of talents who joined the Motown organization in 1960 as the A&R director. This was an industry term standing for "Artists and Repertory" — the person responsible for acquiring both songs and singers and deciding which songs were for which artists.

There was a barbershop on Twelfth Street called Rene Mullins House of Style. Stevenson used to get his hair cut there, and so did Gordy. Mullins packed in more customers than he could cut. So he introduced them to one another and kept them busy socializing until he could get to them. One day Stevenson started talking about how much he liked Jackie Wilson's songs. Mickey admired the singer's ability to reach white audiences. Mullins said that he should meet the man who wrote his songs, and thrilled Mickey by taking him to a man waiting in a corner — Berry Gordy Jr.

The two men got along well and Gordy said he was starting a new company, and so Mickey went to Hitsville U.S.A. for an audition. Gordy listened to him sing his original songs and told him that he liked the songs. Mickey thought he was about to get an offer when Gordy added, "Your voice is shit."

At the time Hitsville U.S.A. was not the great Motown but a start-up studio that might or might not succeed. Mickey was not about to be insulted, and started to leave. "I was getting out of here. I don't need this," Mickey remembered, when Gordy then told him that he was impressed by how much Mickey knew and offered him the A&R job. Mickey's response as he remembered it was "A&R? What the fuck is that?"

This was another thing they had in common. In Gordy's autobiography, he confessed that he wasn't sure what the title meant either. But he knew that he was supposed to have one, and he was certain that this was the person he wanted to comb the Detroit streets and bring him talent. He liked the flashy way Mickey dressed and the hip way that he talked. "Mickey was street," Gordy later said. "Much more street than I was. I could see he was definitely an Eastside graduate, while I was still sort of that Westside boy at heart." There was that critical divide in black Detroit between the homey Westside and the faster, more hip Eastside. Somewhere around Woodward Avenue, the easy rural southern ways seemed to be traded for those of the harder, faster northern city. This, Gordy thought, was the man to work Detroit and find its raw talent.

Actually Stevenson grew up on the Westside, two blocks from the Eastside, where I-75 now is, in a neighborhood some fifteen blocks away from Hitsville U.S.A. He was born in the South, and his family had migrated from Alabama to Detroit by way of Chicago. His father was a tap dancer and his mother a singer named Kitty Brown Gale Stevenson. Kitty also wrote songs. She thought of herself as a blues singer but sang with a sixteen-piece orchestra, Todd Rise and His Orchestra. They played at the Detroit clubs with headliners such as Dinah Washington.

Like many other Detroit teenagers, Mickey sang in a high school group, a quartet called the Meadowlarks, who sang songs by the Ravens. It was fashionable at the time to name groups after birds because birds like to sing. He went on tour with the great vibe player Lionel Hampton and suddenly, instead of singing on Detroit streets, he was in a top professional group. "I saw great artists and great shows, great theatrical shows. Great lighting . . . I saw things that coming from Detroit and the Warfield Theater there was no comparison," Mickey recalled while munching on ribs at his R&B and soul food club in Los Angeles, where "Dancing in the Street" chimed out as his cell phone's ringtone.

On tour with Hampton, Mickey was making money, but he sent most of it home because he could get more. "We thought the tour was going to go on forever," he said. Then the tour ended and he went home with no money. Mickey called this "one of the basic lessons of life: the tour does not go on forever." It was a lesson that most of the artists he recruited at Motown would have to learn for themselves.

Mickey went on to sing with groups in New York and Los Angeles. All the while he was writing songs, so that by the time he went to Berry Gordy he was calling himself a singer-songwriter. He had many ideas similar to those of Gordy. He had a preference for jazz musicians over blues because he thought that these were the people who really understood music. He also thought that, given what was going on in politics, society, and music, the time was right for a strong black-owned studio that produced black music aimed at white audiences. But he failed to get the financial backing for such a company. He had established himself in Detroit living over Denny's Show Bar in the downtown club area. He liked living over a club:

I could bang on my piano and no one could bother me cause they got a band downstairs. You know to a normal person you'd go insane. But for me it was great. I could hear the bands downstairs and I could play as loud as I wanted to upstairs. So the musicians — I knew quite a few of them and they would say to me, "I want to borrow some money," and I'd say, "I just saw you work on the weekend and you're broke. You got a problem."

"No, man, I didn't get paid. . . ."

"I'll go get your money for you. You give me 15 percent." . . . I'd go to the club owner and say, "Pay the guy. . . . I'll see to it that they are there on time. They play, you give me 15 percent." So I made a deal on both ends, so now different musicians come to me. I end up working with the best in the city. These were guys who could really play. But they weren't readers, but they were playing R&B and rock 'n' roll.

Gordy was right. Mickey was streetwise and he knew the music world. He also knew how to find talent. He explained that he was always looking for what he called "the gift. The ability to sing or write, whatever it was, and if it was a one-time thing, could they repeat it. Give you something else. You strike me as a talented writer and I hear your song, I'd say, 'Okay, do something else.' "

Another key element to the building of both

Motown and "Dancing in the Street" was a smooth-voiced young man from Washington, DC, who looked sculpted as a black Adonis, named Marvin Gaye. The original name was Gay, but Marvin added an *e,* partly from a fear of being thought homosexual and partly to distance himself from a volatile relationship with his preacher father named Gay, a violent and sexually ambiguous man who secretly dressed in women's clothes.

Marvin grew up in segregated Washington, DC, a fact of life that filled him with anger from an early age. This was the city in which the great contralto Marian Anderson, a child prodigy who came out of the black Baptist church, was refused a concert booking at the most prominent concert hall, Constitution Hall, because the theater, owned by the Daughters of the American Revolution, not only had segregated seating but would not allow a black artist to appear.

First Lady Eleanor Roosevelt resigned from the DAR in protest, and the NAACP pressured Secretary of the Interior Harold Ickes to arrange an open-air concert for Anderson on Easter Sunday 1939 on the steps in front of the Lincoln Memorial. The concert, which drew seventy-five thousand people and was listened to on the radio by millions, established those marble steps as a venue of black protest. The concert took place a week after Marvin Gaye was born, and he grew up hearing the story repeatedly from his father.

As a child Marvin felt a connection to Marian Anderson. He believed that he was "destined to be a singer," a conviction that he always claimed had come to him through dreams. He had other idols such as gospel star Mahalia Jackson. But as he grew to adolescence, he developed a different idol. Years later he told his friend and later biographer David Ritz:

My dream was to become Frank Sinatra, I loved his phrasing, especially when he was very young and pure. He grew up into a fabulous jazz singer and I used to fantasize about having a lifestyle like his — carrying on in Hollywood and becoming a movie star. Every woman in America wanted to go to bed with Frank Sinatra. He was the king I longed to be. My greatest dream was satisfying as many women as Sinatra. He was the heavyweight champ, the absolute.

In 1959 at the age of nineteen, Marvin

went to Chicago to become the newest member of a group called Harvey and the Moonglows. Harvey was Harvey Fuqua, a savvy musician, eleven years older than Marvin, who had sung backup for Bo Diddley and had coauthored a successful song, "Sincerely," with Alan Freed. Fuqua became Marvin's mentor.

The Moonglows recorded only a few songs with Marvin, including singing backup for Chuck Berry. Only once did Marvin sing a lead, on "Mama Loochie," which was written by Gaye and Fuqua.

The Moonglows were a victim of that decline of R&B and rock 'n' roll in 1959 and 1960, when America seemed to be waiting for the new sound. The group disintegrated and Gaye and Fuqua drifted from Chicago to Detroit, looking for a future. Gaye was still hoping Fuqua could lead him on a path to black Sinatradom.

Gaye and Gordy met at a Hitsville Christmas party in December 1960. Gordy, laughing in the sound booth with Mickey Stevenson and Smokey Robinson, just wanted to continue with his Christmas party, which was going on throughout the little Hitsville house, when his sister Gwen started to drag him away to hear this new talent that he just had to hear. "My sisters were always promoting somebody," Gordy recalled. Gwen was as always very insistent. She took him looking for her latest find, Marvin Gaye, a thin and handsome young man who they found slouched on a piano bench playing a jazzy tune.

"Berry Gordy, how you doin', man?" said Gaye, without looking up from the keyboard.

Gordy's first impression? "He was cool. Real cool." Which is funny, because Gaye's first impression of Gordy was "the coolest dude I'd ever met." They instantly liked each other. Gordy asked Gaye to sing, and he loved what he heard, later describing his voice as "pure, mellow, soulful, and honest."

Gaye thought the ex-fighter had "a short man's complex," and recognized his tough and competitive nature, and even as he moved to the Motown inner circle, he predicted that they were "destined to clash." But he saw Gordy as a man who knew how to seduce "beautiful world-class women" and how to make world-class money, which were two of Gaye's central interests.

Motown from the outset was a Gordy family business, just like the grocery store, the plastering company, and the printing business. The four Gordy sisters, Esther, the oldest and most accomplished, Loucye, who died in 1965, and Gwen and Anna, the intriguing women who moved through Detroit like stars, were all strong players in the new company. Esther, the vice president in charge of management, was the second most powerful figure in the company. By 1966, according to a *New York Times Sunday Magazine* article, ten members of the Gordy family were on the Motown staff.

Fuqua, who had guided the shy and impressionable Gaye, had a plan. Gwen, who had dragged Berry to meet Marvin, was to be his wife. She had recently broken off with Billy Davis. At the same time, Harvey would marry Anna. Such things rarely go according to plan, but incredibly the plan still more or less worked. Anna, thirty-seven, seemed enthralled by the twenty-year-old Marvin Gaye. They had their wedding reception at the 20 Grand. Fuqua adjusted and married Gwen instead.

Was this a cynical career move by young Gaye? He told David Ritz, "From a professional point of view, I have to say — and I hope this doesn't sound too cold — that I knew just what I was doing. Marrying a queen might not make me a king, but at least I'd have a shot at being a prince."

Anna saw her young husband as a tremendous talent and worked hard on developing him. She was his mentor, teacher, and guide. It was not surprising that Gaye would have such a marriage, coming from an abusive and violent father but a mother to whom he was devoted. As a child he used to have a fantasy about robbing banks so that he could support his mother. He did have a lifelong relationship, often violent, with prostitutes, and it is not known if that continued during his marriage. But as Marvin became the kind of crooning sex symbol he dreamed of being, he shunned the young women who chased him and was devoted to his wife, who in turn, was devoted to him. His marriage, his tie to the Gordy family, and to the broader Motown family, probably provided the warmest, most secure nest he ever knew.

Meanwhile, Harvey Fuqua, married to Gwen, who was herself always promoting someone or pushing some group, became head of promotion for Motown. It was all in keeping with the way the Gordys ran Motown, an incestuous little company built on marriages, romances, and affairs. Gordy was always marrying or having affairs with the talent. His sister Loucye married the saxophone player Ron Wakefield. Their oldest brother Fuller's daughter Iris married producer and songwriter Johnny Bristol. Mary Wells, while still a teenager, married another teenager, singer Herman Griffin. Mickey Stevenson married Kim Weston. Smokey Robinson married Claudette Rogers, the lone female singer in his group, the Miracles. Her cousin Bobby Rogers, who also sang with the Miracles, married Wanda Young of the Marvelettes. Georgeanna Tillman of the Marvelettes married Billy Gordon of the Contours. Berry Gordy would even chastise his young artists for dating outside of the company, telling them that there were many good choices within the company and no need to look outside.

Originally Anna and Gwen had their own label, "Anna." Sometimes when the sisters tried to interest Berry in new talent he would say, as he did to Gwen at the Christmas party, when she dragged him to Marvin Gaye, "Why don't you put him on your label?" But they kept pushing talent toward their brother, and eventually it was all the same company. Hitsville U.S.A.'s first breakthrough record was produced on the Anna label. The song "Money," written by Berry Gordy, was a song about the obsession with money. Chroniclers of Motown have made much about how this early song was about money. It seemed to be a presentation of Gordy's values. Gordy always denied this, saying the song was supposed to be funny.

But Berry Gordy is not to be confused with Harold Battiste, starting up a black company to help black artists. Battiste, after all, went broke and Gordy was determined to become rich. One of the advantages of picking up raw talent was that you could sign them to any kind of contract you wanted and did not have to pay them well. They were to become famous and Gordy was to become rich.

Motown emerged at a time of transition in both music and the country. Fifties rock 'n' roll had died, and it was an open question what was going to take its place. The goal of Motown was clear in the logo they printed on their record jackets: The Sound of Young America. It was no longer about black or white. The lucrative market was teenagers, and it was biracial. To Gordy crossover was something far more complicated than cleaning up black songs so that they would be acceptable to whites. He saw that if you made the right kind of black music and avoided the controversies of a controversial age, you could have all teenagers as your market, and this could be the most lucrative music market the world had ever seen.

Bo Diddley once commented, "You cannot say what people are going to like or not going to like. You have to stick it out there and find out. If they taste it and they like the way it tastes, you can bet they'll eat some of it."

Berry Gordy's approach was exactly the opposite. He believed that he could identify the exact sound and theme that teenagers wanted. The trick was to invent a sound that seemed new. In an age of change, new is a key to success. Gordy was looking for the perfect crossover music that fused the musicality of jazz and the hard-beat blues of R&B, and bent it to the softness of white balladeers. Jon Landau, in his groundbreaking article on Motown in *Crawdaddy* magazine in 1967, called it "A Whiter Shade of Black," which was both an apt description and a parody on the new, somewhat incomprehensible hit "A Whiter Shade of Pale" by a British band with an equally incomprehensible name, Procol Harum.

Change was the big idea of the 1960s. The election of John Kennedy was change. As historian and confidant Theodore White wrote in 1964 about Kennedy when he first came to office, "His scholars could describe quite clearly what he instinctively sensed: that the pace of change in America was accelerating — industry changing, habits changing, technologies changing." Even the Catholic Church recognized the yearning for change, and in 1964, that great season of change, ordered priests to turn around and face the worshippers instead of the altar and speak the old Latin Mass in English.

Everyone had the feeling, expressed by Bob Dylan in his third album, released only months before "Dancing in the Street," that "the times they are a-changin'." But ironically Dylan's song was written in a very old-fashioned folk ballad style. Berry Gordy understood that in this climate the music would have to change, too, and he would have to introduce "a brand new beat," a new sound. He was in search of the Motown sound. And it had to be a sound that would work well on small transistor radios and car radios, *their* radios.

He had learned a great deal from the car industry. He learned how to mass-produce, putting out new hit records every week from a pool of in-house talent:

. . . my own dream for a hit factory was quickly taking form, a concept that had been shaped by principles I learned on the Lincoln-Mercury assembly line. At the plant, the cars started out as just a frame, pulled along on conveyor belts until off the line. I wanted the same concept for my company, only with artists and songs and records. I wanted a place where a kid off the street could walk in one door an unknown and come out another a recording artist — a star.

Gordy even borrowed the phrase *quality control* from the car industry for a board that reviewed every recording to make sure that it was flawless — or flawlessly in line with Gordy's ideas. Nothing was to be left to chance. Another idea from the car industry: You were not just offered a General Motors; you could choose between a Chevy, a Buick, or a Cadillac. Hitsville U.S.A. offered a variety of labels. The labels gave the illusion of choice, so that the public and the radio stations did not feel that they were getting all their music from one company — Tamla, Miracle, which became Mel-o-dy, VIP, Gordy, Motown, and several others. Detroit had long been called Motor City, but the phrase "Motown" was Gordy's invention.

Like the auto manufacturers that had their own companies to make ball bearings, axles, and paint, Gordy established a network of ancillary companies. The Motown Record Company produced records. Hitsville U.S.A. owned the studios. Jobete Music was the true cash cow, a publishing company that controlled rights to the songs. International Talent Management Inc. (ITMI), the in-house management company, supposedly represented the artists but actually signed them to contracts that kept them under the control of the larger company.

Motown was built on training raw talent. A bare frame of a street singer could go through the Motown plant and come out a Cadillac of a performer. Young hopefuls knew the company could do this for them and that they probably could not do it without the company.

The backbone of Detroit's native music talent was the public school system. The black population of Detroit insisted on extensive music education in the schools so that any Detroit graduate with an interest in music graduated reading music and with a basic knowledge of music theory. Starting in the 1940s and even earlier, Detroit produced important musicians such as the Jones brothers — Thad, Elvin, and Hank — and Ron Carter and Tommy Flanagan in the jazz world. And as Gordy mentioned in his autobiography, kids in Detroit grew up with upright pianos in their homes. Martha and the Vandellas, the Supremes, and Wilson Pickett all got their starts harmonizing in the school yards, lots, and alleys of Detroit.

The Reverend C. L. Franklin's New Bethel Baptist Church was an important center for gospel, nurturing not only the reverend's daughter Aretha but visiting stars such as Sam Cooke. Franklin also drew the Reverend James Cleveland as choir director. A great gospel performer in his own right, sometimes called "the King of Gospel," Cleveland had a huge influence on Aretha Franklin and other locals. He was one of the innovators who had brought jazz and pop into gospel solos and choirs and turned church music into popular music.

In 1960, in Detroit, there were no important record companies. Successful local artists such as Della Reese and Jackie Wilson went to other cities to cut records. But as Motown's reputation grew, it became a magnet for Detroit's black immigrants and their children.

Success for a black company meant selling not just to the black 10 percent of the market but to the white 90 percent. By now, as Mickey Stevenson pointed out, the idea of crossover was not so much making songs that appealed to white people — they had already done that — but songs that appealed to white radio programs. Part of that was to create a groundswell among young people. Stevenson said:

> I've had people . . . say that when they were growing up and wanted to hear Motown music they were not allowed to hear it in their homes. But someone would tell them about it and at night they would pull the cover over their heads and listen to the Tempts or the Four Tops. . . . If something starts taking off underground, if it's hot you can't stop it.

The white radio stations had to be courted carefully and a largely white promotion and sales force at Motown was masterful and without a whiff of payola at the height of the scandal. Cousin Brucie said, "Gordy was a tremendous businessman, and he was surrounded by tremendous businessmen."

Though Motown was having great successes with male groups, Gordy had a particular interest in recruiting young women, because he believed that this Motown sound, this ultimate crossover music, would be best with female voices. White people did not find black women threatening, as they sometimes did find black men. All-female acts were in no way a break with tradition, since many stars of the blues were women, and they had a strong presence in gospel and in jazz singing. There were the all-girl bands such as Maurice King's, and Phil Spector and other R&B producers were having great success with girl groups. Motown, to a large extent, was built on recruiting and developing teenage Detroit girls who became the young women in evening gowns known as "the Motown divas."

Motown's first female star was Mary Wells, a local girl whose single mother supported her with housecleaning work. Mary, who suffered debilitating childhood illnesses, sometimes helped her mother clean. A serious science student, she graduated from that legendary factory for athletes and musicians, Northwestern High School, at the age of seventeen, but her dreams of being a scientist were deferred by the growing legend of Berry Gordy, Tamla Records, and Jackie Wilson.

Wells found Gordy at the 20 Grand Club and tried to sell him a song she had written for Jackie Wilson. Gordy asked her to sing the song, and then recorded her, when she was still age seventeen. According to legend, he had her do more than twenty takes. Her song, "Bye Bye Baby," made it to number 8 on the R&B chart and in 1961 reached number 45 on the white pop chart. This was what Gordy was looking for.

That same year, Wells, now eighteen, became the first Motown female to make the Top 40 chart with "I Don't Want to Take a Chance," a song written by Gordy and Mickey Stevenson, which rose to number 33.

The next female discovery was Kim Weston, who came from an infamous black ghetto by the Detroit River known as Black Bottom, which she still says "has the best spirit in Detroit." She attended Miller High School, which produced Della Reese and jazz great Milt Jackson. There she attended girls' voice class, instructed by George Shirley, the first black to sing tenor leads at the Metropolitan Opera. At Shirley's classes she met fellow student Martha Reeves.

Singing in a local church, she was invited to make a demo recording, which found its way into the hands of then singer, later Motown songwriter, Eddie Holland, who brought it to the attention of Mickey Stevenson, who signed her at age nineteen and later married her. Mickey Stevenson wrote her first hit, "Love Me All the Way," which peaked at number 24 on the R&B chart and also made it to 88 on the pop chart.

Martha Reeves's parents lived in rural Alabama. Her father played guitar and her mother sang, and that was how they courted. They married at the age of fifteen and were sharecroppers, able to live in the shack they called home only as long as they delivered the required amount of harvested crops.

They left and the father, Elijah, or E.J., worked various part-time agricultural jobs. When Martha, their first daughter and third child, was born, they were living in a two-family house in Eufaula, a cotton-trading town of about six thousand near the Georgia border. Jobs were scarce, and a cousin who had moved to Detroit sent word that there were good jobs to be found there. The Reeveses moved north when Martha was not quite a year old.

The extended Reeves family all lived in a three-bedroom house — if you counted closets with beds — on Illinois Street on the Eastside. From a very early age, Martha's parents took pride in her singing. At the age of three Martha and two brothers won chocolate-covered cherries in a singing contest. As early as the third grade Martha was getting the solo parts in school productions and was thrilled by her ability to please people with her singing. In high school she distinguished herself in the school choir, and in her senior year she sang the soprano solo in a performance of Handel's *Messiah* to an audience of four thousand at Ford Auditorium.

Martha recalled her high school days, unconsciously quoting from "Dancing in the Street," which was something that occurred in her speech from time to time. She said, "There was music everywhere. Amateur clubs, parks, street corners. They taught how to read music in the public schools and gave you instruments to take home and practice on and taught how to sing and had choirs that performed. We jammed on street corners."

The high school kids loved to harmonize and practiced it on the street and in parks and lots. Some groups earned reputations. There was a well-known group called the Street Corner Gang, which really started on a street corner. A lot of groups formed around the city. Martha and her friends sang after school in a park across from the high school. They called themselves the Fascinations. Another group was called the

Del-Phis. They were originally five girls. Then one left and was replaced by a man. The man left, and so did two other girls. Then it was down to Rosalind Ashford, Annette Beard, and Gloria Jean Williamson. Gloria invited Martha to join the group. This was fun for high school but did not earn a living for any of them when they graduated. Martha and the Del-Phis went their own ways.

The Reeves family by now had their own Eastside house. E.J. had worked in a Packard factory and then landed a solid job with the city waterworks. When Martha graduated from high school, she took a job with a local dry cleaner, City Wide Cleaners, which had six locations around Detroit, all of which she worked at as a substitute clerk, filling in for the days off of the regular clerks.

In 1961, now twenty years old, Martha entered a talent contest. The prize she won was an appearance for three nights at the 20 Grand during the 5:00 to 8:00 happy hour. She was well aware that careers had been made at the 20 Grand. And, adding to her excitement, for three nights she had her own private dressing room.

On her last night, Mickey Stevenson, whom Reeves described as the "knight in shining armor" of her career, came to the club. He would go to such amateur happy hours looking for young talent.

Martha was a bit depressed that night, thinking of going back to the dry cleaner, standing in the light with a friend's ID because she was underage. Mickey heard her sing a two-song set with no R&B — Bart Howard's 1954 pop standard "Fly Me to the Moon" and "Gin House Blues," a blues classic first sung by Bessie Smith. When she finished the set, she was heading back to the dressing room, her final treat before the dry cleaner, when a tall, suave stranger held out his hand to help her down the backstage steps and said, "Your name is Martha. Martha what?"

She said, "La Vaille," which was how she had been billing herself — Martha La Vaille. He handed her a card and told her to come see him. The card said "William Stevenson, A&R director, Hitsville U.S.A., 2648 West Grand Boulevard."

She had never heard of Hitsville or of Motown. In 1961, not many people had. She actually knew a lot of their records from Detroit radio. Martha listened to R&B on WCHB, one of the first black-owned stations in the country. But she also listened to CKLW, a Detroit Top 40 station, and the ABC affiliate WXYZ. All three were abuzz with Motown songs, and Martha had become a fan of Mary Wells, the Miracles, and the Marvelettes, even though she did not know who produced them.

All Martha knew at that moment was that this man, Stevenson, in his tailored silk suit, looked "as if he had just starred in a movie." He looked like her ticket out of dry cleaning. The man told her to come to Hitsville U.S.A. for an audition. He said, "I think you have something."

She tucked his card into the bodice of her dress and walked coolly to her fabulous temporary private dressing room, and was careful to close the door before dancing and shrieking with excitement. On her way home, she decided to quit her job at the dry cleaner. She woke up early the next morning and took the bus across that dangerous Woodward Avenue border to the Westside.

She was surprised to see that the company was simply a Detroit house not unlike the one she lived in, except that it had that carved blue-lettered sign announcing Hitsville U.S.A. In the cramped reception area Mickey Stevenson was called and told that she was here to see him. Martha could hear his response: "Who?"

Mickey explained to her that she was not supposed to just show up. She was supposed to call the number on the card and make an appointment for an audition. They were held on the third Thursday of every month.

But then the phone rang and he asked her to answer it as he ran out of his office. She answered a number of calls, met singer-producer Clarence Paul, settled a pay dispute for James Jamerson and drummer Benny Benjamin, and by the end of the day, when Paul drove her home in his Cadillac, she was the new A&R secretary.

Mickey Stevenson told the story differently. He did not like auditioning but did it constantly:

I used to have auditions at one time almost every day. . . . I would audition everybody . . . but at the time, I didn't know how to audition. You start with a song that's terrible and I'd say, get out of here. That ain't no song. I was rude. I was inconsiderate, but not intentionally. I didn't know how to handle it. I learned over a period of time to say, "That's a nice song but we're not ready for you right now." One of those kinds of lines. I used to say, "Get out of here. What is this?" Or your song ain't nothing, but your voice is good. By the end of the week I'd be going through a hundred people, or a hundred fifty people. . . . They came from all over. They started in Detroit, but as we got larger, they would come from Chicago, Ohio, all the way from New York they would come to join this black company. They have a chance to do something here. So it became that. It became a way out. Well, I couldn't turn them down when they came from all over the place. I had to stop and listen. But to some of them I would say, "Let me ask you a question. You got in your car and drove three hundred miles to bring me this bullshit?" I look back, boy, was I terrible. But out of every hundred of them, and I'm tired of listening, somebody would walk in there and blow me out the box.

Stevenson said that Martha Reeves constantly showed up to audition. The way he told the story, he already had a secretary who came to like Martha and would say to him, "Oh, that girl is here again." Stevenson recalled, "I thought she had a good voice, not great, a good voice. She had a unique sound."

One day he had to run out of the office and he asked her to answer the phone. He was impressed with her efficiency, and since his secretary was about to leave he offered her the job. According to Mickey, Martha said, "I won't be nobody's secretary." So Mickey made her his assistant.

According to Martha, she worked there for three weeks with no discussion of pay until her father insisted, "You better get some of that man's money or you won't be going back to his company." So she asked Stevenson and he started paying her thirty-five dollars weekly.

For Martha, the salary wasn't the goal. She could see that once you found a place in this company, opportunities would turn up. She would wait for hers. She was not the only local girl doing this. Mary Wilson, Florence Ballard, and Diana Ross were also drifting through the little house looking for chances. Their upbringings had been similar to Martha's. Mary Wilson was born in the Mississippi Delta, Flo Ballard was born in Detroit of parents from Mississippi, and Diana Ross was born in Detroit and knew her neighbor Smokey Robinson as a child.

Wilson grew up with the Reverend Franklin's three daughters and listened to them sing at their father's church. When Mary was fourteen years old, in 1958, she entered a local talent contest. Florence Ballard was another contestant and the two started talking about how to advance their singing career. It was not an uncommon conversation for black kids in 1958 Detroit. A year later, in the eighth grade, the two, now close friends, joined a girl quartet put together by three male singers from Alabama including Eddie Kendricks, who later became the star falsetto tenor of Motown's the Temptations. The male group, the Primes, wanted an accompanying sister act called the Primettes. The Primettes were Ballard and Wilson and a big-eyed girl Wilson had met occasionally who lived catty-corner to Wilson's home in the Brewster Housing Project — Diana Ross. The fourth singer changed several times but the three stayed together. Flo Ballard, who was thought to have the strongest voice, sang lead, and the Primettes came to be thought of as Ballard's group.

When school was out for the afternoon, the group hitchhiked across town just to hang around at Hitsville, looking for a chance. Martha Reeves knew Wilson and Ballard because they had all been in the music program at Northeastern High School together. Motown occasionally used the Primettes as backup for Mary Wells, changing their name to the Supremes.

Meanwhile, Martha said in an interview that she got her first recording when union rules required an additional vocalist on a session. But her Motown career was really launched in July 1962, when the A&R office was asked to arrange backup for Marvin Gaye's first R&B album. Gaye had endless talents. He was a good drummer and an excellent pianist and he played on a number of the earlier Motown recordings, including Stevie Wonder's early albums on the Tamla label when Stevie was only eleven and twelve years old. Gaye was also a good songwriter, and Gordy saw this as his greatest talent, and was constantly pushing him to write songs. But Gaye resisted this. "I didn't want to be one of the cats behind the scene," Gaye told Ritz. "I wanted to get out front."

So with some reluctance Gordy let him record albums of pop standards. They did not sell well. He had failed as the black Sinatra. "Be a songwriter," Gordy insisted. But Gaye, who as he once predicted, argued more with Gordy than anyone else — he could, because he was family — persisted. Now he was recording an R&B album.

Motown recordings were often put together with whoever was available. Can you go in the studio and sing backup? We need someone for hand clapping. This was why young hopefuls liked to be there.

Martha arranged the backup by calling in her old group, Rosalind Ashford, Annette

Beard, and Gloria Jean Williamson, who were then hired for five dollars a side. The four of them were asked to come up with a background for a song written by Gaye and Stevenson called "Stubborn Kind of Fellow," which many said was a good description of handsome Marvin Gaye. The four stood behind Gaye and improvised, all five on the same hanging microphone. The song was Gaye's first hit, reaching number 8 on *Billboard*'s R&B chart, which at the time was labeled "the black singles chart," and 46 on the white pop singles chart. The song not only made Gaye famous, it made the backup singers a group.

Here the story diverges into conflicting versions. According to Martha, Gordy called down the stairs and told them they had an hour to come up with a name for the group. According to Martha, she made up a combination of the Detroit great Della Reese and a street in her neighborhood, Van Dyke Street — the Vandellas. The explanation is plausible because Martha was always a big Detroit booster, but it is not the way the other Vandellas remember it. According to Rosalind Ashford:

Gordy said you have half an hour or I come up with the name. After a half hour he shouted down, "Have you got a name yet?" He said, "You are going to be called the Vandellas." I never knew what it meant. Everybody called us the vandals. They joked that a vandella was a female vandal.

"Stubborn Kind of Fellow," followed in December by "Hitch Hike," launched a string of hits for Gaye with the Vandellas on backup. This success almost guaranteed that the Vandellas would soon get offered their own song, especially given Gordy's interest in developing girl groups. They recorded two songs that year, neither of which were hits, but the following year, 1963, they got a song from the unstoppable songwriting team Holland-Dozier-Holland.

Eddie Holland was with Berry Gordy almost from his start as a successful singer. Gordy admired Eddie's powerful tenor and thought he could make him a star. But Eddie had a dread of public performance. Gordy was also impressed with his "look-alike brother" Brian, who seemed to have a profound understanding of music. Gordy thought Brian might end up another Smokey Robinson. Brian was considered one of Motown's best early songwriters, most famous for "Please Mr. Postman," sung by the Marvelettes, which was a number 1 hit in 1961. Lamont Dozier sang for the Anna label and later for various Motown labels. In March 1963 they decided to team up, with Dozier and Brian as composers and Eddie as the principal lyricist and arranger. Together they wrote some two hundred songs, including many of Motown's biggest hits between 1963 and 1967.

Their first song, "Come and Get These Memories," was also Martha and the Vandella's first Top 40 hit. It was followed by "Heat Wave," which made number 1 on the R&B chart and number 4 on the pop chart. Martha and the Vandellas were stars. The song had a driving beat and an irresistible dance rhythm, and Martha Reeve's voice had an almost mystical urgency. This sound was to become the Vandellas' trademark.

Motown was developing a sizable stable of stars, and Thomas "Bean" Bowles, the lanky reed player, came up with the idea of a Motown touring company, the Motown Revue. He booked ninety-four one-night stands in three months, traveling on a bus with the words Motor City Tour printed on it. Martha and the Vandellas, Mary Wells, Marvin Gaye, Smokey Robinson, the Temptations, the Supremes, and twelve-year-old Stevie

Wonder all went on the road in the fall of 1962.

The tour went to New York and Washington and the Midwest but was also to sweep through the heart of the Deep South at the height of the civil rights movement. Though most of them had southern roots, few knew the reality of being black in the South. Gaye had grown up in segregated Washington, DC, but not the Deep South. Most had never been there, or had moved when they were too young to remember. Martha Reeves had gone back to Alabama a few times with her family. They would switch to less comfortable cars at the back of the train before they crossed the Mason-Dixon line, and when they got to their relatives, they quickly went to the family farm and stayed there until they had to leave.

"You didn't talk about it," said Martha. "You didn't say, 'Hey, they hate us down here, so be careful.' When I went down to Alabama with my family, my parents kept us close to the farm. They ground their own corn and made wonderful corn bread and grits."

Mary Wells, without thinking, took a sip from a white-only water fountain, and at first when a crowd started to gather, she thought that it was because she was recognized as a star. In Montgomery, Alabama, they were playing to a segregated audience that was surrounded by plainclothesmen with clubs. Anyone who tried to stand up or, worse, dance, would get clubbed. Finally Smokey Robinson stepped to a microphone and asked the men to stop clubbing people and to back off. They did, and the audience started dancing, and soon the blacks and whites were no longer separated.

By the early 1960s, Freedom Rides — black people sitting in white sections of buses to challenge the legality of segregated buses, the tactic initiated by Bayard Rustin in the 1940s — had become a central tactic of SNCC. Motown toured the South at the height of the SNCC Freedom Rides, and a busload of northern-looking black people appeared to southern police exactly like Freedom Riders. The Motown Revue would pull into a town, expecting crowds of fans, and instead would be met by police with shotguns. In Montgomery, Alabama, they performed to a racially integrated audience on a baseball field. As they left, gunshots were heard, and the tour group later realized that there were bullet holes in their bus sign and in a window.

In the urgency of the 1960s, when Motown was accused of ignoring the politics all around them, some of the artists would point to such incidents and say that they had been involved in civil rights. Martha said, "We were always political. We sold love in front of segregated audiences. That's political." But she also admitted to having no interest in taking on the South while on that tour. "I was traveling on a bus trying to sell music and being accused of being a Freedom Rider," she said many years later.

But many Motown artists began to reflect on what Mary Wilson called "the Motown bubble," the way they lived in Detroit in their Motown world and were completely ignoring the important things going on in the larger world.

The Motown bubble was becoming a troubling issue as the political and social conflicts of the 1960s heated and became ever more polarizing. For Gordy and many others in music, the lesson of the 1950s was to avoid controversy. But in the 1960s, people wanted to know where you stood. As Elvis Presley demonstrated, to avoid controversy was to risk irrelevance. Could Motown really be "the voice of young America" and say nothing about the issues of the day that were consuming young Americans?

Gordy wanted to be revolutionary without

being controversial. He wanted, as Robespierre complained to the Convention in 1792, "a Revolution without a revolution." Motown broke all kinds of taboos about race and sex, but Gordy did it with the understanding that breaking taboos had become fashionable. Songs were not about change or about the issues of change. They were about love and dating and sex and infidelity. But for black people to be singing about these things to white people, and for white couples to be dancing to black people talking about love and even sex, was a strong political statement that the time for integration, for tearing down racial barriers, had come. The statement was always made very carefully. Motown would be about integration by the way it did things, but not by what it said or, to use a popular phrase of the day, by direct action.

With few exceptions, Motown people did not participate in the civil rights movement. They did not go south to march. But it was all about integration in its way. As Amiri Baraka pointed out, blacks in America were always so marginal that "merely by being a Negro in America, one was a nonconformist." Motown moved black out of the marginal and into the mainstream. It was the model set down by Booker T. Washington, not the one by W. E. B. Du Bois.

Gordy was not, as is often suggested, apolitical. In 1957 he supported Charles Diggs Sr.'s successful bid to be a black U.S. congressman. In 1963 he created another Motown label called Black Forum, whose stated purpose was to present "ideas and voices of the worldwide struggle of black people to create a new era." Starting with Martin Luther King Jr., Black Forum recorded speeches and talks by an increasingly controversial lineup of black activists, including Langston Hughes, Amiri Baraka, and Stokely Carmichael.

Nationally, the civil rights movement reached its height in the early 1960s. It had grown from a hard local struggle in southern communities to a movement garnering national and international attention. Martin Luther King Jr., a rebellious political activist still in his early thirties, was becoming a major figure. In 1964 he would become the youngest recipient of the Nobel Peace Prize. Soon he would be representing one of two opposing factions that would splinter the movement. But by 1963 he and the movement had become so recognized that it would have been at best very odd for a leading black enterprise to take no interest in it.

How could a black-owned music company

in an increasingly black city not be part of this movement, especially since the movement was linked to music? Just as music was an integral part of the black church, it was central to the civil rights movement. In African religions that seek to bring spirits to possess worshipers, it is believed that only through music can the spirits be brought down to people. Folk songs and traditional hymns like "This Little Light of Mine," and "We Will Overcome" — "will" changed to "shall" by the movement — became songs of the movement, so-called freedom songs. James Farmer reworked a thirties trade union song "Which Side Are You On?" and even Ray Charles's "Hit the Road Jack" became "Get Your Rights Jack." Freedom songs were recorded and sold and performed in concert halls, including Carnegie Hall, and what started as comfort for scared people marching and locked in southern jails became popular culture. In 1962 folksinger Pete Seeger advised SNCC to form their own singing groups and raise money for the organization through concerts and recordings. Cordell Reagon and Bernice Johnson, who later married, formed a quartet called Freedom Singers.

It was Seeger's contention that all great political movements had to have their own songs. In history this has usually been true. The American, French, and Russian Revolutions, as well as the American labor movement, all had their songs of inspiration. In October 2011, at the height of the Occupy Wall Street movement, in which thousands camped out in Manhattan's Zuccotti Park and in most other major American cities as well as numerous others around the world to protest the abuses of big banks and finance companies, the *New York Times* music section ran an article with the kind of astute sense of history that is rare in newspapers. They wrote that though this movement appeared to be sweeping across the world, it lacked songs. The article quoted an array of historians and music critics questioning if this movement could survive without its own songs. The civil rights movement, however, had songs.

Much of the music industry, though surprisingly little of it R&B, came out for civil rights. Harry Belafonte was a close supporter of King, as was Joan Baez. When a March on Washington was announced for August 1963, Josephine Baker flew in from Paris. Bobby Darin, Peter, Paul, and Mary, Marian Anderson, Dizzy Gillespie, and Mahalia Jackson were all there. So at the march, folk, jazz, rock, classical, and gospel were all represented.

For Detroiters, an earlier march in June up Woodward Avenue, with King delivering an address at Cobo Hall, was the pivotal historic moment. Particularly moving was a section of King's speech when he said, "I have a dream . . ." Sponsored by Reverend Franklin and other community leaders, a huge crowd filled the hall. The march was one of King's first attempts to move the civil rights movement north, to point out that northern urban blacks were also denied their rights, a move that in time cost him some northern supporters. As he often did that year, King pointed out that it was the one hundredth anniversary of the Emancipation Proclamation, and yet "The Negro in the United States of America is still not free." It was a poignant moment in a city where blacks cheering the proclamation in 1863 led to white violence. The blacks fought back in the first of several notable Detroit "race riots." This had been the moment when the city council decided that Detroit needed a police force. In Detroit the police force was created to control African Americans.

Gordy recorded the King speech and released it on an album titled *The Great*

*March to Freedom* on Motown's Black Forum label. This was Motown's official recognition of support for the civil rights movement. Gordy even traveled to Atlanta to present King with a copy of the record. Gordy had decided to unabashedly tie Motown to civil rights or at least the Martin Luther King strain of it. This did not stop King from suing Motown for copyright infringement, though the suit was later dropped. The album was released on August 28, 1963, the day of the historic march on Washington, DC.

Gordy sensed correctly that 1963 was a historic moment for the civil rights movement but miscalculated the importance of King's rally in Detroit. Though it seemed huge in June, it was dwarfed by the press coverage of 250,000 people attending the rally in Washington in August. The key line of Gordy's recording, the "I have a dream" passage, is always remembered from King reusing it in Washington.

The March on Washington is a good example of how history is not so much a record of what happened as of how it was reported, and most of the established press reported it as a show of unity and a triumph for both the movement and the Kennedy administration. E. W. Kenworthy for *The*

*New York Times* reported, "It was the greatest assembly for a redress of grievances that this capital has ever seen." That may have been true, but historian Howard Zinn wrote in *The Nation* that, having come from the brutal reality of SNCC work in Mississippi, "I felt a certain air of unreality about the March on Washington."

SNCC was always a bit different from the rest of the civil rights movement. SNCC was kids in blue jeans questioning the leadership of older people in suits. It had begun in February 1960, when four students from a black college in Greensboro, North Carolina, sat down at a segregated lunch counter and refused to move. Spontaneously throughout the South young blacks staged similar sit-ins. On April 17, black student protesters met in Raleigh, North Carolina, and founded the Student Nonviolent Coordinating Committee, SNCC, always pronounced *snick*. They were to be an independent group of student activists. In June they sent a letter to Martin Luther King Jr. informing him of their existence. King hoped they would become an active youth wing of his Southern Christian Leadership Conference, but they wanted to remain independent, and Ella Baker, a fifty-seven-year-old veteran organizer who was an official of King's SCLC, met with two hundred SNCC activists and urged them to remain independent. They valued King, especially because press coverage is essential to make nonviolence work, and wherever King showed up, the press followed. But they laughed at his exalted position. They called him "the Lawd." And they disdained what King called a tactic of "calm reasonableness."

They were extremely active in sit-ins and Freedom Rides that challenged the illegality of segregated interstate buses. SNCC went where other groups wouldn't. Their courage and energy brought new recruits to the movement by the hundreds. But they paid a price for their daring, being regularly killed, beaten, and arrested.

Zinn, an active supporter of SNCC, wrote that the word that most characterized them was "impatience." They were impatient with the Kennedy administration, which did so little to enforce federal laws on integration and did virtually nothing to protect protesters in the South, and they were impatient with the civil rights establishment and its leaders, who had few successes. In truth, while they were being beaten and killed and the FBI stood by watching and the press was giving tremendous coverage and the nonviolent movement was earning admiration around the world, very little integration was taking place and few southern blacks were able to vote.

The original SNCC plan was in the best SNCC tradition, to stage a sit-in in Congress to protest their inaction. This was illegal and the protesters would be arrested, but the idea was to bring in wave after wave of protesters. There was also to be a sit-in at the Justice Department to protest their failure to protect and defend the rights of black people in the South.

In the end the sit-ins were replaced by a huge rally at which King did more or less what he had done in Detroit. The only truly militant speech to make it to the podium, the only one that really challenged the political establishment, was by SNCC chairman John Lewis. At twenty-three, the youngest person on the podium, he said that when he started, he "wondered if I'd be able to speak at all." But he said that by the time he finished, he felt "lifted . . . by a feeling of righteous indignation." He said that "American politics is dominated by politicians who build their career on immoral compromising" — youthful candor from a future U.S. Congressman. Deleted from the speech under pressure from the movement's establishment was much harsher language, including "We will not wait for the president, the Justice Department, nor the Congress, but will take matters into our own hands and create a source of power, outside of any national structure, that could and would assure us a victory." Had Lewis not been censored, his speech might have been remembered as the birth of the black power movement.

Another SNCC activist, Michael Thelwell, wrote in the French black review *Présence Africaine,* ". . . somewhere along the twisting road that stretched between the first ideas for the March and the abortion of those ideas that was finally delivered in Washington on August 28 lies the corpse of what could have been a real step forward in the struggle for Negro rights in this country."

But how many people ever read *The Nation* or *Présence Africaine*? In the end it was a march, not a sit-in, a polite legal action that Kennedy could endorse and that said little about the anger of those fighting for black rights in a movement that had experienced assassinations, church bombings, and even children murdered.

Bayard Rustin talked of creating theater that could somehow touch people. The

March on Washington did just that, but the anger that was covered up seethed underneath. Black nationalist leader Malcolm X said of the March, "It was like putting Novocain in a sore tooth. If the tooth hasn't been pulled or fixed, it's hell when it wears off."

As 1964 approached, the year of "Dancing in the Street," the Novocain was about to wear off. But in 1963 Motown sold $4.5 million worth of records. Three songs by Martha and the Vandellas were on the Top 100, along with Marvin Gaye, the Miracles, Stevie Wonder, Jackie Wilson, and even the Supremes, with "When the Lovelight Starts Shining Through His Eyes," a Holland-Dozier-Holland song. It was the Supremes' first hit, barely making the chart at 99. Elvis Presley's "Devil in Disguise" was 100.

Some small measure of racial integration had come — at least to the music world, because at the end of 1963 *Billboard* decided that there was no longer enough difference between the sale of records to whites and blacks to continue maintaining a black R&B chart.

# CHAPTER THREE: SUMMER'S HERE

In 1964 events swirled ever faster. Only a few months passed between April, when President Johnson announced in Chicago his plan to build "a great society of the highest order" that would end poverty, and the early summer, which Johnson called "the summer of our discontent." So much was happening by summer that to say "summer's here and the time is right" was bound to be open to many interpretations.

Society became desperate for explanations — for books or songs or something to explain what all this meant. The first big upheaval that set the stage for 1964 happened in the final weeks of 1963 — President Kennedy was publicly murdered. Kennedy, rightly or wrongly, had become such a central symbol of the spirit of change in America that it was difficult not to wonder if he had been killed in an attempt to stop change. In contrast to the ideas of change sweeping the country, Kennedy was a fairly conservative figure — a dedicated cold warrior whose foreign policy revolved around taking on the Communists, and far from a champion of civil rights, which his administration was forever struggling to comprehend and react to. The March on Washington had been a demand that he do more.

Despite this, he was young, and after eight years of Eisenhower, Kennedy seemed the embodiment of change, so that when he was killed, the question often asked was, who had tried to stop the change? Was it really just a drifter named Lee Harvey Oswald? Other theories abounded, especially after a nightclub owner with known Mafia ties, Jack Ruby, shot and killed Oswald before he could attempt to explain his actions. To clear up all of the speculation, the new president Lyndon Johnson commissioned an official inquiry into the two shootings, headed by Supreme Court Chief Justice Earl Warren.

The American public spent the first eight months of 1964 anticipating the Warren Report and the rest of the year refuting its findings that both Oswald and Ruby had acted alone. Even the murdered president's brother Robert Kennedy, who anticipated the Warren Report in June by saying he believed that Oswald was simply a deranged person acting on his own, did not quell the speculation that flourished throughout the summer.

By the spring of 1964 the tragedy of Kennedy's death had moved to a different part of the collective brain of an increasingly angry America. No longer was it just a tragedy, it was seen as a sign of the times that there were ruthless people who would stop at nothing, and so they also must be ruthless to stand up to them.

The Kennedy assassination marked the end of an era of optimism spurred not so much by the social change that a celebrated few were struggling to achieve as by economic growth. Under Eisenhower, the economy had grown comfortably, at a rate of 2.5 percent a year. But under Kennedy, growth doubled. Between 1960 and 1964, the gross national product, the sum value of American goods and services, had leaped by 25 percent.

Detroit participated in that growth. In an April 1964 meeting with stockholders, General Motors reported that retail deliveries of cars and trucks in the past month were the highest in the history of the company.

In February 1964 *Life* magazine published

an article titled "The Emptiness of Too Much Leisure." By 1964 Americans had more leisure time than ever before. It may be typically American to view this as a problem. Europeans were gaining far more leisure time and worrying less about it. The problem came largely from the success of the trade union movement in obtaining living wages for a forty-hour week, although some research indicated that many Americans worked longer to take advantage of greater overtime pay. In the United States a group of prominent social and political scientists gathered for a conference called "Leisure: A Challenge to Present-day America." Dr. James C. Charlesworth, president of the American Academy of Political and Social Science, warned that leisure "is growing much faster than our capacity to use it." He recommended the establishment of departments of leisure in each state government and the compulsory teaching of "leisure skills" in the public school system. But there was some evidence that Americans were figuring it out. The sporting goods industry reported a $20 billion increase in sales over the mid-1950s.

In 1964 there was a great push to sell endless new gadgets to the new leisure class. In June the First Lady, Lady Bird Johnson, launched the first "see-as-you-talk" commercial telephone service for Bell Telephone System. The service was between Washington, New York, and Chicago. The rates, still high by today's standards, were astounding for 1964. The first three minutes cost $16 between New York and Washington, $21 between Chicago and Washington, and $27 between Chicago and New York. The First Lady explained that it was always a great pleasure when her daughters called her when they were away, and now being able to see them would be "an added dividend." But people didn't like the new "picture phone." They thought the equipment was too bulky and too hard to use and the picture was too small. It was discontinued. Surprisingly there were not a lot of complaints about the cost.

Of course the issues of too much leisure, sporting equipment, and picture phones had not reached the poor, the unemployed, and the majority of black Americans in urban ghettos and southern share-cropping farms. One idea that would be increasingly discussed in the 1960s, that there were two Americas, was evident in the leisure problem.

When on the day of Kennedy's death Lyndon Baines Johnson took the oath of office, the age of optimism had brutally ended, but the demands for change were still there. For Johnson in 1964 the first order of business was to show that his administration was continuing the work of the fallen president. The ambitious Kennedy had launched fifty pieces of legislation that were still tied up in congressional committees. The most pressing piece of business was the Civil Rights Bill. The demands only a few months before of 250,000 people on the Capitol Mall could not be forgotten. One week after Kennedy's death, Johnson had begun calling civil rights leaders to reassure them, starting with Roy Wilkins of the relatively moderate NAACP, then Whitney Young of the Urban League, then Martin Luther King Jr., and then James Farmer. From moderate to radical, though he never made it all the way over to SNCC.

On February 10, the House passed the bill that had been discussed, debated, and reworked for the past eight months. The bill was the most far reaching into the private lives of American citizens in American history. Its primary task was to ensure blacks the right to vote in all fifty states with the same registration requirements as white people. It also made it illegal to discriminate on racial grounds in public places such as restaurants, restrooms, barbershops, gas stations, theaters, clubs, and dance halls. It gave the Justice Department the authority to desegregate schools and established an Equal Employment Opportunity Commission to act against job discrimination.

Many of the most contentious parts of the bill were rights already guaranteed outside of the South. For example, one of the most controversial parts of the bill was the provision against job discrimination. Though seldom enforced, such measures already existed in twenty-five out of the fifty states but in no southern states. With good reason, the Civil Rights Bill was seen as being aimed at the South. This put the Democrats in a difficult position in a presidential election year, because Democrats, John Kennedy included, won elections with a solid block from the South.

American politics had been frozen in its Civil War configuration. Southerners continued to vote for Democrats because in the years leading up to the Civil War their party had fought for the right to southern slavery. The Republicans, on the other hand, were despised in the South and embraced by northern African Americans — the only blacks who got to vote — for they represented the party of Abraham Lincoln. In Detroit as in most of the North the first politically active blacks were Republicans.

In 1964, the entire political configuration started to change. It was first seen in Alabama in 1962, when a Republican came within 6,800 votes of taking a Senate seat from the Democrats. No serious national political strategist failed to notice that race. The Civil Rights Bill, if passed, could cost the Democrats the South.

On June 19, at 7:49 at night, the bill passed the Senate by a vote of 73 to 27. It was one of the rare occasions in history when every senator voted. Most of the votes against it were from the South, but a notable exception was Senator Barry Goldwater of Arizona, a leading contender for the Republican presidential nomination who also voted against the Civil Rights Bill.

Nor did all blacks cheer the new law. Before it was passed, heavyweight champion Muhammad Ali, who had announced his membership in the fast-growing black nationalist group, the Nation of Islam, said, "The bill won't change the hearts of the slave masters, and like the counterfeit money it is, if the Negroes tried to spend it, they would be arrested."

Cassius Clay's winning the heavyweight

title on February 25 in Miami and becoming Ali was a major event of 1964. This was still a time when heavyweight champions mattered. The current heavyweight, Sonny Liston, was not much of a standard-bearer. He was known to have underworld connections and he himself had a criminal record, having served time for armed robbery. But he was a brutal puncher and a fearsome-looking opponent. Almost everyone expected him to easily defeat the young Cassius Clay, and many people openly looked forward to it, because Clay was brazen and outspoken. He was an early rapper, composing humorous rhymes to talk about his fights. In short, he was what was known in the South as an uppity Negro. Bookmakers took seven-to-one odds that Liston would win.

No one seemed to notice that Clay was actually not only faster than Liston but larger than he was, and he easily dispatched the champion in six rounds. But there was more to this fight. In his corner was black nationalist leader Malcolm X. At a press conference the following day, Clay announced with Malcolm X that he had joined the Nation of Islam and had changed his name. So now the heavyweight champion of the world was a militant black — what was known as a "Black Muslim." This was as clear a sign as any that there was a new kind of change in black America. A few days later Malcolm X announced that he was leaving the Nation of Islam and was forming his own group, and that 1964 was to be the bloodiest year ever in the civil rights struggle.

After his victory, the unpredictable Muhammad Ali shouted from the ring to Sam Cooke, who was at his corner, and called him "the greatest rock 'n' roll singer in the world."

What was Sam Cooke, the gospel singer turned R&B star, known for sweet, harmless tunes, doing with Malcolm X and Muhammad Ali? Was he, too, turning militant? Was this to be a new age for R&B? A few months earlier, Cooke had recorded "A Change Is Gonna Come." Moved by all that was happening, he felt that he, too, should speak out. But it worried him to be openly political, and he considered softening the lyrics, playing it safe, like Motown.

By the spring of 1964 it was clear that change was going to come in the unfinished business of the Civil War, racial integration. Author James Baldwin described the coming change as "the achievement of nationhood, or, more simply and cruelly, the growing up of this dangerously adolescent country." In May a black student was attempting to be the third ever at the University of Mississippi. The first, James Meredith, had been able to attend only by force of National Guard troops in 1962. Meanwhile, Ross Barnett, the governor of Mississippi, arrived at New York's City College and attempted to deliver a speech on the dangerous "mongrelization" that the Civil Rights Bill would cause, but was pelted with raw eggs by students.

Also in May, tensions marked the one-year anniversary of the military occupation of Cambridge, Maryland, by National Guard troops. Americans had come to watch the approach of summer each year with dread because it had become the season of such racial strife. The vice mayor of Atlanta, Sam Massell, warned in late May that "boycotts, the pickets, and sit-ins will be mild compared to the strife that may descend on our cities if we don't promptly show good faith in seeking equitable solutions."

This was true not only in the South. New York City seemed particularly ripe for some kind of social explosion. In April, at the opening of the 1964 World's Fair, young blacks announced a "stall-in." They planned to drive on the Long Island Expressway, which approached the fair, and then pretend their cars had broken down, causing massive traffic jams. The black leadership in the city urged the young people not to do this, but they went ahead with their plan. They demanded a halt to construction until the industry was integrated, a rent strike, that the school system immediately produce a timetable for integration and the police do the same, and a police review board to investigate abuse.

Surely this was going to be a long, difficult summer.

Suddenly it seemed white people who had more or less ignored black people wanted to know everything about who the Negroes were and what they wanted. Books explaining Negroes were in demand, and studies were regularly commissioned. On June 7, 1964, *The New York Times Sunday Magazine* published an article by a black novelist, John Oliver Killens, titled "Explanation of the 'Black Psyche,' " which made the supposedly startling revelation that "the Negro is different, and his aim in America is not to be like the white man, but to be himself, to make his own contribution, in a free and equal society."

Two University of Chicago sociologists

got some press attention for a study of 721 black families and 839 white families in which they found that "contrary to what may be the popular stereotype, almost no Negro respondents reported that they would encourage their child to marry a white person." This integration idea was turning out more complicated than most whites expected.

Meanwhile, the front pages of newspapers were filled with news on the United States spending ever more money and sending ever more military "advisers" to bolster a corrupt and repressive South Vietnam against a Communist North Vietnam.

The year 1964 was supposed to be one of civil rights, but even as the public increasingly focused on the "Negro problem" it became apparent from Lyndon Johnson's own taped conversations, released after his death in 1973 at only age sixty-four, that he was agonizing increasingly about Vietnam. Only weeks before Kennedy's death, a coup in Vietnam had taken the life of the first South Vietnamese president, Ngo Dinh Diem, installing a regime possibly more brutal, corrupt, and incompetent than the one he replaced. Kennedy had resolved to disengage from Vietnam after he was re-elected. Like Johnson, he saw a tough anti-

Communist stance in Vietnam as vital for the election.

Johnson saw the situation as a disaster in waiting and recognized that sending troops meant huge numbers of casualties and no way out and an unwinnable war that would be politically unpopular. In early March, a State Department report reiterated what French president Charles de Gaulle had been privately telling the United States, that a bombing campaign would be ineffective, neither weakening the resolve of the north nor boosting morale in the south. With no good alternatives, Johnson was obsessed with what had become known as "the domino theory," by then a ten-year-old idea from the Eisenhower administration, that once Vietnam fell to the Communists, the rest of Southeast Asia and maybe even more of Asia would fall one by one to the Communists. The Communist doctrine claimed that their ideology was the future, and eventually the rest of the world would follow. Nowhere was this idea taken more seriously than in Washington. In March Johnson asked his defense secretary, Robert McNamara, about the world's view of Vietnam. "Why aren't the Russians as interested in this as we are? Why aren't the French and the English? Why do they want the Commies to take over all of Southeast Asia?"

In his private conversations, Johnson asked friends and advisers for help with what he saw as a "mess." But he couldn't let all of Asia fall. In June 1964, the CIA produced a study authored by Sherman Kent, an intelligence analyst, that stated that the domino theory was a myth and if Vietnam were to fall to the Communists, no one other than possibly Cambodia would follow. In Johnson's inner circle it was known as the "death of the domino theory memo." Unfortunately Johnson ignored it. History disproved the domino theory. In the end, and millions of lives later, South Vietnam would fall and Asia would not follow.

The future was not looking bright for Detroit or for most other urban areas. Money was leaving the cities, and this had grave implications for the overwhelming majority of Detroit's blacks. White people were leaving for the suburbs, a 1960s growing phenomenon in northern cities known as "white flight." At the same time black immigration to Detroit had dropped off because of a lack of jobs caused by factories moving away as well. As a long-term consequence of this trend, in 1990 Detroit had half as many jobs as it had in 1960. Detroit began losing population. The 1960 census showed a 9 percent decline in total Detroit population. Charles Roemer, a member of the city planning commission, shrugged off this news, saying, "The gloss of the suburbs will wear off." In Detroit, subsequent years would prove him wrong, as white flight increased. In the 2000 census, whites were only 12.3 percent of Detroit's population.

The 1960 census showed that the city was 28.9 percent black, almost double the black percentage in the 1950 census. In 1960, more than 35 percent of the workforce was black, but only 3.3 percent of the police force. In 1961, Mayor Louis Miriani ordered a crackdown on crime, which resulted in a widespread harassment of blacks by the white police force. In the mayoral election blacks organized behind a thirty-three-year-old unknown white lawyer, Jerome P. Cavanagh, the son of a Ford worker, and the sizable black vote elected him, marking the beginning of black electoral power in Detroit.

Even though Detroit car sales were up, there were largely unheeded warning signs. Smaller foreign cars had made the first sign of inroads in the market, gaining 10 percent of car sales by the early 1960s. In June 1964, the Connecticut State Police released a report that the new, smaller cars were not as safe as the Detroit giants. Studying 1,300 accidents, they concluded that the smaller car crumpled every time it hit a big one. According to the director of the project, A. J. White, when a big and small car collide, "it's like a sledgehammer hitting a tack." This was good news for Detroit automakers, who liked to make them large and were starting to worry about smaller imports. And it was good news for Motown, since every new star purchased a safe sledgehammer in the form of a very long and befinned Cadillac. They lined West Grand Boulevard near the studio day and night. In 2012 Martha Reeves still had one.

But bad news for Motown came from the Public Health Service in Washington. The "baby boom" was over. In March there were fewer babies born than in any March since 1955, and the total from March 1963 to March 1964 was significantly less than that of the year before. The Public Health Service could not explain why this was happening, but for the music industry in time this might mean fewer teenagers buying their records.

Trouble was brewing and there was a fear in many sectors for many reasons that the good times wouldn't last. Perhaps the general mood of the country was expressed by Grayson Kirk, the president of Columbia University, who told the graduating class: "Our country has rounded a corner in its history; the road, which led to that corner, no longer beckons us ahead with the same legible signposts that guided our fathers. In one sense the American dream is over."

Nineteen sixty-four was a presidential election year, and the first declared candidate was trumpeter Dizzy Gillespie, who announced his candidacy at the time of the 1963 march. He said that if elected, he would rename the White House "the Blues House." For his cabinet he promised to appoint Duke Ellington as secretary of state, drummer Max Roach as secretary of defense, Charlie Mingus as "minister of peace," Peggy Lee as secretary of labor, and Miles Davis as director of the CIA. He promised to appoint Mississippi governor Ross Barnett to direct the U.S. Information Service. Malcolm X was to be attorney general and Alabama governor George Wallace was to be deported to Vietnam. Among his campaign promises were free health care and education. Lest anybody thought he was joking about all of this, he sold Dizzy for President buttons and sent the profits to James Farmer's CORE and Martin Luther King's SCLC.

In hindsight few presidential elections have had a greater impact on the future of U.S. politics than the 1964 presidential election. Lyndon Johnson, who had been an incumbent for only months, was the uncontested Democratic nominee — at least once it was clear that Robert Kennedy would not run — a fill-in for the murdered president. In fact, it was one of the least planned presidential campaigns of modern history. President Kennedy had conducted only one meeting about the 1964 campaign, and Johnson had not been present. Logically, given the depth of the emotional wound from the killing, the Republicans should have put forward one of their prominent liberals and argued that he could better carry the Kennedy mantle. But Republican voters were rejecting the leading liberal, New York governor Nelson Rockefeller, in the face of issues of war and peace and civil rights, because he had divorced. Others, such as Pennsylvania's William Scranton and Michigan's George Romney, never caught on enough in the face of an insurgent right-wing movement that coalesced around Arizona senator Barry Goldwater.

The Republicans had never had a candidate like Goldwater before. Traditionally, the central argument between Republicans and Democrats had been government involvement. Democrats wanted government programs and Republicans didn't, though they initiated them anyway. It was a relatively small difference.

But Barry Goldwater, out to steal the South from the Democrats, opposed the Civil Rights Act. While Robert Kennedy in his commencement speech at Marquette University was praising the "genuine and intense concern with social justice" of the college generation, Goldwater at Pennsylvania Military College claimed that he was the "voice of reason" against "impatient spirits who . . . make social changes an end in itself." He appeared to be calling for an end to civil rights and an end to the kind of social programs that had kept Democrats in power in every election since 1932, with the exception of the eight years of Eisenhower the war hero. Goldwater also wanted to end efforts to live peacefully with Communist nations. He denounced "the illusion of coexistence and peaceful accommodations." Between the United States and the Soviet Union, a relationship called the Cold War, which had been a nuclear-armed staredown for the past two decades, Goldwater was speaking at a particularly sensitive moment because the reform-minded Soviet leader, Nikita Khrushchev, had been trying to ease relations with the United States.

Goldwater said that NATO commanders in Europe should be given the authority to use nuclear weapons on their own initiative. Goldwater even urged the use of "low-yield" nuclear weapons to defoliate South Vietnamese forests.

Usually American presidential races are decided more on differences in personality than on differences on issues. That was certainly true in the previous election between Kennedy and Richard Nixon. But this election was to be about huge differences on the main issues.

In 1964, even if the birthrate was slacking off, seventeen-year-olds became the largest age group in the United States, a group deemed too young to vote for another four years but eligible to be shipped to war in only one year, and a group who felt the one voice that could express what they thought and felt was music. The race was on to sell them records.

By 1964 Hitsville U.S.A. had become the hit factory that Gordy had planned. His assembly line found talented youngsters — to use a favorite Ed Sullivan word — kids fresh out of high school, or in a few cases even younger.

Gordy now had a staff in place hired, with specific skills for the assembly line that would turn gifted street singers into polished nightclub performers. Motown artists wore glittery tuxedos and dreamy pastel gowns of chiffon and sparkles and satin with gold lamé. They sometimes brought in designers such as Helen Duncan, who designed satin pantsuits for the Vandellas, and they had a hair-stylist named Betty Bullock. If the hair couldn't obtain the look the designers wanted, there were styled wigs. The fashionable Gordy sisters played a key role in designing what were known at Motown as "the uniforms," especially Gwen, who ran a department called Special Projects.

Cholly Atkins was a nightclub singer in the 1930s. He became famous appearing with the great tap dancer Charles "Honi" Coles in an act billed as Coles and Atkins. When rock 'n' roll started to dominate in the 1950s, it seemed that his era of elegant, formally dressed club performers was over. In fact it was, but Berry Gordy gave it a brief respite in the first half of the 1960s. When Gordy was starting Hitsville U.S.A.,

Cholly Atkins was working at Harlem's Apollo Theater. It was that lull after rock 'n' roll when everyone was trying to find the next new thing. Atkins started helping young acts that he liked at the Apollo. Soon he had his own studio in the building where *The Ed Sullivan Show* was shot, and acts went to him to pick up a few steps. Starting at the very beginning, in 1959, especially at the urging of Harvey Fuqua, whose Moonglows had learned steps from Atkins, Motown would periodically work with Atkins until they hired him full time to choreograph all of the Motown acts.

Early Motown acts were occasionally awkward. Martha Reeves struggled with her microphone cable. But by 1964 smooth-moving acts were a Motown characteristic. Much of the look of the Supremes, perhaps Motown's smoothest act, was the result of the hand gestures and over-the-shoulder poses devised by Cholly Atkins. Atkins told music writer Nelson George that he took R&B acts "and prepared them for that transition from chitlin circuit to Las Vegas."

That transition was what Motown was all about, taking black talent and making it something that was still black but with universal appeal, an act that played the Apollo but, as integration slowly took hold, could also play Las Vegas. Atkins worked for Motown in a department called Artist Development. Among the other key figures in this department was Maurice King, whom Berry Gordy had lured from the Flame. King was eighteen years Gordy's senior and he always insisted that the young artists call him "Mr. King." He not only taught them music theory but prepared them for club performances with such details as the patter between sets.

A key component of the Artist Development department was Maxine Powell, who knew the Gordys from their print shop and was lured away from her finishing school to Motown. She told the artists that they were being trained to perform in Buckingham Palace and the White House. Over time a few of them have appeared at those venues. She taught them social graces and manners and that what she called "body communication" was "an art." She also taught them how to give interviews without ever saying anything with the slightest negative suggestion about Motown. Even today, former Motown artists, full of complaints about their treatment, many of them having even taken Gordy to court, are careful to consistently praise Motown and Berry Gordy.

Powell was also a bargain hunter, scouring

the sales racks for bargain dresses, often in wrong sizes, which she would then tailor to the singers. She worked especially with Motown's women, such as Kim Weston, Martha Reeves, and the Supremes. Looking at recordings of the Supremes' successive appearances on *The Ed Sullivan Show* over the years, one can see Powell's work on Diana Ross. At first she was an uncontrollable ham, mugging outrageously to the camera, but Powell gradually smoothed these impulses into a more subtle performance. Diana Ross called Maxine Powell "the woman who taught me everything I know."

Powell also worked with the men. She tried to keep the Temptations from sweating too much. Marvin Gaye, wandering Hitsville in hats and shades and pipes, insisted that he was already too cool to need Miss Powell. She did think he was better than most, more polished and well mannered, but pointed out that he had bad posture and sang with his eyes closed, and she worked with him on that.

"I am here to help you skip to the bank," she would tell them.

According to Powell, when she met Martha Reeves she was "like the rest of them, crude and rude and speaking street language." But she said that Martha became "a great lady." She and Martha Reeves remained lifelong friends in Detroit, even though Reeves still called her "Miss Powell." Even decades after Motown, in her nineties, Powell remained a serious bargain hunter, terrorizing the local Walgreens with her weekly newspaper coupons, ordering around the staff, demanding to know where the listed items were, and insisting on the advertised sale prices. Then she would give a sweet smile. She mobilized the entire sales staff in her search for discounts. No one argues with a tiny nonagenarian in a large hat with a sense of mission.

When Miss Powell was interviewed for this book, Martha said she was over ninety-five, but Powell would not give her age. "If I told my age, people would start asking if I have arthritis or something. I don't have nothing, I'm not on any medicine," she explained. She was a tiny woman not much more than four feet tall but a powerhouse in her way. She poked with a jabbing left to make a particularly urgent point. She still picked up some work when people came to talk to her about Motown. She would give them some pointers and they would end up hiring her.

Ivy Jo Hunter said of Maxine Powell, "She made show business look like show business." In a 1970 article in the London *Sunday Times,* Philip Norman wrote, "Songs like Marvin Gaye's 'Through the Grapevine' or Martha and the Vandellas' 'Dancing in the Street' have all the sharp style of the urban Negro at his best." That was the goal.

But it took time to arrive at just the right style and the right sound. Jon Landau, in his 1967 *Crawdaddy* article, pointed out that the Motown of 1963–64 was far more musically sophisticated than the earlier recordings. They developed an extremely strong percussion beat and an extremely simple and clear melody line. Back when Martha and the Vandellas were backing up Marvin Gaye, they established a pattern of the backup coming in high-pitched at the beginning of every sentence, usually with "oohs." This, too, became a trademark of Motown songs.

By the summer of 1964 they were there. A key turn in this route was the upheaval caused by Mary Wells. In April 1964, Mary Wells's "My Guy" rose to number 1 on the *Billboard* chart, a fact that seemed to confirm the magazine's decision to have a combined black and white singles chart. The song had been written and produced by Smokey Robinson, who was unofficially in charge of Mary Wells. But shortly after this, she demanded a new contract with a better share of royalties. She used the loophole that she had signed her previous contract at age seventeen, and now that she was no longer a minor because she had just turned twenty-one, the old contract was no longer valid. She could not get the terms she wanted and left Motown, signing a far more lucrative deal with 20th Century Fox Records.

It was a huge blow for Berry Gordy, who had always assumed that once anyone was within the nurturing embrace of the Motown family, no contract issue would make them want to leave. He started rewriting Motown contracts to avoid any other escapes. It was a tremendous upheaval to lose their biggest female star, the key player in developing the "Motown sound." It was also a huge blow for Smokey Robinson, who now had to compete with other songwriters and producers for emerging female stars.

Part of Gordy's formula for success was constant competition within the family. Artists competed with one another to get songs. On the road, the bigger the hit, the later in the act an artist appeared on the bill. But positions could be changed by the size of applause, which was carefully calibrated every night. Producers were hooked up to artists based on the proven chemistry of the match. Chemistry meant having a hit. As soon as a record was produced that was not a hit, the artist got a new producer. Even Berry Gordy and Mickey Stevenson produced under these rules. Nothing short of a hit was acceptable at Motown. The same applied to songwriters. If an artist had a hit, the writer of that song had an option on the artist's next recording, and other writers would have to prove that they had something better. There was even competition for studio space. Mickey Stevenson recalled:

> We worked at home, Hitsville, where we all felt at home. We had the kitchen working — chili cooking. You could go back and get a cup of chili so you didn't have to run home. Don't lose your spot. You lose your spot, they look for you, you're not there, you lose your spot. We were going round the clock. Instead of going home, you be in the kitchen with the chili.

Now even beyond the usual competition was the competition for which producer with which song was going to make which female singer the next Mary Wells. Mickey Stevenson's idea for the Mary Wells replacement was his wife, Kim Weston, but she did not do well with the Smokey Robinson song she was given, "Looking for the Right Guy." Later in the year Mickey did produce a number of hits with the help of Holland-Dozier-Holland, with Kim replacing Wells on Marvin Gaye duets.

Martha Reeves was also in contention, but Gordy had another idea. The Supremes' last song had been their first hit in eight recordings, and on the road their amateurism next to the Vandellas was obvious. Yet they were the group Gordy focused on. Gordy's idea was that rather than having the strongest voice, Flo Ballard, as the lead he would bring up the skinny, big-eyed girl with the soft voice who mugged and hammed her way through the songs. Diana Ross would carry the group with charisma. Lamont Dozier, who often supervised the backup, started moving the microphone farther away from Ballard, lest even in backup she overpower Ross. Gordy became fixated on developing Ross to the point that the other female singers, including Kim Weston and Martha Reeves, were growing resentful. Ivy Jo Hunter recalled once suggesting to Gordy that someone else could sing a song better than Diana, "and Berry turned a different shade of dark" and asked if he meant the phrasing. Ivy said, "No, she just has a better voice." And Berry was silent.

There were unconfirmed rumors of a sexual romance between the two. At least it was unconfirmed until 1994, when Gordy detailed their lovemaking in his autobiography — apparently he was unsuccessful on their first night — and Ross gave the book possibly the weirdest blurb ever to appear on the back of a book: "I also wish he had told me he loved me, as he says in the book. Maybe things would have been different — and maybe not."

Gordy was famous for his several marriages and various affairs. His brother-in-law Marvin Gaye called him "the horniest man in Detroit."

But there was not a great deal of complaining because at Motown, even more than most places, there was no arguing with success. In the spring of 1964 the Supremes released "Where Did Our Love Go," which reached number 1 on the *Billboard* chart. Their next four songs all hit number 1: "Baby Love," "Come See About Me," "Stop! In the Name of Love," and "Back in My Arms Again."

Like "Where Did Our Love Go," all of them were Holland-Dozier-Holland songs. They were all songs about love, with tremendous crossover appeal and no real edge in those edgy times. They were an escape with a hard beat and a soft melody well suited for what had become the soft sound of the group. And there was an additional key to their success. Gordy and his company pushed their records harder than any other Motown recordings.

By 1964 Motown and American R&B was confronted with a sudden and powerful new challenge. In the top 100 songs of 1963 in which Martha and the Vandellas had three hits and the Supremes one, the new British group, the Beatles, had seven hit records, and in the month of February 1964, when they visited the United States, 60 percent of records sold were by the Beatles. Another British group, Gerry and the Pacemakers, also had a hit, as did the British group Freddie and the Dreamers, with "I'm Telling You Now." Also at number 39 was Dusty Springfield with "I Only Want to Be with You." Springfield was one of a number of white British singers who took up American R&B in that period when it appeared to be fading in the United States. Springfield, who became a great champion of Martha and the Vandellas in Britain and a close friend of Martha Reeves, intuitively understood R&B and this was evident in her evening gown costuming, her singing, the hard-driving beat, the backup singers, and the sound track with brass and strings. She would have easily fit in at Motown despite her peroxide blond hairdos.

Though the Beatles named themselves after a white American group, Buddy Holly and the Crickets, they too were clearly influenced by black music, especially in their early songs. Most notable was their use of slides into falsetto, as in "I Want to Hold Your Hand." There were also the Chuck Berry guitar riffs. Almost all the new British music had these old African American devices.

In 1964, that year of Motown and the Beatles, Little Richard wanted to revive his career and found that he had been forgotten in the United States. He went to England and toured with the Beatles. To the English he was still a star.

On the Beatles' first American tour, eight days in February, they were known to young fans but not widely known in America. They wanted to pose with the then–heavyweight champion Sonny Liston, but he grumbled that he did not want to be seen with those "sissies." So they tried for the contender, the long shot still known as Cassius Clay, even though he would probably be beaten and forgotten. It was prefight and good publicity. Clay was working out at the Fifth Street Gym on Miami Beach. He stayed in the black section of downtown Miami and ran the few miles to the gym as part of his workout, hoping the police didn't stop him running along the causeway. A black man running was considered cause for suspicion.

The Beatles, too, were on Miami Beach at the last stop of their tour at the Deauville Hotel. Clay, always appreciative of comic moments, agreed to pose with them. They climbed on each other to try to be as big as him. In one shot he jolts all four of them lined up with one punch. It was silly and good publicity and everyone was happy, but when the four left, Clay walked over to Robert Lipsyte, a cub reporter for the *New York Times* sports page, whose lack of seniority drew him the coverage of the unlikely contender. Clay leaned down and asked Lipsyte, "Who were those sissies?"

A lot of people did know who they were. The four played to 3,500 at the Deauville, almost 3,000 at New York's Carnegie Hall, and 8,000 at Washington's Coliseum, and their appearance on *The Ed Sullivan Show* became one of his most famous broadcasts. They were all premier venues, but when they returned in the summer they would need bigger spaces, giant stadiums.

More British invasions were planned. While the Beatles were poor kids from Liverpool, the core of the group to be known as the Rolling Stones were two very middle-class kids named Mick Jagger and Keith Richards. Jagger's father was a gym teacher who expressed disappointment that Mick never realized his potential as a cricketer. "He could have been a great athlete," the older Jagger once said. The two grew up together in Dartford, Kent, in south-eastern England. Nevertheless, they were greatly influenced by Chuck Berry and Little Richard — whomever they could hear from those few movies that made it over, because the BBC kept them off the radio.

And then, just when they started getting the music at the end of the 1950s, the music seemed to stop. Keith Richards said in a 1972 interview with David Dalton of *Rolling Stone* magazine about the end of the 1950s, when they were starting: "By that time, the initial wham had gone out of rock 'n' roll. . . . They'd run out of songs in a way, it seemed like." The Rolling Stones decided to take up where America had left off. Not only were they to make music in the R&B and rock 'n' roll traditions, but — unlike the Beatles — in the style of Chuck

Berry, Jerry Lee Lewis, and later James Brown, they moved onstage and made themselves a visual spectacle. Jagger, as it turned out, was an athlete after all.

They were one of the first white groups to sing with blacks, doing an opening act for the Ronettes on their 1964 English tour. Although the Ronettes, two sisters and a cousin, had mixed parentage and were light skinned, they were considered black.

Another musical mini-step toward integration took place at the hands of a British singer in 1964. Adam Faith, an Englishman with carefully combed straight blond hair, at first glance seemed whiter than Pat Boone. But he had adopted some of the vocal distortions of blues — or of Elvis Presley's adaptation of blues — and moved to a hard beat. In 1964 he recorded "It's Alright" with the backup sung by two black brothers, the Isley Brothers. Though only backup singers on this recording, they had some standing as black stars. They had previously had doo-wop hits and in 1966 would become Motown stars with the Holland-Dozier-Holland song "This Old Heart of Mine." In fact, at the time of the recording the black backup singers had a bigger name in America than did the British lead singer. The Adam Faith song was only released in the United States, where with its simple lyrics screamed and shouted to a driving rhythm, it became a racially integrated Top 40 hit. Perhaps of more significance, the integrated aspect of this 1964 hit was rarely discussed.

The Rolling Stones came to the United States in June 1964 with a new R&B that was harder and edgier, and faced screaming teenagers on a three-week tour that was the beginning of a growing reputation in America.

There can be no doubt that Motown would have sold more records were it not for the British groups, especially the Beatles, but Motown did hold its own, and in 1964 the record industry was once again thriving, due largely to both Motown and the Beatles. It was the British that gave the popular music world a sense that something new was happening, the new music that deejays like Cousin Brucie were looking for, and that sense of excitement also helped Motown as they perfected their sound. Motown had cordial relations with their British rivals, though the Beatles' management irritated Gordy by negotiating low prices for Motown song rights. Motown groups, including Martha and the Vandellas, toured the UK and got the same kind of screaming reception that the Beatles got in the United States. They were feeding off each other's excitement and selling a lot of records. Martha Reeves said, "The Beatles came here and they did *Ed Sullivan* and they became big here, but there was always the idea of an exchange, so we went to England and we were big there. It was never a competition. We were complimentary and we sang each other's songs. I sang 'Eleanor Rigby.' "

By May the press was getting more interested in a few hundred young people who preferred freedom songs. In fact their struggle was becoming so famous that the music was bringing substantial record sales. It had always been part of Bob Dylan's repertoire. The Kingston Trio, a San Francisco folk group, regularly had Top 40 hits and included in their pop folk albums occasional songs from the civil rights movement, such as Dylan's "Blowin' in the Wind." By 1964 so many other groups were doing freedom songs that the trio faded. The Freedom Singers themselves, the civil rights singing group, were selling records. Peter, Paul, and Mary, who also sang at civil rights events, recorded their first album, *Peter, Paul and Mary,* in 1962, and it was a number 1 hit for seven weeks. Pete Seeger, who had been blacklisted in the 1950s, reemerged as a civil rights singer in the 1960s, popularizing "We Shall Overcome," while being directly involved with SNCC. He was also enormously popular by 1964, as was Joan Baez, who was equally famous for her recording of "We Shall Overcome."

In June 1964, the Mississippi Freedom Summer began with great national interest. SNCC leader Bob Moses had been developing his ideas on a campaign to register black voters in Mississippi since 1960. SNCC was strongly divided on whether this was the most worthwhile effort, given the unlikelihood of success. The idea of bringing in hundreds of volunteers from the North, mostly white, was particularly controversial. At the heart of SNCC's success was its ability to find and nurture local black leaders. There was a fear that the whites who would join would be well educated and would tend to take over the movement. But unidentified assailants regularly murdered local black activists in Mississippi, and these killings drew little attention. Attacks on white northerners would not go unnoticed, and these northerners would draw northern news media and then the federal government would have to start protecting civil rights workers.

As the volunteers were being trained in Ohio, Mississippi was preparing its violence. In February the Ku Klux Klan, a relic of the past, was resurrected in Mississippi. Before the volunteers even arrived, there was an increase in beatings and other violence directed at organizers in Mississippi. The state highway patrol was increased by two hundred men. The Mississippi legislature gave municipalities greater power to make arrests. The distribution of leaflets on economic boycotts was declared a felony. Local police increased personnel and acquired more firearms.

Meanwhile three hundred volunteers arrived at a well-greened campus in Oxford, Ohio. They were told to expect beatings, shootings, and arrest. For SNCC workers, that had become a way of life. Years later John Lewis estimated that he had been arrested forty times while campaigning for civil rights.

When not singing freedom songs, the volunteers took self-defense workshops in which they were taught in the event of an attack how to curl up on the ground in a fetal position with knees tucked up as close to the head as possible. They also learned to lock arms and sway as they sang freedom songs. They were advised not to carry watches, pens, contact lenses, glasses, or more than ten dollars in cash. They were never to go out alone, especially at night. They were also schooled to avoid offending local customs by swearing, slights to religion, drunkenness, or women wearing pants. Though the volunteers were an interracial group, mixed dating was absolutely to be avoided.

Volunteers were screened for correct attitudes. They had to understand that they were to defer to local leadership. Glory seekers and those with what was called "a John Brown complex," the desire to be a charismatic crusader, were to be avoided. In the end, seven hundred volunteers were sent south. While the average young American was listening to Motown and the Beatles, these seven hundred with their own songs were an elite. The average family income was 50 percent above the norm. Ninety percent of them were white, but that was also true of America as a whole. Almost half were from Ivy League or other elite colleges.

The world they went to could have been a planet away from the Motown bubble, where they were polishing etiquette, vying for studio space, and singing love songs aimed at appealing to an integrated market.

The hypothesis that the abuse of these all-American northerners would stir a huge response did not take long to confirm. On June 21, when the project was just getting started, a volunteer and two CORE organizers working with the Summer Project disappeared in the area of Philadelphia, Mississippi. Had it only been James Chaney, a local Mississippi black who had joined CORE the year before to work on voter registration, the rest of America would have taken no more notice than it had with the dozens of other blacks killed and missing. But with him were two white organizers, Michael Schwerner, an Ivy League–educated New Yorker with some experience as a CORE organizer, and Andrew Goodman, also from New York, a volunteer with the Summer Project.

Goodman had arrived only the day before. The three were sent to investigate the burning of a church where Chaney and Schwerner had urged the black congregation to register a month earlier. It was one of twenty black churches that were fire-bombed in the summer of 1964. The three were arrested and released, and then they vanished.

President Johnson and Attorney General Robert Kennedy responded to a huge public outcry. The disappearance of the three had been a front-page story around the country. The FBI resisted involvement, but under enormous political pressure from the administration, they took on the case, setting up an FBI office in Philadelphia with one hundred and fifty FBI agents who questioned about a thousand people, half of whom were thought to be KKK members. Hundreds more, including Navy divers, were sent to search for the bodies. Divers found seven other bodies of local civil rights workers whose murders had drawn little attention, but no one could find the three for whom they were searching. Meanwhile, the drama made almost daily news throughout the country.

On July 16, in a world somewhat closer to Motown, an off-duty policeman became involved in a dispute between black summer school students and a white supervisor in Harlem. The officer shot and killed a fifteen-year-old boy who the officer said had attacked him with a knife. A crowd of young blacks began smashing store windows. This led to days of violent conflict in both Harlem and Bedford-Stuyvesant, the leading black neighborhoods of New York. The expected "riot" season had begun.

*Life* magazine reported, "The worst fears come true as New York's Negro ghetto erupts." The press struggled to understand the phenomenon, which they tended to see as Negroes run amok and police defending law and order or, as the *Life* headline put it, "A Rampage and the Bullets of the Law." A photograph showing a bleeding black man with a clearly horizontal wound across his temple explained that he was grazed by "one of the hundreds of bullets fired into the air by police to disperse rioters." Aside from the fact that such a horizontal wound could not have come from a bullet fired into the air unless the victim was an unlucky sky-diver, the article doesn't even question the use of bullets for riot control. But even this reporting suggests that there was something more profound going on. "What sets the New York riots apart from past racial up-heavals," the article stated, ". . . is rather the blind desperation of the rioters. They have gone — or, as they feel, been driven — beyond reason." Even the magazine's own photos of clubbing and shooting suggested that it was the police who had run amok. A week later, the National Guard was called in to control a black uprising in Rochester, New York. In August there were similar disturbances in New Jersey — in Paterson,

Jersey City, and Elizabeth — and in Chicago and Jacksonville. It could spread anywhere that had a large black ghetto, and every city was braced for a summer explosion — Philadelphia, PA, Baltimore and DC, can't forget the Motor City . . .

Meanwhile in Detroit, with the Beatles at their heels, Motown was still searching for the perfect sound for young America. Among the more recent Detroit people who had come to Motown looking for opportunities was Ivy Jo Hunter, a horn player. While Gordy and Stevenson had been picking up talent in the local clubs, Hunter was away in the Army. When he returned to Detroit in the winter of 1963, he found work shoveling snow. He also sang R&B in local clubs. He occasionally helped out young groups and was overheard by Hank Cosby, a saxophone player at Motown, giving tips to one group. Cosby recognized that this small man with a fast and mischievous sense of humor had a deep understanding of music. Hunter's response to the offer of a job at Motown was, "It pays better than shoveling snow." That was about as high a praise for Motown pay as was ever heard.

Neither he nor Martha Reeves could exactly remember this, but they thought they had once gone out on a date. They had met at a rent party, a common practice in urban black communities where people would throw a party in their own home and charge admission for music and dancing or sometimes gambling. The goal was to earn enough money to pay the rent.

In 1964, just as that throbbing summer of discontent was getting started, back in the Motown bubble Hunter worked on a song with Mickey Stevenson and Marvin Gaye. Stevenson and Gaye had done many songs together, and Hunter would go on to do songs with Gaye, and songs with Stevenson, but this was the only song the three did together. The exact evolution of the song is unclear. Stevenson was interviewed in Los Angeles and Hunter in Detroit, and they had slightly varying stories. Gaye died tragically in 1984, shot to death by his troubled father.

The one thing Stevenson and Hunter both agree on is that Gaye contributed the phrase "dancing in the street." He, of course, did not invent the phrase. In past centuries it was a common expression connected with carnivals, especially in black culture. Dancing in the street was celebrating. In law, the phrase was best known for the response of a celebrated First Amendment scholar, Alexander Meiklejohn, to the Supreme Court's landmark decision that *The New York Times* could not be responsible for damages for an ad criticizing the Montgomery, Alabama, police in their handling of a civil rights demonstration. *Sullivan v. New York Times* held libel to a higher standard of proof to avoid inhibiting freedom of the press. When Meiklejohn learned of the unanimous court ruling he said, "It is an occasion for dancing in the street." The statement stuck to the decision, and over the years is frequently quoted in essays both for and against the Supreme Court ruling. It is a phrase that sticks.

At Motown, songs were not written the way Rodgers and Hammerstein did, combining a composer and a lyricist. Everybody did a bit of everything. "Once you start writing," said Mickey Stevenson, "it comes as a collaboration." He could not give any specifics on who wrote what, but he did say, when asked about the meaning of the song, that it had come to him and Gaye when driving through the city on a hot summer day, watching kids of different races playing by fire hydrant water spouts. Gaye said to him, "Dancing in the street." So to Stevenson it was a song about integration.

Hunter recalled that most of the song was

written in the attic of the home of Mickey Stevenson and Kim Weston. "I was writing this melancholy song, and Marvin Gaye was listening and said, 'That's no melancholy song, that's dancing in the street.' "

According to Hunter, the other Gaye contribution was that he named the cites in the song, selecting urban centers that had important black communities, including his hometown, Washington, DC. After Gaye listed several of these, Hunter said, "Can't forget the Motor City." And it went into the song just like that.

There was already a tradition, especially in black music, of songs listing American cities. Probably the most famous was Chuck Berry's "Sweet Little Sixteen," which mentions Boston, Pittsburgh, Texas, San Francisco Bay, St. Louis, and New Orleans. It even contains the line, exactly like the one in "Dancing in the Street": "Philadelphia, P-A."

There are also conflicting versions of how Martha Reeves came to sing this song. It is agreed that she just happened to be in the studio on the right day. It also seems to be true that Kim Weston had been offered the song first. Guitarist Joe Messina recalled that "Kim Weston" was the artist name on the music he was handed for the session.

The story that Kim Weston did not want the song and that Marvin Gaye seized on Martha on a whim as a replacement is at best an exaggeration. When interviewed, Kim Weston denied turning down the song, and said that she wanted it. Furthermore, Martha, in her autobiography, said that she initially did not like the song. Later in an interview, she backed off slightly from that, saying that it was just a momentary feeling. "I was not impressed. I don't want to dance in the street. I want to dance on a big stage or a big elegant ballroom."

Mickey Stevenson said that his wife had been assigned the song. The track had already been made, and they needed a demo tape for Kim to study. This was the usual practice. The artist would spend two days studying the song with the tape before the recording session.

Stevenson said he had never intended it for Martha. But she was extremely professional and reliable. Late one night, according to Stevenson, they wanted to make the demo tape for Kim, and Martha was still there. Stevenson said that he and Marvin Gaye and Ivy Jo Hunter were in the studio working on a demo tape on top of the finished music track. After hearing the track with Paul Riser's arrangement, Gaye and

Hunter were concerned that Kim Weston's usual heavier approach was not well suited for the light feel of the song.

Kim Weston, later in life still living in Detroit in poor housing and long separated from Stevenson, still remembered being offered the song. She recalled being in the kitchen cooking when Stevenson and Gaye burst in full of excitement and announced, "We've got your next hit."

The three ran up to the studio in the attic and played it on the piano and sang it.

"I loved it," said Weston. "They wrote it for me."

Mickey said, "Okay, what we will do is, we'll dub somebody in on it, let Kim take the record, and study the voice and know what we're looking for." Although Martha Reeves has always remembered Marvin picking her for the song, and he may have been the one who approached her, Stevenson recalled that she was his idea. It would have been his decision. In any event, they were only looking for someone to make the demo and not the final record. According to Stevenson, they had Reeves listen to the song twice. Then she sang it.

According to the oft-repeated legend, she tore through the song brilliantly, and then they had to tell her that they had made a mistake and failed to record it. So they did it again. This myth was destroyed in the fall of 2011 in her old Eastside family home, a two-story white-shingled, purple-trimmed house with a yard enclosed by a chain-link fence. No one lived there anymore and it might have been just one more abandoned building. There was no market for selling such homes. There were many abandoned, boarded-up, decaying houses in the neighborhood.

Martha was sentimental about the house where she had grown up, where she learned to sing at the kitchen sink, the oldest girl of eleven children, assigned to washing the dishes; the house where she used to play with the child Stevie Wonder to keep him out of everyone's way at the studio. The house is full of posters of concerts and recordings from the 1960s and 1970s and shelves of scrapbooks. Martha liked to go there to think and to talk. We were sitting on the lumpy old furniture in the living room and she was explaining about how they failed to tape the first take and how she had to do it again, and how this irritated her. As she spoke, she was playing the famous recording. I asked her which take she thought was better, and before she could answer, Hunter interrupted with a sly grin and said, "Look at me. I'm sitting in a studio with an artist you don't want to upset. Do I say, 'Do it again,' or do I say the machine wasn't on?"

Martha slapped her thigh with a look of shock on her face. Forty-seven years earlier she was tricked into redoing a recording and producing her best and most famous work. Not only that, but Hunter revealed another fact that she had never known. She had been "up for a release." At Motown, artists were often the last to know things. "Up for a release" meant that either Gordy or Stevenson had put the word out to the approximately fifteen songwriters that they wanted a new song for Martha and the Vandellas. Holland-Dozier-Holland would have had the option on them because they had written their last hit. But other songwriters could try to steal them away. "Dancing in the Street" was just the song to do that.

Reeves said, "I just sang it the way I felt it." As she sang, she thought about being an Eastside teenager, on a porch, with one of the small portable record players that had become available in the 1950s, playing 45s while kids danced to the music out on the street. When she finished the second take, she looked up at the small and crowded control room, where Gaye, Stevenson,

Hunter, and the engineer, Lawrence Horn, were. Martha said, "When I saw grown men up in the window slapping each other, I knew."

That is not exactly how Stevenson remembered that moment in the booth. Martha's voice was just as he had observed at her first audition: "not great, but a unique sound." It was neither sweet nor beautiful but it had an undefeatable power that some would call sexy, others edgy, some even said political. Landau called it "a straight, tough soul voice." In the words of drummer Stephen Jordan, "Her voice was pleading and not super aggressive. It makes you feel good." It had that element of the church music with which she had grown up. Whatever that force was, it had never been more evocative than on the recording they just made.

But Stevenson had a problem at home with Kim Weston, to whom he had promised the song. He remembered:

She finished the song. Ivy Jo looked at me. Marvin Gaye looked at me. And they both said at the same time, "What you going to do, William R.?"

I say, "What you mean?"

They say, "You know exactly what we mean."

"It do sound like a hit, don't it?"

Ivy Jo, who had a huge bush of hair, a giant head on a small body because he had vowed not to cut his hair until he had a hit, said, "Sound like it? I'm going to the fucking barbershop."

Then Stevenson said, "Well, I got to take this into Kim."

To which Gaye replied, "And do what? You are the A&R man. Your word is the best song goes on the best person. Isn't that your word?"

Stevenson had established a sacrosanct rule that the artist who had shown herself or himself to be the best singer for a song was the one who got it. He had always insisted that it didn't matter whose toes got stepped on, including his own. If you could show that you were the best singer for the song, you got it. Now that moment had come.

According to Kim Weston, the reckoning that Stevenson was dreading never happened. The next time she heard the song was when she heard Martha and the Vandellas singing it on the radio.

The record was produced quickly. There were no stops or doctoring in the four-track studio. The Funk Brothers' track was one of the best they had ever done. Despite that, the few musicians who are still alive don't recall the session. It was just one of many. Asked if he remembered the session, during an interview in 2012 back in his home in Gore Springs, Mississippi, guitarist Eddie Willis said, "Man, we did thousands of sessions." Joe Messina thought he remembered that it was a short session with not many takes. Some Funk Brothers tracks took nine hours to produce, but not this one.

Paul Riser, a twenty-year-old Detroit trombonist schooled in classical music, arranged it. He had been asked to join Motown in 1962 as an eighteen-year-old trombonist just out of high school.

One of Riser's most important contributions was the introduction. After drums and bass briefly "set the groove," as they almost always did, two trumpets, Johnny Trudell, whom they had found at the Flame, and Floyd Jones, blasted a fanfare. The trumpet blast is the first thing to grab the audience. Martha Reeves said that as soon as she heard the trumpets, she started to feel good about the song. She also said that in fifty years of touring with the song, as soon as the audience hears the trumpets, they get excited.

Motown did not do many brass introductions. But there were other unusual characteristics to the track. The drumming was different. This was partly because the track was not done with their usual drummer, Benny Benjamin, but with Fred Waits, who had played with blues greats such as John Lee Hooker. Waits was born in Mississippi and came to the University of Detroit on a scholarship to play flute. Motown found him, and he played drums in 1963 on Stevie Wonder's first hit "Fingertips," which also featured Marvin Gaye's drumming. After Motown he went on to work with bebop jazz greats such as Sonny Rollins.

Benjamin, especially on Holland-Dozier-Holland songs, had developed a distinctly Motown sound of hitting hard on every beat. But Waits hit the second and fourth beats very hard — really slammed them. Waits was known for his elaborate fills, the part of the drumming that propels the song forward after a pattern is established. He hit very hard on the cymbal, although some, including Ivy Jo Hunter, recall Jack Ashford being dubbed in with tambourine and stick cracking on the downbeats like gunshots. The downbeats crash loud and hard throughout the song and drive it forward. According to Stephen Jordan, a leading R&B drummer who had been a student of

Waits, the drum picks up tempo slightly so that the song gradually gets slightly faster and gives a sense that it is rushing to its conclusion.

James Jamerson was also unusual, basically playing one chord, switching the emphasis to the offbeat, known in music as syncopation. After the session, he said, "That was the most fun I ever had playing one note."

The trumpet introduction is the fanfare before the announcement. The announcement begins "Calling out around the world." This is the hook, the phrase that grabs the listeners. The trumpets are the hook before the hook. The hook should be as early in the song as possible. Mickey Stevenson said, "The hook locks you in. After I give you the hook, I can take you different places and bring you back." Stevenson remembered that when they were writing the song, "Calling out around the world" were the first words written. The rest of the song grew out of the hook.

Repetitive phrasing, or as Frank Sinatra put it, "imbecilic reiteration," is also part of the R&B formula. If you listen carefully, the phrase "dancing in the street" is repeated twenty-six times in this two-minute, thirty-six-second recording, or more than once

241

every six seconds. A 45 rpm record could hold three minutes on a side, but if the recording was longer than two minutes and forty-five seconds, deejays became very reluctant to play it.

After Martha sang, the Vandellas were called in to dub in a background. Annette Beard, married and pregnant, decided to give up being a Vandella and had been replaced by Betty Kelly; this was her first recording as a Vandella. Rosalind Ashford recalled not being in the studio but having been called in to do the recording, which is further evidence that they were not planning on having Martha and the Vandellas sing it. She remembered being taken into a side room to learn the song. She said that she and Betty Kelly learned it very quickly and then went into the studio with notes she had written on a piece of paper. She said, "It said things like 'ooo' four times, then four 'ahs,' then 'dancing in the street' three times."

They rehearsed a little more than an hour, according to Ashford — Betty Kelly remembers it being at most forty minutes — before making the recording. Ivy Jo Hunter sang along with them, and they did it in only a few takes.

Rosalind remembers loving the song. "I

assumed it would work. But I didn't think whether it would be a hit. I just knew it would be a good song."

Stephen Jordan said, "The whole thing was something supernatural. It couldn't happen again. That's the beauty of records. You can catch a moment — this was a watershed moment."

Gordy agreed as soon as he heard it. This was what he had been working toward. He called it "the song that seemed to tie everything together." He said that "the goal to hook people in the first twenty seconds was never accomplished better."

It was released on July 31, while the Vietnam problem and the presidential election were heating up and Chaney, Goodman, and Schwerner still had not been found in Mississippi. In New York, Cousin Brucie was so excited about the song that he aired the promotion copy even before the release date. He recalled:

The record industry at the time was really boring. Motown sent me this song and said it was a new good-time R&B Motown release — a good party song. . . . We had nothing to play. We had British stuff. Motown gave us something to play. When I started out, I was told I couldn't play "too Negro." They didn't think blacks were any market. But this was new. It was exciting. It had energy. It was black. It was R&B but it was very palatable to lily whites' pink ear. It didn't challenge us. That's what Gordy did.

The B side, "There He Is (At My Door)," is almost a throwaway. It did not make much of an impression, since it was already two years old, and next to the sparkling new sound of "Dancing in the Street," the B side seemed to emphasize how much the Motown sound had evolved since 1962. The song by Eddie Holland, Lamont Dozier, and Frank Gorman, predating the famous Holland-Dozier-Holland team, had first been recorded by the Vells, a group in which Gloria Jean Williamson sang lead and Reeves was one of the backup singers. For this B side, Reeves's lead was dubbed in so that she is actually singing backup for herself. But the song, though no longer remembered, got a huge ride by being on the flip side of "Dancing in the Street."

Slowly, "Dancing in the Street" started to have an enormous impact on the young people who heard it — the slamming back-beat, and the bell-like brightness of the sound. Jazz guitarist Pat Metheny was not even a teenager when he first heard it. "I remember that song vividly, coming out that summer. I was nine years old. That spring my grandfather, my dad's dad, gave me a transistor radio, which I kept tuned to WHB Top Forty radio in Kansas City."

Later, as a jazz musician, he appreciated it even more. He was not an R&B musician, but this music had jazz in it. He especially noted the bridge, a musical term for a passage of different characteristics that moves a song from one verse to another. The bridge on "Dancing in the Street" slips to a minor key and has been singled out by many musicians, including Keith Richards. Mention "Dancing in the Street" to any musician and he or she will often reply, "That bridge!" When Pat Metheny recalled the song, he said, "Just that bridge in 'Dancing.' The bridge switches to minor. In the past thirty years there haven't been a lot of tunes with that many chords."

Jon Landau, then a leading critic of R&B music, was interviewed on tour with Bruce Springsteen whom he manages. He said, "There are some records that are so perfectly constructed, when I hear them, I can't think of anything that would improve them — 'Johnny B. Goode,' 'Like a Rolling Stone'

— 'Dancing' is one of those records. The record is perfect."

On August 2, two days after "Dancing in the Street" was released, America changed. At the time, according to polls, the leading issue in the United States was civil rights. Lyndon Johnson and Congress had earmarked a huge part of the federal budget for social spending on the programs that were to build Johnson's "Great Society." At the beginning of the year, Khrushchev had announced that he was reducing his military, and Johnson planned to do the same. "And I'm taking that money and putting it into poverty," Johnson told California congresswoman Helen Gahagan Douglas on the first day of 1964. By the end of the year, Khrushchev would be replaced by the more aggressive Brezhnev, but Johnson's plan had really fallen apart before that, on August 2. The United States had been avoiding war with North Vietnam but finding small ways to harass them. They trained and armed South Vietnamese, establishing a fleet of fast Norwegian-made patrol boats in Da Nang, a harbor in northern South Vietnam. From there, the American-trained units would raid the coast of North Vietnam, carrying out small acts of sabotage, blowing up bridges, radar stations, whatever they could find. To make these raids effective, the units needed logistical information, which was furnished by a long-standing Navy spy operation, known to the military as covert Operation 34A, destroyers that slipped into the territorial waters of the Soviet Union, China, North Korea, and North Vietnam to gather information on coastal activities.

The North Vietnamese wanted to slap the little boats that were raiding their coast but these boats were too fast to be caught. And so the North Vietnamese sent three torpedo boats after one of the destroyers in North Vietnamese waters in the Gulf of Tonkin, the U.S.S. *Maddox,* which reported that the three exhibited the "apparent intention of torpedo attack." It is not clear if they actually attacked. The *Maddox* suffered no damage, though a later Pentagon investigation claimed to find torpedo shell fragments. The *Maddox* counterattacked, damaging two of the enemy boats and destroying the third. She then retreated to the fleet in open waters, but was then ordered back to the Gulf of Tonkin with a second destroyer.

The mood was surprisingly light in the White House when President Johnson was briefed on the incident. There was a discussion with Secretary of State Dean Rusk about denouncing the incident as "an unprovoked attack," but Johnson was reminded of the 34A operation that he had approved, and it wasn't certain if they really could call it unprovoked. With one of his typical metaphors, Johnson compared the situation to going to the movies in Texas with "a pretty girl." Johnson described it as a hand starting at a girl's ankle and slowly moving up. "You move it up further," said the president, "and you're thinking of moving a bit more, and all of a sudden you get slapped. I think we got slapped." He said that he would reprimand but not retaliate, despite the urging of the new ambassador to Saigon, General Maxwell Taylor, to take military action. And to the surprise of his advisers, he moved on to other subjects.

On August 4, the United States reported that the North Vietnamese had attacked the two destroyers. A later message said that there was no visual confirmation of an attack and that the radar may have misinterpreted weather conditions. It was not clear that there was any attack at all. In fact, twenty years after the war that was about to start had ended, the relevant North Vietnamese military authorities confirmed that they had ordered the first attack, but there had been no second attack.

On August 5, U.S. aircraft carriers, in retaliation for the fictitious second attack, struck North Vietnam and sank an estimated thirty North Vietnamese ships. On August 7, Congress authorized Johnson to use military force against North Vietnam however he saw fit. Not one member of the House opposed the resolution, and only two senators voted against it — Wayne Morse of Oregon and Ernest Gruening of Alaska, both Democrats. Morse called it "a historic mistake." As the conflict expanded into full-scale war, the Senate was still holding hearings to determine if the second attack ever took place. Most historians who have examined the evidence have concluded that it didn't. There was also little mention of the fact that the attacked vessels had been spying in North Vietnamese territorial waters or that they were engaged in sabotage against North Vietnam. And so began an eight-year war in which millions died, including fifty-eight thousand Americans.

Federal agents searched around Philadelphia, Mississippi, throughout June and July. They found the car belonging to the three, but no bodies. Finally they started offering $25,000 for vital information and, acting on an informant's tip, they found the three bodies buried in an earthen dam on a farm. The two white men had each been dispatched with a quick bullet to the heart, but Chaney, the black man, had been severely beaten and then shot three times. And yet Freedom Summer went on. The murder of the three did not cause any volunteers to leave the South. The project that succeeded in registering only a few black voters did much to mobilize the consciences of whites and blacks in the North to support the movement and also to make SNCC more militant and distant from King's Southern Christian Leadership Conference.

History was made twice in the summer of 1964 in the same large stadium six miles outside of San Francisco called the Cow Palace. It had been built by Franklin Roosevelt's New Deal in the 1930s. On July 13 to 16, while Motown was putting together the perfect record in Detroit and while the people of Harlem were in combat with the police, the Republican Party was holding its national convention to nominate Barry Goldwater. Journalist Theodore White wrote, "No one can yet define accurately what happened to the Republican Party at San Francisco — whether the forces that seized it were ephemeral or were to become permanently a majority that would alter and perhaps end the Republican Party as known through a century of American history. This will become clear only as the years throw perspective."

Now, with the hindsight of decades, we know that the Republican Party did survive but as a completely changed entity. The liberal wing led by Nelson Rockefeller was shunted aside for archconservatives. No reforming liberal would ever get the Republican mantle again. The party became belligerently militarist, anti-union, and anti–civil rights. This was not a platform that the leading Republicans, men like Rockefeller, Javits, and Keating in New York; Lodge in Massachusetts; or Scranton in Pennsylvania would ever run on. But they were out. In San Francisco, the new western party had overthrown the eastern establishment and built a western/southern party.

Some of this platform was clearly on the losing side. Not one congressman who voted for the Civil Rights Bill was defeated in 1964. But eleven of the twenty-two northern congressmen who had opposed it were defeated that fall. Protests outside the Cow Palace were for civil rights but also against it, some cursing Earl Warren, the Republican-appointed Supreme Court

251

justice who had led landmark integration decisions. There was also a Beatles fan carrying a "Ringo for President" placard.

The Beatles themselves kicked off their summer twenty-three-city one-month American tour with a concert at the Cow Palace on August 19 to a crowd of 17,130 people. *Billboard* had already announced in July, "Britain's Beatlemania Has Spread to America!" On September 6 they performed at Detroit's Olympia Stadium to thirty thousand screaming fans. In terms of the size and enthusiasm of the audiences, it is considered the biggest tour in rock 'n' roll history. In the huge crowds, teenage girls fainted from hyperventilating, fans pressed so forcefully that people were bloodied. The four were hidden in an ambulance and rushed to the airports, their only way of escaping to the next town. It was sometimes terrifying. John Lennon said, "Can't sing when you're scared for your life." Ringo, the oldest Beatle, had just turned twenty-four years old.

The Democratic Party's nominating convention in Atlantic City from August 24 to 27, the coronation of President Johnson, which should have been uneventful, was as much of a watershed as the Republican convention at the Cow Palace. Present were 5,260 delegates and 5,500 people from the news media. The drama that Johnson didn't want came from 68 delegates sent from Mississippi by an organization called the Freedom Democratic Party. Since black people were completely excluded from the delegate process in the state of Mississippi just as they were from the general election process, a group of activists led by SNCC formed their own party, which selected its own delegation and demanded to replace the regular Mississippi delegation. The delegates were blacks and whites, maids and schoolteachers. As one of their leaders, Charles Sherrod, of SNCC put it, "Ordinary people with an extraordinary story to tell." America had come a long way since the March on Washington the year before. Thanks to the Summer Project, people in the North had some idea of the brutality that these people faced in Mississippi. They told their stories — horror stories of beatings and screams and prison torture and burnings — to the press, and it was hard to ignore them.

On the other hand, Johnson thought that a fight over this or even the refusal to seat the regular delegation would be a political disaster that would cost him the entire

South in the upcoming election. For three days the credentials committee tried to find an acceptable compromise, but these scarred veterans of Mississippi were not interested in compromises. The final offer was that two delegates at large would be seated with voting rights, the regular white Mississippi delegation would be seated but had to swear loyalty to the ticket, and that in 1968 no delegation would be seated that deprived blacks of a vote.

The press hailed this as a great victory for the Freedom Party because they understood so little about these people of SNCC. They had faced beatings and jails and death, and getting seated at the convention was the only acceptable result. Their response, of course, was a sit-in. They illegally sat in the Mississippi chairs, locked arms, and refused to move. Many, including old-time civil rights leaders such as Bayard Rustin, said that it was a mistake not to accept the compromise.

In hindsight it was probably the Democratic Party that made the mistake. The South was already lost, and there were other supporters now at risk. Sherrod said, "In the South and the North, the black man is losing confidence in the intentions of the federal government. . . . The seating of the

Mississippi Freedom Democratic Party would have gone a long way toward restoring faith in the intentions of our government for the many who believe that the federal government is a white man." Soon a large wing of the civil rights movement would break away from the program of nonviolence. A new organization, the Black Panthers, would be formed, and a new militancy would usher in harder, more violent times. Many black people felt attacked by the Republicans and betrayed by the Democrats. Soon the phrase "dancing in the street" would have another meaning for a different time.

H. Rap Brown, a SNCC activist who would soon lead the organization away from nonviolence, was at the convention and said of the compromise, "So all the liberals, 'our friends,' turned against us." According to Brown, "The convention was a classic example of the lack of a vehicle for the redress of grievances for black people."

In the fall Johnson defeated Goldwater by 43 million votes to 27 million, one of the great landslides of American presidential history, but it should have been sobering that 27 million people actually voted for a candidate who wanted to use nuclear weapons and opposed civil rights. Goldwater carried the entire South. In Mississippi, 87 percent of the people allowed to vote — an estimated 91 percent of blacks were denied the vote — cast their vote for Goldwater.

Also that fall, SNCC volunteers returned from Mississippi to their college campuses with new lessons learned. Berkeley became the first of many college campuses paralyzed by student protest led by SNCC veterans.

When "Dancing in the Street" was first released, the Beatles' "A Hard Day's Night" was number 1 on the *Billboard* chart. By August 15 *Billboard* listed "Dancing in the Street" as a "hot" up-and-coming record. On August 22 it entered the Top 100 chart at number 68. At the time the number 1 hit was "Where Did Our Love Go" by the Supremes. By September 19 "Dancing" had entered the Top 10 at number 10. The Supremes had dropped to number 3, and "The House of the Rising Sun," by the Animals, was number 1. By October 3 "Dancing" had reached number 3, overtaking the Supremes, who had dropped to number 19. Indicative of the interests of Motown with Martha and the Vandellas on the rise, the studio ran a full-page ad for the descending Supremes on the page opposite the chart. On October 17 "Dancing in the Street" was number 2 on the chart. Number 1 was "Do Wah Diddy Diddy," the British Manfred Mann's cover of an American song. "Dancing" never beat the British record to make number 1 but it was already a classic.

A bad year for many people, 1964 was a great year not only for Martha Reeves, who got through it in "the Motown bubble" — in a recent interview she said she had never heard of the organization SNCC — but for Motown, which released sixty single records, of which 70 percent hit the Top 100 chart and nineteen were number 1 hits.

By the end of the summer of 1964, the entire tone of the 1960s had changed: America was almost a different country, and "Dancing in the Street," born on the cusp, one of the few Motown songs that was not about love and heartache, was going to make the transition to the new and much more harsh America.

On December 11, 1964, Sam Cooke died, shot by the night manager of a shady motel in south central Los Angeles after a dispute with a prostitute. A coroner's jury ruled it justifiable homicide after a fifteen-minute inquiry. Angry young blacks picketed the motel. Conspiracy theories on who killed Cooke and why spread like theories on the Kennedy assassination, but no one turned up any evidence of such plots. Eleven days after Cooke's death his most prophetic song was released, a fitting cap to the year, "A Change Is Gonna Come."

The legal scholar Alexander Meiklejohn, who had been dancing in the street in August, died in December, a saddened man. He had been a close friend of Andrew Goodman and his family. The Gulf of Tonkin resolution also filled him with despair. When depressed, he always tried to find quotations that would cheer him up. In the fall of 1964 he had quoted from Bertolt Brecht's *Messingkauf Dialogues:* "There is an essential gaiety. If it is not lighthearted, it becomes absurd. You can achieve every shade of seriousness by means of ease, but none without it. No matter how fearful the problems plays handle, they should always be playful."

Isn't the same true for songs? In the next few years, the brightness of "Dancing in the Street," the party song, would be used to arrive at darker things more appropriate to the times.

# CHAPTER FOUR:
# THE TIME IS RIGHT FOR DANCING IN THE STREET

In 1965 one of the first signs of that change that was gonna come was on January 30, when *Billboard* announced that it was reinstating its rhythm & blues chart for black record sales because it saw that the difference between white and black tastes in records was once again significant.

This was not encouraging for Motown, which both artistically and commercially had gambled on the future of integration. But integration, the theme of a decade of civil rights struggle, was no longer the shared goal of Afro-America. The ideals of black nationalism, that blacks should look to each other and not depend on whites, were gaining popularity. Ten years earlier, novelist-anthropologist Zora Neale Hurston — always an iconoclast who called the literary scene in the Harlem Renaissance the "niggerati" and referred to W. E. B Du Bois, often suspected of middle-class values, as

Dr. Dubious — went too far when she wrote an article criticizing *Brown v. Board of Education*. Her point that it was insulting to suggest that blacks could not have good schools on their own would have resonated with some by 1965, but in 1955 was unacceptable. She was denounced by fellow African Americans and, worse, cheered by southern racists. Her once-prominent career was over, and she ended her days in her native central Florida working as a maid. One client realized one afternoon that his cleaning woman was the writer profiled in the magazine he was reading. She died unforgiven, in obscurity.

But by 1965, many black leaders openly questioned the goal of integration. Wouldn't blacks be better off with their own successful institutions such as Motown? This was Hurston's question, but after a decade more of experience with integration, more blacks were asking it.

Major League Baseball was an example. Segregation led to the creation of about two hundred all-black professional baseball teams. They had black coaches, black managers, and black owners and were the leading black entertainment — according to some historians, a bigger draw than even music. Black baseball produced some of the best players and some of the best teams in the history of the sport. Then, in 1946, Major League Baseball was integrated, starting with Jackie Robinson and Larry Doby. A handful of Negro League stars were picked up, such as Satchel Paige, who pitched for Cleveland on the 1948 World Series Champion Cleveland Indians. Soon white Major League Baseball was skimming off the best of the black players, and black baseball lost its fans and was no longer commercially viable. But at no time has Major League Baseball offered more than a fraction of the jobs in baseball that the Negro Leagues had. There was only a smattering of black players, a few black coaches, rare black managers and general managers, and no black owners until 2012, when basketball star Magic Johnson became owner of the Dodgers. So some could ask, why was this progress? And although this was an example of successful integration, by 1964 most attempts such as schools had had little success.

Nor was there still wide acceptance of the tactic of nonviolence. In fact, it had always been a questioned approach. Martin Luther King Jr., who owned numerous firearms, was talked into nonviolence largely by Quaker Bayard Rustin. Among nonviolent civil rights activists in the Deep South, the shotgun was a common piece of household equipment that proved useful in scattering advancing Klansmen in the night. A distinction was made between the tactic of nonviolence and the necessity of self-defense. But even Mohandas K. Gandhi made that distinction. Following Gandhi's example, nonviolence was used as an aggressive tool of activism and was never passive.

Among black militants there were always skeptics. In 1959, activist Robert F. Williams was suspended from the NAACP for six months after he declared, "We must meet violence with violence." There had always been numerous blacks who scoffed at King and felt his movement was not accomplishing anything. Some were the young people who joined SNCC, but there were many others. In 1963, after leaving the Great March in Detroit, King went to New York, where a young black crowd outside a Harlem church pelted him with eggs.

It was not without reason that the youth questioned the efficacy of the movement. In 1964, ten years after the landmark *Brown v. Board of Education* Supreme Court decision officially integrated schools, in the eleven states of the old Civil War Confederacy, 1 percent of black public school students attended integrated classrooms.

As the nonviolent civil rights movement endured beating after burning, after lynching, after shooting, this idea of violence for violence was gaining currency. Also gaining currency was the phrase "black power." The term had first been used by author Richard Wright in 1954 as the title of a book about the Ghana independence struggle. Malcolm X had used it. It was only in 1965 that it came into wide usage. The term, often misunderstood, summed up the idea that rather than petitioning the white establishment for their rights, black people ought to build their own power base through economic success, which had been Booker T. Washington's argument. Berry Gordy, who tried to steer clear of black power politics, was in fact a black power ideal. Black power combined Washington and Du Bois, who thought blacks should be political activists. But this new movement found Du Bois and his NAACP to be far too soft, focused on having blacks aspire to white values. The black power movement was nationalist, infused with the idea that blacks were different, an African American nation within the American one. And like SNCC from the start, it had the impatience of youth. It carried the idea "we have waited too long." And

Malcolm X added the phrase "by any means necessary."

History teaches that every act of violence precipitates others until it is hard to say where it all began. But at least it can be said that the assassination of Malcolm X in February 1965, shot at least seven times at the beginning of a talk in a ballroom in Manhattan's Washington Heights, at age thirty-nine, was an important step in turning the mid-1960s to violence. He was thought to have been killed by gunmen from the Nation of Islam, the group he had broken away from in 1964. His troubles with this group and its leader, Elijah Muhammed, started when Malcolm X had made this same observation about violence and history. He had referred to the assassination of President John Kennedy as the "chickens coming home to roost." Elijah Muhammed disapproved of the remark. The point Malcolm X was making was that allowing violence against black people in America created the climate that made Kennedy's assassination possible.

Malcolm knew that violence. In his boyhood, Malcolm's father had been killed, according to unconfirmed rumor, by white racists, and an uncle had been lynched. Malcolm converted to the Nation of Islam while serving prison time for breaking and entering. A young man of great political skill who could bundle together a confusing array of contradictions, he nonetheless advocated violence. He did not believe in the nonviolent tactics of the civil rights movement, and told every black person to own a firearm. In an interview published by the *Village Voice* four days after his death he said, "Only violence or a real threat of it will get results."

Yet there was a clear sense that the violence toward Malcolm X would unleash even more violence. Marvin Gaye said, "I loved Malcolm's strength and his truth-telling. When they cut him down, I felt the loss inside my soul, and I knew that an age of terrible violence and suffering had just begun. I knew what my people were feeling — all the pent-up rage and anger. I felt it, too."

Robert F. Williams continued with his fiery rhetoric. In 1962 he published a book, *Negroes with Guns,* in which he said, "All those who dare to attack are going to learn the hard way that the African American is not a pacifist, that he cannot forever be counted on not to defend himself." In July 1965, Williams, at a poorly attended speech, said, "We are now in the year of fire." Using an increasingly common phrase, he predicted "a long, hot summer." In fact he called for it. "Let our people take to the streets in fierce numbers and meet violence with violence. Let our battle cry be heard around the world: freedom, freedom, freedom now — or death."

The prediction about summer proved true just as the same prediction from Malcolm X the summer before had.

What *Billboard* had recognized when they reinstated the R&B chart was that blacks and whites still had very different ways of looking at things. In a 1961 essay titled "The Black Boy Looks at the White Boy," James Baldwin explained his friendship with Norman Mailer, saying that although he greatly admired him and had a deep fondness for him, the two writers could never truly understand each other because of the difference between being black and being white. Baldwin wrote, "There is a difference, though, between Norman and myself in that I think he still imagines that he has something to save, whereas I have never had anything to lose."

Amiri Baraka saw the white-black relationship often stuck in a historic view from slave times in which whites tend to see blacks as childish and blacks see whites as foolish.

The one thing that seemed clear was that whites and blacks saw through different lenses. One of those differences between the white perspective and the black was how the summer urban riots, which were becoming a regular event, were viewed. To the blacks they were insurrections, violent protest, uprisings that if not exactly planned had an idea and a goal behind them. The goal was to alarm the white man. It was Malcolm X's idea of the value of violence. But whites saw only riots — violent chaos from an angry people, disorganized or perhaps incapable of real organization. Evidence for the black point of view was the pattern in which white property and interests in the ghetto were attacked while those of blacks were left unharmed. This reality was obscured by the fact that the violent police response always left far more black victims than white.

The division was never neat. Some whites also saw insurrection, including political activist Tom Hayden and even CBS News, which used the same word to describe these outbreaks. On the other hand, Martha Reeves was one of many blacks who simply saw these events as riots.

■ ■ ■ ■

The violent outbreak in black Los Angeles should not have been a surprise. There had been several earlier outbreaks of violence, all of which were aggravated by a harsh, violent response from the Los Angeles Police Department. By the summer of 1964, the office of Governor Pat Brown had discussed a detailed report on the explosive situation in South Los Angeles. From the white point of view, it all erupted in August because of a heat wave that had kept the temperature in the nineties. This is also part of a racist stereotype that endured through the 1960s, that black people got out of control in hot weather. Actually the heat wave broke during the uprising, and most of it occurred in somewhat cooler weather. The violence of August 1965 spread throughout South Los Angeles, but was named after its epicenter in a neighborhood called Watts.

For black people, even traditional civil rights leaders who deplored violence, what happened in Watts was understandable. Bayard Rustin said that Watts was caused by a "rebellion of Negroes against their own masochism and was carried on with the express purpose of asserting that they would no longer quietly submit to the deprivation of slum life."

It is interesting that since that uprising made Watts famous, whites have constantly expressed surprise that Watts is not a crowded urban area of high-rise tenements but a sprawling zone of houses on wide palm tree–lined boulevards. In 1992, President George H. W. Bush toured the area after another violent outbreak and declared with great surprise, "This is open and rather pretty." It had also been supposed that crowding made Negroes act the way they did.

Other suggestions were "brain disease" and "weak character." An article in the 1967 *Journal of the American Medical Association* titled "Role of Brain Disease in Riots and Urban Violence" by Vernon H. Mark, W. H. Sweet, and F. R. Ervin, all respected doctors, asked why, if the cause of the violence was the conditions in the ghetto, all the ghetto dwellers didn't riot, but instead only a minority. Is there a brain disease in the Negro population that causes these outbreaks? Dr. Mark spoke to President Johnson and to his Kerner Commission, which was investigating the riots. George Todt, a conservative columnist for the *Los Angeles*

*Herald Examiner,* opined that the root of the uprisings was "the weak character traits in uncivilized human beings."

It was also proposed that the riot was caused by the writings of James Baldwin. And it was also suggested that the popularity of the song "Dancing in the Street" had encouraged black people to take to the streets. This idea comes primarily from the observation by fans that during the riots this very popular song at the time was never heard on the radio. Had it been banned because it provoked rioting? No radio station ever said so. The song just wasn't played, and the rumor persisted. Even if only a rumor, this was the first time it was suggested that the song had a second meaning.

This idea that "Dancing in the Street" caused violence came out of the broader idea that black R&B radio was being blamed. One of the favorite scapegoats was the popular LA black deejay Magnificent Montague. Montague was known for his flamboyant rap and for unconventional practices, such as playing a favorite song fifteen times in a row. Berry Gordy said of Montague, "Once you heard his outrageous oratory, you wouldn't forget it or him." He was particularly remembered for saying as he started a record, "Feel the heat I'm send-ing to your soul. Burn, baby, burn!" Monta-gue had just arrived that year at KGFJ from New York. "Burn, baby, burn!" was already his trademark. Fans would call in and say it, and he would gratefully respond with "Burn, baby."

During the Watts uprising, white people started complaining that Montague was inciting black people to arson. In fact, people on the streets of Watts would shout, "Burn, baby, burn." The police went to his studio and demanded he stop using the word *burn.* By the third day of the uprising he agreed not to say it.

It was true that his phrase had become a slogan for violence in the street, a fact that even decades later was deeply painful to Montague. Often white journalists reported the use of the slogan without even knowing from where it had come. Throughout the 1960s, the phrase remained on the streets in black areas where there had been upris-ings. In 2008, when Republican vice presi-dential candidate Sarah Palin chanted, "Drill, baby, drill" to call for offshore oil drilling, she probably knew even less about the origin of the phrase than did the white reporters in Los Angeles in 1965. She did not mean to be invoking a phrase about the meaning of R&B soul, much less about black nationalism and urban uprisings, which she would have termed "rioting."

The German philosopher Arthur Schopenhauer wrote, "All truth passes through three stages. First, it is ridiculed. Second, it is violently opposed. Third, it is accepted as being self-evident." Popular culture seems to find a similar path from enthusiastic expression to violent opposition to banal jargon — from emotion to jargon to nothing more than a pleasing rhythm. This, too, was the trajectory with which "Dancing in the Street" was destined to struggle.

What did set off the violence was the arrest on August 11 of a twenty-one-year-old high school dropout named Marquette Frye with a juvenile record for suspected drunkenness. Frye, born in Oklahoma, the third of four children, moved to Los Angeles at the age of ten with his mother, who remarried there. According to Marquette, he and his brother Ronald were celebrating Ronald's discharge from the Air Force, drinking vodka and orange juice with two women they knew. On the way home they were stopped by the California Highway Patrol, who were about to let them go, when a second car pulled up with an officer who allegedly taunted Marquette, and he argued back. A crowd formed, and they were joking with the police, exchanging words but light-heartedly. But when Marquette's mother, who lived nearby, arrived, she angrily derided the police for harassing her son, whereupon one of the officers twisted one of her arms behind her back, lifted her by the twisted arm, and put handcuffs on her, causing her to cry out in pain. Then, according to Marquette, the crowd got "boisterous." An officer hit Marquette with a hard blow to the head. The patrol car door was slammed on his leg. And he was hit in the head again as they drove him away, leaving an angry crowd behind.

The police said that they had to use force because he was resisting arrest; however, Frye was five feet seven and 130 pounds. The situation rapidly ignited, and six days later 34 people were dead, 1,032 people injured, and there was more than $40 million in property damage. Most of the property damage was to white establishments accused of discriminatory practices. Most of the deaths and injuries were to blacks.

In addition to 934 officers of the LAPD, 718 officers from the Los Angeles County Sheriff and 2,300 California Army National Guardsmen were called in to quell the disturbance. The brutality with which the uprising was attacked caught national attention, as did Police Chief William Parker's observation that the rioters were like "monkeys in a zoo."

Many of the responses to Watts indicated that the uprising had successfully made its point. Journalist Theodore White, by no measure a radical, wrote in the *Los Angeles Times* on August 22, only a few days after South Los Angeles was subdued, "Modern Negro violence is not simply rioting but a form of guerrilla warfare." Although he urged "new weapons and tactics" to face this new threat, he also stated, "It is at this time perhaps necessary to find out how to create some form of Negro self-government coupled with Negro responsibility in the big cities, which will give Negroes that sense of control over their own destinies that all men so dearly require."

The office of California governor Pat Brown obtained funding from the legislature to give job training to five thousand people in South Los Angeles, which quickly created almost that many jobs, and though that barely made a dent in unemployment in the area, it was an impressive start.

Watts had a profound effect on Marvin

Gaye, which in turn would impact on Mo-town:

> I remember I was listening to a tune of mine playing on the radio, "Pretty Little Baby," when the announcer interrupted with news about the Watts riot. My stomach got real tight and my heart started beating like crazy. I wanted to throw the radio down and burn all the bullshit songs I'd been singing and get out there and kick ass with the rest of the brothers. I knew they were going about it wrong. I knew they weren't thinking, but I understood anger that builds up over the years — shit, over centuries — and I felt myself exploding. Why didn't our music have anything to do with this? Wasn't music supposed to express feelings? No, according to BG, music's supposed to sell. That's his trip. And it was mine.

In the spring of 1966 Trinidadian-born, New York City–raised Stokely Carmichael was elected leader of SNCC. A man of mischievous wit and elegant speech, he emphasized the break of SNCC from Martin Luther King. The slogan "Freedom Now" was to be replaced with "Black Power." He simply had had it. In June 1966 he was arrested in Greenwood, Mississippi, during a march with Martin Luther King and other civil rights leaders. In a now-famous speech he said, "This is the twenty-seventh time I have been arrested — and I ain't going to jail no more!" Then he added, "The only way we gonna stop them white men from whuppin' us is to take over. We been saying freedom for six years and we ain't got nuthin'. What we gonna start saying now is Black Power!" The crowd roared back the new slogan "Black Power!"

Carmichael turned on its head the old civil rights refrain, What do we want? And the answer: Freedom!

Don't be afraid. Don't be ashamed. We want black power. We want black power. We want black power. We want black power. We want black power. That's right. That's what we want, black power. And we don't have to be ashamed of it. We have stayed here and we've begged the President, we've begged the federal government. That's all we've been doing, begging, begging. It's time we stand up and take over. Take over.

In September 1966, *Liberator,* a black power journal from Harlem, published an editorial by Daniel H. Watts:

> Young Stokely represents the best in our Afro-American youth, he is daring, courageous and creative. He along with hundreds of others had travelled the long and painful road of non-violence and turn the other cheek, before they had discovered that preacher King had them in one big trick bag, consisting of awards, degrees, money and medals for King and bruised, battered and dead bodies and raising frustration for Black people.

This was a new civil rights movement that rejected the older, nonviolent one that King had led. Martha Noonan was an SNCC activist from Detroit with a music background. Her mother was a singer and classical pianist. She first went south to Mississippi, and Georgia in 1963. Martha said, "I thought I could sing until I went south. Those incredible voices from church singing." So she learned the freedom songs, but she never led them.

She was more of an R&B girl from Detroit anyway. In 1963 she had an idea that Motown might do a fund-raiser for SNCC. She met with Berry Gordy, who received her cordially and turned her down.

Martha did not participate in the Freedom Summer project because she thought it was a mistake to bring large numbers of people to Mississippi when they had been doing well with local grassroots leadership. She stayed with SNCC after Carmichael, whom she had worked with several times, took over.

Carmichael came to Detroit for a rally as SNCC's new leader. SNCC organizers told Martha and a friend of hers that they were to introduce Carmichael by singing freedom songs. Martha had never done this before, which made her a little uncomfortable, but she knew the songs and she had a voice. She had attended many SNCC rallies in the South, where the songs had been sung.

So Martha and her friend sang until Stokely Carmichael came onstage and turned to her and said, "We don't sing freedom songs anymore."

Mortified, Martha became silent until after the rally, when she walked up to Carmichael and said, "You could have told me that before!"

After the rally, as was usual after SNCC rallies, there was a party. At SNCC parties they played R&B music. But it was mostly a newer, politically edgier R&B, such as Chicago-born Curtis Mayfield's "Keep On

Pushing" with the Impressions, released by ABC-Paramount only a month before "Dancing in the Street." It made it to number 10 on the *Billboard* chart, behind the Supremes and the Vandellas, but it had a political edge that was now more suited to the times. It was also the song that introduced Barack Obama for his address to the 2004 Democratic Convention that made him a political star.

The new R&B of the mid-1960s was making the old Motown songs of requited or unrequited love, such as those by the Supremes or Smokey Robinson, seem slightly old-fashioned. But "Dancing in the Street" was different. SNCC rallies still played "Dancing in the Street." Noonan said, "It was very upbeat, positive music which did reflect the spirit of the time that change was coming and it was going to be better. It was in the air, a good time to be born. I thought it had to do with black unity."

Movements needed songs, and just as the civil rights movement had its freedom songs, this new breakaway movement needed its own songs, and these were to be R&B, especially "Dancing in the Street." The new movement did not care if Martha Reeves and Motown were backing them any more than the civil rights movement worried about whether or not the old-time authors of their freedom songs would have approved of their movement.

These were difficult times for Motown. The Washington versus Du Bois argument was smoldering, and Gaye was increasingly taking up the Du Bois argument for activism. Stevie Wonder began raising money for the civil rights movement. Kim Weston left Stevenson and Motown and recorded a stirring rendition of "Lift Every Voice and Sing." This song, from a 1900 poem by the principal of a segregated school, written to introduce Booker T. Washington at the celebration of Lincoln's birthday, was later set to music and has become known as the "Black National Anthem." To this day blacks will sometimes stand when the song is played. Having their own national anthem is as good a piece of evidence as any that there are two separate Americas.

In the mid-1960s not only music but all of the arts were separating into black and white visions. In 1965, Amiri Baraka, who had been LeRoi Jones until 1967, left his home in Greenwich Village, where he had been a hip ex-beatnik writer, and moved to Harlem to lead what he called "the Black Arts Movement," an artistic wing of the black power movement, in which blacks would create their own literature, theater, and poetry, rather than be exploited by the white literary establishment.

Their art would express a black perspective, something totally distinct and apart from white art. The movement went beyond art to the fashion of wearing African-style clothes and the emergence of "soul food" restaurants. While Baraka saw all of this as part of a political program that would give political power to blacks through "a radical reordering of the Western cultural aesthetic," polls consistently showed that these cultural manifestations of black separatism were far more popular in the black population than was the black power political movement itself. Even those who did not agree with the political aspirations of black nationalism wanted to see a celebration of a distinctly black culture. One of the most important accomplishments of this movement was the emergence of black studies programs in most universities. This was the most popular of all the manifestations of black power.

But Gordy still operated in the belief that black art flourished only when it reached out to include white audiences. This was a simple mathematical calculation. He had arrived at a formula that was working. He told anyone who would listen that they could not argue with his success. In 1963, when he met with Martha Noonan he told her, "I played a little different and people liked it and we got other people who played differently and a million people like it."

He was pleased to get the black market as long as it wasn't at the expense of the far larger white market. He wanted to show white people that in the age of dangerous, angry black people, of black power, and ghetto rebellions, Motown blacks were neither angry nor dangerous.

The non-threatening black was becoming a big seller. In 1965 Bill Cosby became the first black star of a television drama, *I Spy*. Cosby was the epitome of the black who showed no anger, no anxiety, nothing to indicate he had experienced abuse and descended from centuries of worse. It was a difficult role for people who grew up in northern ghettos or the Jim Crow South. As Baldwin once wrote of his own background, "Escaping Harlem is like an animal that escapes a trap by amputating a leg. You always leave something behind." But for those who could do it, such as Marvin Gaye, who always struggled with it, it was a formula for success. Even in the next century, Barack Obama, in order to be elected president, had to convince the public that he was without anger.

Motown wanted Bill Cosbys, too. Gordy, in his zeal to prove the harmlessness of "Dancing in the Street," despite its African drumming and African-style call-and-response harmony, would shoot film shorts of Martha and the Vandellas playing to all-white crowds. Martha would wear a wide, bright smile that was not in her eyes. You could see her face strain to hold on to the smile while belting out a song of such strong emotion and force. In one film, the Vandellas wore suits with broad, vertical stripes and little matching hats so they looked like some kind of candy striper volunteers singing in a park. The park had only happy children with lollipops and balloons, and all of them were white.

"The only place you don't feel the tension in the music of 1966," said Montague in his 2003 autobiography, "is in Detroit, where Berry Gordy is managing to go the other way and make Motown less black, less tense, and more controlled."

Gordy was not the only one trying to keep his artists away from the trouble of the 1960s. Beatles manager Brian Epstein forbade the four to talk about the Vietnam

War, which got bloodier every day. Epstein would not allow Vietnam questions at press conferences. But Lennon and Harrison would speak on the banned topic anyway. And with their album *Revolver,* the acoustic guitar and folk sound of the previous one, *Rubber Soul,* were replaced by a hard electric sound, almost similar to Stokely Carmichael's replacing freedom songs with R&B. Likewise, songs such as "Eleanor Rigby" were much edgier than the cheerful pieces that had made the Beatles stars. In what belongs in the annals of premature obituaries, *Time* in September 1966 ran an article titled "Is Beatlemania Dead?" The article noted that their latest tour, which had still brought in staggering quantities of money, did not draw as big a mob around their hotels, possibly, the article noted, because three of the four had gotten married. They were still banned from a Texas radio station, and in one concert in Memphis, the free Christian protest rally against them drew more people than the music concert. *Time* also noted, presumably with irony, that while two girls threatened to jump out of the twenty-second floor of a fifty-story Manhattan building in honor of the four, in the old days they would have chosen the top floor.

"Eve of Destruction" was released in July 1965 as the B side of "What Exactly's the Matter with Me." The A side was quickly forgotten as the B side moved up the charts. Written by nineteen-year-old P. F. Sloan, several groups turned it down before Barry McGuire, who had just left the folk group the New Christy Minstrels, agreed to record it. The song listed many of the events of recent years that had darkened the times and the music, including racism and violence. The clear underpinning was the war in Vietnam — the maelstrom Johnson once described as unwinnable, into which he was pouring more and more American troops. The song concludes that the end of the world must be near. Bob Dylan had already made the point more eloquently. Despite the huge sales and angry denunciations from right-wing groups, neither the music nor the words showed much finesse. Even musicians sympathetic to the message criticized it artistically. Folksinger Phil Ochs, a constant presence at antiwar rallies with his song "I Ain't Marching Anymore," applauded the message but not the artistry. Paul Simon told *Rolling Stone* that it was an example of how bad a protest song could be. Still, apocalyptic visions had become trendy.

In September *Time* reported that with "Eve of Destruction" at the top of the charts and

with a dozen more songs of protest snapping close behind it heralds a radical change for rock 'n' roll. Suddenly the shaggy ones are high on a soapbox. Tackling everything from the Peace Corps to the PTA, foreign policy to domestic morality. They are sniping away in the name of "folk rock" — big-beat music with big-message lyrics. Where once teenagers were too busy frugging to pay much heed to lyrics, most of which were unintelligible banshee wails anyway, they now listen with ears cocked and brows furrowed. The rallying cry is no longer "I wanna hold your hand" but "I wanna change the world."

Meanwhile, "Dancing in the Street" was well on its way to being a standard. The first of many covers was already coming out the year after the song was released. It was always part of Gordy's financial plan to have his songs covered, and covers have made him very wealthy, even though they have not always been a triumph for the artists picking up the songs. Drummer Steve Jordan said, "Covers are great. Songwriters hope to have lots of covers of their song. But you have to choose your covers. Some songs, the recording is so strong, you are just setting yourself up for disaster. With this one, the original will never be topped." So far that has proved true.

In 1965 "Dancing in the Street" was so popular in Great Britain that there were five British covers of the song. The 1965 album *Kinda Kinks,* by the British group the Kinks, was an example of how performers set themselves up for disaster. The Kinks had become stars the year before with their hit "You Really Got Me," but although they were known for working with R&B, their version of "Dancing in the Street" with no particular interpretation, and without Martha's voice or horn arrangements or a distinctive rhythmic groove, was a surprising demonstration of how dull this song could be.

Another barely remembered cover was by the Rokes, a British group that moved to Rome and became extremely popular in Italy singing British and American R&B hits in British-accented Italian.

Petula Clark, at thirty-three, was already a seasoned professional, partly because she began her singing career at the age of nine.

By 1964 she was in danger of being a has-been when she came out with "Downtown," which electrified people all over the world and made her an international music star. She was a singer who could belt out an R&B song and did a rousing version of "Dancing in the Street" that further popularized what was already a hit song in the UK.

At almost the same time, Cilla Black recorded the song. Ironically, given her love of black American music, Cilla Black was born Priscilla White. She grew up in Liverpool and knew the Beatles, who befriended and promoted her. For Black's first break, an audition for Beatles' manager Brian Epstein, with the Beatles playing backup, she chose Gershwin's "Summertime" from *Porgy and Bess.* The Beatles played it in a key that was impossible for her, and the audition was a disaster. A second chance went better.

As for many of her generation of British female vocalists, including Petula Clark and Dusty Springfield, covers of American R&B were a mainstay of her repertoire. Like her mentors, the Beatles, she did a great deal with her voice, although her body barely moved, a fact that seemed underscored by the way her sprayed hair was equally motionless. Cilla Black hit stardom in 1964 with a Burt Bacharach song made famous by Dionne Warwick, "Anyone Who Had a Heart." In the UK charts, Black's cover rose higher than Warwick's original. She also sang a number of Beatles compositions and had a number 1 hit with "You're My World," an English-language cover of the Italian hit "Il Mio Mondo."

In 1965 she recorded "Dancing in the Street" as part of a campaign to become popular in the United States. "You're My World" had hit number 26 on the American *Billboard* chart. But Cilla Black did not enjoy touring in the United States, and retreated to her native England, where she has remained a star ever since, though she is little known in the United States.

The fifth 1965 British cover of "Dancing in the Street" was by an American group. The Walker Brothers, three Americans who were not brothers and none of whom was born with the name Walker, were unknowns who formed the group in 1964 and moved to the UK on the theory that the Brits loved American rock 'n' roll. They were right, and by 1965, when they sang "Dancing in the Street," a number of their covers had made the top 10 on the British charts, though the Motown song was not one of them.

There were also two notable covers of

"Dancing in the Street" in the United States that year. Brenda Lee made the U.S. charts thirty-seven times in the 1960s, making her one of the five top-selling pop music artists of the decade. She is only one of the surprises of this top five 1960s list. The only ones that are not a surprise are the Beatles and Ray Charles, the creator of soul, the consummate fusion of black music — gospel, blues, and R&B. But he is the only black among the top five sellers. Elvis Presley, whom young people in the 1960s considered a has-been, was still a top seller with his Las Vegas–style ballads. And as surprising as Brenda Lee and slightly higher in sales was Connie Francis, an Italian American who had tried out most genres. In 1965 Brenda Lee recorded "Dancing in the Street" in her strong but somewhat tinny voice, backed up by a close imitation of Riser's arrangement, complete with trumpet intro and a slamming 2/4 beat.

The Everly Brothers, the melodic duet who harmonized on parallel melodic lines and were both accomplished acoustic guitar players, did "Dancing in the Street" in the sweet sound for which they were known. To realize how strong the edge is to the Martha and the Vandellas original, the Everly Brothers offer a version that really does sound like it is about nothing but dancing.

In 1966 the Brits were at it again with the Red Squares, a hard-sounding electric band, covering "Dancing in the Street." But this was also the year of one of the song's most successful covers, by the Mamas and the Papas. Their producer, Lou Adler, who had also coproduced "Eve of Destruction," Sam Cooke, and many others, said, "The first time I heard 'Dancing in the Street' I became a fan of Martha and the Vandellas." When he opened a nightclub in LA, Martha and the Vandellas was one of the first acts that he booked. "When I first heard the song I thought it was really uplifting." But he added, "I always felt that there was room for another interpretation." He added that when whites sing R&B, it is immediately a different interpretation. The Mamas and the Papas often covered black artists with their own interpretations. Usually they changed the tempo. "But with 'Dancing in the Street,' said Adler, "you couldn't really change tempos. Instead the interpretation was 'They just had a lot of fun with it.' " And the Mamas and the Papas had a very different concept of harmony than the call-and-response style of Motown girl groups.

The result was a song that was very bright and energetic, with a sense of fun. At times in the history of the song it seemed a safer, more accepted interpretation than the original. It also became a signature song of the Mamas and the Papas.

From June 16 to 18, 1967, Adler and Alan Pariser produced the Monterey Pop Festival, at the outset of what became known on the West Coast as "the Summer of Love." The event was billed as "three days of music, love, and flowers." The new California music, "the San Francisco sound," cemented its reputation to ninety thousand people with such groups as Big Brother and the Holding Company, Country Joe and the Fish, the Grateful Dead, and the Jefferson Airplane. Most of the San Francisco groups had not even cut a record yet. A brilliant, little-known guitarist who had built his reputation in Britain, Jimi Hendrix, as though his music wasn't spellbinding enough, concluded his set by literally setting his guitar on fire. Here Otis Redding, a southern blues and soul singer, secured his white fan base and became a star. Sadly, six months later he would die in an airplane crash, and his recording "(Sittin' On) The Dock of the Bay" would become the first posthumous number 1 hit.

How to close this first of the great open-air rock festivals of the 1960s? Adler had the concert end with the Mamas and the Papas singing "Dancing in the Street." It was forever after said that "Dancing in the Street" was the great closing number. For Martha Reeves, it was the number they came to hear and the one the audience waited for, but for almost any artist it was the song that would leave the audience energized.

In 1967, H. Rap Brown, born Hubert Brown in Baton Rouge, Louisiana, became chairman of SNCC. He had acquired the nickname "Rap" from his fiery rhythmic speaking style, which made him one of the early rappers.

By then every summer was approached with dread or excitement, depending on the point of view. In the spring and summer of 1966 there had been forty-three violent uprisings in U.S. cities, almost all of which had begun over the treatment of a black person by the police. Brown said, "These rebellions are but a dress rehearsal for real revolution." The summer of 1967 promised to be the longest, hottest one ever.

During the summer, H. Rap Brown often spoke in urban black neighborhoods from the roof of a parked car. Sometimes the car had music playing, and often that music was

Martha and the Vandellas singing "Dancing in the Street." He did this in Cambridge, Maryland, in Detroit, and in numerous other stops. The song would energize the crowd and give his rally a partylike atmosphere.

There were more than 120 violent uprisings in American cities that year, most of them in the summer. Some of the most violent were in Cambridge, Maryland, Minneapolis, New York, Milwaukee, Cincinnati, and Tampa. But two of the worst and most remembered were in Detroit and Newark. Unknown to Reeves, the theme song of these disruptions around the country, or " 'cross the nation," just like "Burn, baby, burn" in Watts, was "Dancing in the Street." Strangely, the uprisings, too, often took on a party spirit. It can be seen in press photos of the incidents — people standing around, laughing, taunting the police. And this was the atmosphere this song helped create. The record would be played. People would sing it. They would refer to what they were doing as "dancing in the street." Radical leader Tom Hayden, who was in Newark as an organizer at the time of that city's explosion, said of "Dancing in the Street," "It certainly was a beat in Newark during the years I was there." Martha Reeves had been right when she insisted that this was a party song. But this was a different kind of party.

On July 12 the Newark police's rough treatment of a black taxi driver led to six days of violence in which twenty-five people were killed, including a white police detective, a white fireman, and twenty-three black people, two of whom were children.

On July 23, 1967, Martha Reeves had a ten-day engagement at Detroit's Fox Theater, where Elvis Presley had first appeared in Detroit in 1956 to fifteen thousand screaming fans in three nights. One night, while she was performing "Dancing in the Street," a man in the wing started waving his arms furiously to get her attention. When she finished the song, she went to the wing and the stage manager told her that Detroit was literally in flames. A dispute with police, she was told, had erupted, and angry crowds were smashing storefronts, looting, and setting entire city blocks on fire. Reeves was told that rather than go into her next number, the hit "Jimmy Mack," she needed to tell the audience what was happening and get them to leave calmly and go home. "It was very scary," she later said, but she did talk the audience into leaving quietly.

The city's Afro-American population

seemed to have made good on H. Rap Brown's threat when he had visited earlier in the month. If "Motown doesn't come around," he warned, "we are going to burn you down."

By 1967 there was a great deal in Detroit that needed to come around. There were discriminatory housing practices that kept blacks in third-rate dwellings, an "urban renewal" project that bulldozed black neighborhoods to build highways, and a brutal, largely white police force.

The spark that set off the Detroit riots was on Twelfth Street, an almost entirely black neighborhood where the Funk Brothers often worked out passages for the next day's track at the Chit Chat Lounge. Though no survivors can recall, it would be a great irony if the celebrated track for "Dancing in the Street" had been worked out at the Chit Chat, where the Detroit riot of 1967 that tied itself to the song began. The club was beloved in the neighborhood, and when Twelfth Street was leveled by violence, the Chit Chat was untouched.

As whites left for the suburbs, the neighborhood had gone from one third black in 1950 to 96 percent black in 1960. It was happening all over Detroit, which by 1967 was 40 percent black. But the police force was largely white and known for harassing young blacks, using words such as *nigger.* The vice squads were particularly infamous, and one such group raided a Twelfth Street club expecting to round up a handful of people. Instead there were eighty-two people inside celebrating the return of two Vietnam veterans. Hugely outnumbered, the police decided to attempt to arrest all eighty-two. The situation erupted so rapidly that the police lost control of the city and federal troops were brought in the next morning. After five days of fighting for control of the city's black neighborhoods, 43 people were killed, 1,189 injured, and more than 7,000 people were arrested. Almost four out of five victims were blacks shot by police or National Guardsmen. In one of the most famous incidents, the subject of John Hersey's *The Algiers Motel Incident,* the police shot three unarmed black teenagers in a hotel. The youngest victim of the violence was Tonya Blanding, a four-year-old girl shot in the chest with a .50-caliber bullet from a tank that opened fire on her housing complex when they mistook the lighting of a cigarette for sniper fire.

But there were also a few white victims, including the oldest person to be killed, Krikor Messerlian, a sixty-eight-year-old

Armenian immigrant who was beaten to death with a baseball bat by a gang of young blacks as he attempted to protect his shoe repair shop with a ceremonial sword late the first night. One twenty-year-old black, implicated in the beating, was one of the few people charged with a killing.

Amiri Baraka, who was arrested in the Newark uprising and charged with resisting arrest and possession of an illegal weapon — charges for which he was sentenced to three years in prison, although the conviction was reversed on appeal — wrote about the rationale for the summer violence, which he called "the magic dance in the street." In a piece called "Black People!" he wrote about the sentiment that if you are black, the white man "owes you anything you want" and "you can get it, no money down." Smash windows and take it, says the piece. "Dance up and down the street." That was the street language of 1967.

Martha Reeves had been near the scene of riots in performance not only in Detroit but when she appeared in Newark, and in Myrtle Beach, when Cambridge erupted again. She was disturbed by the way she believed her song was being misused in this terrible violence. Nothing could have been further from who Martha Reeves was. She loved singing "Dancing in the Street," because to her, "the song is something you want to say to people. It says, 'Have fun.' "

Later that year, after black urban uprisings had swept the United States, Martha Reeves went to Britain on tour. She was glad to escape America and what to her seemed deplorable violence. To her complete shock, in London reporters followed her with questions about her involvement in the riots. At one London press conference she broke into tears as a reporter asked her if "Dancing in the Street" was a call to arms. "It is a party song," she insisted. She was horrified that she would be associated "with people rioting and burning."

But clearly there was another way of looking at the song, and to many people it was much more than a party song. It is often said that radio stations banned the song, but no one has come up with a concrete example of a radio station outlawing it. In any event, at the time radio stations were not banning songs. Since the payola scandal, they had taken the decisions away from the deejays. The station had weekly music meetings, at which a list of possible records was put together. The deejay had no say in this. Cousin Brucie said, "In 1963 we were told not to bring in records anymore. They were all supplied by the program director, and deejays voted on the ones they brought in. If I suggested something not on the list, they would say 'That's not here, Brucie.' "

"Dancing in the Street" may have been turning up less on urban radio lists in the summer of 1967, but no one had to give a reason. There were few attempts at an outright ban of a song by an American radio station anymore, and if there were any, they usually failed. In 1968 an El Paso, Texas, station banned all records by Bob Dylan because it was too difficult to understand the lyrics and there might be offensive hidden messages. So the station played covers of the songs by artists with clearer diction. The same year, during the violent National Democratic Convention in Chicago, Mayor Richard Daley's attempt to ban the Rolling Stones' "Street Fighting Man" famously backfired into a local hit.

To those for whom "urban insurrection" and "dancing in the street" were synonymous, such as Amiri Baraka and H. Rap Brown and their followers, Martha Reeves's party song was subversive and radio stations might have seen it the same way. But mostly they appeared not to because it could also be seen as just a "party song." How can two such radically different interpretations of a song be explained?

To some, the song was clearly about revolution in the street. Certainly it was to H. Rap Brown, who used it almost as the battle song of urban uprisings and a way to stir the crowd. He even got them dancing to the song against his fiery rhetoric. He corresponded from his cell at ADX Florence super-maximum security prison in Colorado, where after a lifetime of arrests and convictions, some of them highly dubious — including a 1995 arrest for shooting a man who later recanted, saying he had been pressured by the authorities to lie — he was serving a life sentence for the 2000 killing of a policeman, which he denies having done. Brown, who converted to Islam and used the name Jamil Abdullah Al-Amin, said, "About the significance of 'Dancing in the Street' as an anthem for movement in the sixties; when viewed in the context of the struggle, it is part of the catalogue of inspirational and iconic message music that defined an era."

He went on to quote from the eighteenth-century English poet William Cowper's "Human Frailty": "But oars alone can ne'er prevail / To reach the distant coast; / The breath of Heaven must swell the sail, / Or all the toil is lost." Brown understood that to lead he had to inspire, and that "Dancing in the Street" was an invaluable tool for this, that it could give that breath of heaven to fill the sails.

The song was using the language of the time, a street language both the songwriters and Brown knew well. At the time Brown was saying that the new fashion for unstraightened hair called the "natural" was meaningless. "It ain't what's on your head," he said. "It's what's in it." Or as Stevenson, Gaye, and Hunter put it, "It doesn't matter what you wear. Just as long as you are there."

Brown was forever using the word *street.* He spoke of the "brother who was taking care of business, the brother who is in the street." Ekwueme Michael Thelwell, a retired professor who had known Brown well from their years together at SNCC, said, " 'Dancing in the Street' was an obvious choice for the movement. I can see how this would happen from the title. The words 'dancing in the street' meant something."

The Living Theatre's benchmark of avant-garde theater, *Paradise Now,* ended every performance in New York and on tour in the late 1960s with the lines "Theater is in the street. The street belongs to the people. Free the theater, free the street. Begin."

Martha Reeves argues that the politically charged word is *streets,* and that people who have the political interpretation often incorrectly call the song "Dancing in the Streets." The song phrase is actually "Dancing in the *Street*" — singular — and *street* does not have the same connotation as *streets.* In the recording, Martha sings "street," but the backup singers reply, "Dancing in the streets," so that there appears to be a dialogue between these two ideas.

It is almost impossible to talk about these summer conflagrations without the words *street* and even *dancing.* The Kerner Report, the result of a presidential committee to study these summer occurrences, which they wisely labeled "disorders," and named after its chairman, Illinois governor Otto Kerner, reported that in the Detroit disorder, "a spirit of carefree nihilism was taking hold." It quoted one witness observing that young people were "dancing amidst the flames."

Rolland Snellings of SNCC wrote in 1965 of "the coming Black Revolution." According to Snellings, "they are moving to the rhythms of a New Song, a New Sound:

dancing in the streets to a Universal Dream that haunts their wretched nights: they dream of freedom!"

And then there is that telling phrase: "Summer's here and the time is right." And did not "calling out around the world" mean a call for revolution, and didn't the song include a list of cities, each with important black communities that were likely to have "disorders"? What did it mean to be calling out to these cities for people to go dancing in the street now that summer's here and the time is right?

Amiri Baraka, interviewed in 2012, recalled that the song was first released at the time of the Harlem disturbances. "The song comes out at the time of the rebellion in Harlem," he said. "We just moved from the Village to Harlem. That whole idea of revolution. That is what that song was to us. That is what it seemed to be. 'Calling out around the world, are you ready.' That's what we got from it."

In fact, since the song came out just as these uprisings were beginning, it seemed not just to be calling for them but to be predicting them. Baraka said that the song "prophesied the rebellion." After all, the lyrics are mostly in the future tense — "There'll be . . ."

Snellings wrote in *Liberator* in October 1965 following that year's riot season:

WE ARE COMING UP! WE ARE COMING UP! And it's reflected in the Riot-song that symbolized Harlem, Philly, Brooklyn, Rochester, Paterson, Elizabeth; this song, of course, "Dancing in the Streets" — making Martha and the Vandellas legendary.

Notice that this quote dubbing the recording a "riot-song" makes the exact mistake Martha Reeves referred to — he erroneously wrote "streets" in the plural.

When it was pointed out to Amiri Baraka that Martha Reeves, Mickey Stevenson, and Ivy Jo Hunter all denied his interpretation of their song, he said, "No matter what she might think. At that particular time it coincides with people who were dancing in the street. They were the only people I knew who were dancing in the street. It doesn't matter to me what they meant. If you take the words in the context they came in, that's what it came to mean. It was used at rallies by Black Panthers and other groups."

Many people in the music industry agree with this idea about the interpretation of songs. Jon Landau said, "When work goes out into the public the artist interpretation becomes just another interpretation. It's not necessarily the deepest interpretation. It's just one interpretation."

This idea that a song might have two meanings, the lighthearted one for the general public and a political one for the thinking few, was for young white people in the 1960s an intriguing new concept of counterculture introduced by radio stations, which got very uncomfortable about undecipherable rock 'n' roll lyrics. Originally the fear was not so much political messages as the belief that black music held hidden sexual innuendos, which it sometimes did. The most memorable incident of this for white kids growing up in the 1950s and early 1960s was the 1955 hit "Louie Louie." Written and performed by Richard Berry, a black doo-wop singer, the song was a classic example of the mambo craze influencing R&B. Berry took the idea for the song from Cuban bandleader Rosendo Ruíz's "Amarren al Loco." But the lyrics came from a ballad about a Jamaican sailor looking for his lover. Few people ever heard the original recording, but a West Coast group called the Kingsmen slapped together a cover in one take in a garage for fifty dollars in expenses. The recording is full of mistakes and cover-ups and badly used equipment, and as a result the words are completely indecipherable. The song tells of how the sailor searches Jamaica for this girl he cannot get over. What kids, and a lot of radio stations that refused to play it, heard was something like

Da nights and days I sail dad a
Think of girl do dada

What were they saying? Kids sat around with portable record players, which had three speeds, but they could not make it out. Finally a complaint reached Attorney General Robert Kennedy, and he put the FBI on it. What did the FBI do? Exactly what kids had been doing — sat around a record player running it at different speeds. But they dropped the case because they couldn't decipher the words, either. Kids were now even more determined to find out what the FBI couldn't. Different scatological versions circulated and "What are the words to 'Louie Louie'?" remained a topic of young people's conversations for years. This was how white kids learned to listen for hidden meanings in songs.

But for black people the custom of decoding songs came from a very old tradition that was sometimes referred to as "masking" — the black man hiding his true face by the wearing of a mask. This secretive way of sending messages was so embedded in African American culture that, as Amiri Baraka put it in *Blues People*, "In language, the African tradition aims at circumlocution rather than an exact definition. The direct statement is considered crude and unimaginative; the veiling of all contents in ever-changing paraphrases is considered the criterion of intelligence and personality."

This masking became even more of a necessity in slave times. Slave spirituals were often about escape and rebellion, though seemingly about the biblical lessons they had been taught to be de-Africanized — stories of Moses and the Promised Land, the crumbling walls of Jericho. Many songs such as "Steal Away," "Run to Jesus," "Wade in the Water," and the dangerously obvious "Gospel Train" were about the escape route of the so-called Underground Railroad. "Follow the Drinking Gourd" was a reference to the Big Dipper constellation. Following it would lead a traveler north.

Chuck Berry was a great masker; his songs almost always refer to something else. "Johnny B. Goode" was about the possibility of black success even in the South now with the new civil rights movement. So was Sam Cooke's 1960 "Wonderful World," which with his sweet voice seemed at face value to be a high school student saying that he was a poor student, but if his girl would love him, the world would be wonderful. But another interpretation was that if you didn't know biology and you didn't know history — in other words, if you forgot about race and forgot about all that had happened in race history — we could love each other and the world could be wonderful. Cooke did not confirm this meaning. The 1963 hit by the Jaynetts, "Sally, Go 'Round the Roses," for those who looked for masked meanings, was about closeted lesbian love. This interpretation persists, as does another one that it is religious, and yet another that it was about a mental breakdown. The Jaynetts said the song's ambiguous wording was simply a black street rhyme of a kind young girls invented for skipping rope.

Nor was "Dancing in the Street" the only Motown song adopted by the black nationalist movement. When Black Panther Fred Hampton spoke, the crowd would sing back the Supremes' song "Someday We'll Be Together." A number of other Martha and the Vandellas songs seemed to have some radical chic to their driving beats, especially "Heat Wave." Amiri Baraka said of Martha and the Vandellas' hits, "All those songs have reference to explosiveness. Coming out of passiveness. Heat wave. You have the context of the time to give the song its meaning."

But none had the revolutionary standing of "Dancing in the Street." Baraka said it was an anthem "for people hoping for a revolution. We played it all the time." And of course, they were not interested in white covers, it had to be Martha and the Vandellas.

Some white people caught on as well. For white radicals, attempting to decipher the dense lyrics of Bob Dylan was their introduction to the decoding of songs. Dylan's lyrics, while not as indecipherable as "Louie Louie," but far more cryptic, always lent themselves to interpretation. And Bob Dylan, in the best tradition of black masking, adamantly refused to explain his meaning. Radicals from Columbia University's branch of SDS (Students for a Democratic Society), the group nicknamed the "action faction" because they increasingly believed in confrontation as a political tool, found meaning in songs. In 1969 they formed a violent cell called "the Weathermen," a name they took from a line in Bob Dylan's "Subterranean Homesick Blues." The line was "You don't need a weatherman to know which way the wind blows." Dylan, who never expressed interest in political organizing, probably did not intend this, but it was their interpretation.

Conservatives, too, were forever worrying about the uncertain "real meaning" of Dylan's songs. In 1963, when Peter, Paul, and Mary were hitting the British charts with Dylan songs — "Don't Think Twice, It's All Right" and "Blowin' in the Wind" — the right-wing tabloid press was suggesting that these songs hid subliminal messages from the Soviet Union to brainwash young people.

Motown lyrics on the other hand were always crystal clear, but the Weathermen, having caught on to the idea of masking, did not miss the hidden meaning of "Dancing in the Street." To David Gilbert, it spoke to world revolution, country by country. Mark Rudd, one of the original Weathermen, said, "We thought 'Dancing in the Street' was coding for rioting, which at the time we thought of as an act of liberation." And these white revolutionaries, too, insisted on the original recording. "It was definitely Martha and the Vandellas," said

Rudd. "We were Motown purists."

But for black people, the decoding of songs was not new or "counterculture," it was the normal response to hearing a new song. For most of history, with a few exceptions, such as motion pictures during the Joseph McCarthy Senate anti-Communism investigations, white artists had little need for masking, while for blacks it was a necessity. Simply compare what anti-rock forces did to Chuck Berry as opposed to Elvis Presley.

Country Joe McDonald, a white musician who wrote unmasked protest music, especially his dark-humored satire of the Vietnam War, "I-Feel-Like-I'm-Fixin'-to-Die Rag," had little experience with masking. "I grew up with Woody Guthrie," he said. "You just stated the meaning." But he recognized that it was different for black artists. "They could get their asses whipped more easily than us."

White audiences with a different experience tend to look less often for hidden meanings in music. This meant that black songwriters could write a song with a different meaning for whites and blacks. Mickey Stevenson, for one, accepted the idea that a crossover song could change meanings in the crossover. That was why he believed it was important to let people interpret songs the way they wanted. Simply because white people might see it differently, "because they don't come from the place the song comes from."

In the case of "Dancing in the Street," the Weathermen were a white exception because they were deeply interested in the concept of rioting as an insurrection, which fit their ideology of "liberation struggles." Most white people saw a different meaning to "Dancing in the Street" than did black people. Joe McDonald liked "Dancing in the Street," but did not search it for its meaning, even though *street* was a meaningful word. "To me it was just another nice Motown song. Even today when I think of it. It is a very powerful image, dancing in the street. It's working class. The upper class doesn't do anything in the street. They do 'Dancing in the Club.' "

Cousin Brucie, a leading deejay for white radio, said when he first heard "Dancing in the Street":

I thought it was a great party song. Wow, I thought. Motown is really developing and it's sending people out dancing in the street. It was a time of block parties. Block parties were really popular in Brooklyn.

This was a call to a block party. Did anybody have the idea that it was a call to action? I doubt it. But then it was reinterpreted. It got a new meaning, but it also still had the old meaning.

For Sarah Dash, a black musician who sang with Patti LaBelle and Laura Nyro in a famous 1971 cover of "Dancing in the Street," it was very different. "I was always looking for the meaning in songs. I had a journal when I was young. I wrote about what songs meant." So in 1964, when she first heard "Dancing in the Street," it was full of meanings. "I loved 'Dancing in the Street,' " she said. "It was during the civil rights movement. I thought we will be dancing for freedom, for the right to vote, no more prejudice. It was a time when you could actually see black and white dancing together. Calling out, Are you ready for a brand new beat? Now, looking back, it had much more meaning than we knew. A new beat, are you ready to rerecord it in the seventies? It was about freedom for women. For Laura and three black women, it had a lot of meaning."

Dash felt that most people who heard "Dancing in the Street" "were not aware of the subliminal message, the power of vibration. It meant so much to our society consciously and unconsciously."

Most musicians are resigned to being interpreted in ways with which they don't necessarily agree. McDonald said, "Songs have a life of their own and you can't control it." And blacks and whites interpreted differently. The famous conclusion of the Kerner Report was: "Our nation is moving toward two societies, one black, one white — separate and unequal."

If there is a hidden political meaning to "Dancing in the Street," then whose idea was it? Of course it is in the nature of masking that the hidden meaning is always denied, so it is not surprising that everyone involved in creating the song absolutely denies intending any other meaning. Martha Reeves is easiest to believe, because unlike the others, she is a genuinely apolitical person, which may be one of the reasons why her more recent stint on the Detroit City Council for one term proved so uncomfortable for her. "I just want to be responsible for being a good singer," she said. As for the politics of the 1960s — civil rights and black power and the war in Vietnam, where her brother had fought, she simply said, "I wasn't involved."

Mickey Stevenson said that he was political "in that I saw so many unjust things go down." But he insisted his only political message in the song was that all kinds of people could get along together. "Kids have no color," he said, "they would play out there as if they were all brothers and sisters of every creed. So the song comes from that idea. . . . I think that's why the song has outlasted most songs, because it means just that. In Chicago, Philadelphia, Detroit, London — it don't matter — kids all over the world, they don't have this problem. Joining hands, the love train you see, they be laughing with each other and loving each other. Soon they get home and get into the separate bull because they are separate."

Yes, Mickey Stevenson was a very political man, and this was his interpretation. Ivy Jo Hunter also denied any message about rioting. The other person who needed to be asked, the third writer, was the late Marvin Gaye.

Marvin Gaye, who talked about kicking ass with the brothers in Watts, had political passions and was sympathetic to the street uprisings. But like many, he had predicted the assassination of Martin Luther King Jr. "Maybe that's why I stayed away from the area of direct involvement. I wasn't ready to sacrifice my life for a cause." But he might have been ready to slip a well-masked statement into a party song. After the 1965 Malcolm X killing, he certainly pushed Gordy for more politically engaged songs.

Cousin Brucie, who interviewed Marvin Gaye a number of times, said, "When you talked to Marvin Gaye, you knew you were talking to someone political. He was a poet who had an agenda. He realized the only way to spread that agenda was to be light. He was always a gentleman and soft, but you knew the agenda was there."

Gaye later said in his autobiography:

Funny but of all the acts back then, I thought Martha and the Vandellas came closest to really saying something. It wasn't a conscious thing, but when they sang numbers like "Quicksand" or "Wild One" or "Nowhere to Run" or "Dancing in the Street," they captured a spirit that felt political to me. I liked that. I wondered to myself, with the world exploding around me, how am I supposed to keep singing love songs?

This was a profound level of African cultural understanding, the idea that a political message could come simply from

317

the nature of the sound. And it was Gaye who very much wanted Martha Reeves to have the song. Gaye continued to argue for more politically relevant songs at Motown. Soon others joined in, and Gordy began to recognize that the times called for a different kind of music. In 1967 Gordy hired Junius Griffin to be director of publicity. This was a highly significant move because Griffin not only had been a distinguished journalist covering the civil rights movement for *The New York Times* and the Associated Press, but from 1965 until Gordy hired him, he had been working as a speechwriter for Martin Luther King. Gordy said, "Junius was our link to the black community and theirs to us. He kept us in touch with our roots." Though still reserved about political engagement, Gordy recognized that he could not afford the Motown bubble.

Socially conscious, unabashedly political R&B was selling. First there was Curtis Mayfield and the Impressions, whose "Keep On Pushing" was the surprise hit of 1964. As the rest of the music world shifted his way, he became hugely influential, even to Motown artists, especially Marvin Gaye. Like Smokey Robinson, Mayfield sang in falsetto, but he had an unusual guitar sound because he tuned his guitar so that the open strings were sharps rather than naturals. He also played bass, piano, saxophone, and drums. In 1965 Mayfield had a hit with "People Get Ready," and in 1968 with "We're a Winner." He made hit after hit with messages of civil rights and black pride. There was nothing masked about Curtis Mayfield.

By 1968 the hottest black artist was probably James Brown, and he wasn't Motown either. He came out of a southern gospel tradition, and like Motown, had a jazz foundation to his large backup band. He was becoming a huge influence on other artists, including many at Motown such as David Ruffin, Michael Jackson, and Edwin Starr. In 1964 he appeared in a concert film, *T.A.M.I. Show* (Teenage Awards Music International), which used new technology that is considered the forerunner of high-definition television invented by the producer, an amateur electronics expert, Bill Sargent. The other thing this film is famous for is the way Brown upstaged everybody, including Chuck Berry, the Beach Boys, Marvin Gaye, the Supremes, and especially the Rolling Stones, who were supposed to be the stellar closing act but suffered from directly following Brown. Years later, Keith Richards said the biggest mistake of his career was agreeing to follow Brown. Artists from Mick Jagger to Trinidadian calypso star the Mighty Sparrow were imitating not the careful choreography of Cholly Atkins but the wild gyrations of master showman James Brown. In 1966, despite all of Motown's success with crossover music, it was James Brown who was singled out by *Time* magazine, after his second million-selling record, saying, "His rise in the mass market gives a sign that 'race music' is at last becoming interracial."

In 1968, after Martin Luther King was killed, Berry Gordy said, "I couldn't contain my anger." He pointed out that the fallen leader was only one year older than he was. He agreed to put on a Motown benefit concert to raise money for the Poor People's Campaign that King had planned. Gordy even marched side by side with Sidney Poitier, Mary Wilson, and Sammy Davis Jr.

Many people were affected by the King murder. Angry protests and fires burned in 110 cities. James Brown went on television and addressed black communities, asking them to "cool it." The following night, he was scheduled to give a concert in Boston. The new young mayor, Kevin White, appeared onstage with him — White and Brown together, nobody missed that irony.

With tears in his eyes, Brown asked for no violence in Boston and argued with passion for a kind of nonviolent black power. There was no violence in Boston that night, one of the few major black communities in the country that didn't explode.

James Brown met with H. Rap Brown and told him, "Rap, I know what you are trying to do. I'm trying to do the same thing. But y'all got to find another way to do it. You got to put down the guns, you got to put away the violence." When H. Rap Brown was arrested for inciting violence in Cambridge, Maryland, James Brown raised money for his defense fund. James Brown had done the seemingly impossible thing; rather than avoiding politics, he had found a way to bridge the space between the two principal camps of black liberation.

It was not always smooth for him. He supported the presidential bid of Hubert Humphrey, which was not popular with most young blacks, who, if they supported anyone, were for Robert Kennedy. Humphrey, who was deeply involved in the Vietnam War, was seen as the sellout candidate. But that same, volatile year, 1968, Brown released the biggest-selling record by a black artist of the year, "Say It Loud, I'm Black and I'm Proud." Gordy would have never imagined that a record that so clearly expressed the theme of black empowerment, of black power, could be such a huge hit. Some music critics attacked Brown for his black power stance, but as Gordy always liked to point out, you can't argue with success. Even today, black people almost unconsciously repeat the title line.

In 1970, Motown, late in this new game, released several unmasked political songs: Edwin Starr's "War," the Temptations' "Ball of Confusion (That's What the World Is Today)," and "Heaven Help Us All" by Stevie Wonder, who had been arguing for political engagement for almost as long as Gaye had. "War" and "Ball of Confusion" were both written by Starr in collaboration with Harlem-born Norman Whitfield, who had come out to Detroit at age nineteen and worked his way into Motown when the company was just starting. He wrote and produced for Gaye and for the Temptations, and ten years later was a major force pushing the company toward more socially conscious music. Gordy said of him, "He was quiet and shy — not someone you'd think would turn into the boldly innovative producer he later became. . . . He had a fire deep in his soul and a little would come out each time he produced a record."

But despite all these socially conscious hits, Gaye had a political edge that Gordy feared. Marvin had been influenced by his brother Frankie, who was three years younger than Marvin, the pleasant kid who tried to placate their brutal father rather than challenge him, the way Marvin did. He was a talented singer and composer, though without Marvin's drive, his career never blossomed. He was drafted and sent to Vietnam, where he served as a deejay but when he returned in 1970 he told Marvin stories of what Vietnam was like. According to an interview he gave *Rolling Stone* magazine, Marvin had also been disturbed by letters Frankie had sent him from Vietnam. Marvin said, "It was time to stop playing games." He told *Rolling Stone,* "I realized that I had to put my own fantasies behind me if I wanted to write songs that would reach the souls of people. I wanted them to take a look at what was happening in the world."

In 1969, songwriter Al Cleveland, who had some standing in Motown since writing Smokey Robinson and the Miracles' 1967 hit "I Second That Emotion," had a conversation with Obie Benson, the bass singer in the Four Tops who had been deeply upset by seeing police clubbing antiwar demonstrators in Berkeley's People's Park. "I saw this and started wondering, 'What the fuck was going on, what is happening here?' " he later said. Cleveland wrote a song about it that Benson took to his group, but they did not want to sing it. They were still too much in the Motown bubble to see the potential of such a song. But Gaye, after talking with his brother, could see it. He asked if he could rework the song. His contribution seems to have been similar to his work on "Dancing in the Street." He tweaked some lines and gave it a title, "What's Going On."

The song began:

Brother, brother, brother
There's far too many of you dying

He recorded it in June 1970 and finally showed it to Berry Gordy in September. Gordy called it "the worst thing I ever heard in my life" and refused to release it. The Motown quality control department agreed. Gordy thought taking on these issues was a mistake. "Stick to what you do," Gordy told Gaye. "Stick to what works."

When Gaye pointed out that Gordy's whole career had been about trying something different, Gordy's reply could have been a slogan for the company. He said, "If you're gonna do something different, at least make it commercial."

The record was released in 1971. There is a Motown legend that Gaye got the first 100,000 records out without Gordy knowing, but Gordy refutes this. Gordy saw little hope for the record but claimed he told Gaye, "Marvin, we learn from everything. That's what life's about. I don't think you're right, but if you really want to do it, do it. And if it doesn't work, you'll learn something; and if it does, I'll learn something."

Gordy always clung to his father's lesson about learning from mistakes. After the song was released he added, "I learned something."

It climbed the charts rapidly to number 1 on the R&B chart and number 2 on the pop chart.

The sudden disappearance of cover recordings of "Dancing in the Street" after 1966 may have been connected with a reluctance of artists to be associated with rioting, although the revolutionary mantle was never placed on any but the original Motown recording. There was the occasional television appearance, such as the Carpenters' 1968 television debut on *Your All-American College Show.* Eighteen-year-old drummer

Karen Carpenter was the star of the trio, with great drum bridges, and they won a prize, handed to them by the aging Hungarian bombshell Zsa Zsa Gabor, who was a star at the time, though no one could remember exactly why. John Wayne saw the show and said of the young drummer, that's who I want to costar in *True Grit,* but the film ended up going with Kim Darby, already a seasoned actress at twenty-two.

The one notable "Dancing" cover of this period was by Ramsey Lewis in 1967. With his newly rebuilt trio, with Cleveland Eaton on the upright bass and Maurice White drumming to Lewis's light-fingered piano, they brilliantly deconstructed Stevenson, Gaye, and Hunter into jazz riffs and variations. This was their first recording together, and it was pure modern jazz, the song probably unrecognizable to the average Martha and the Vandellas fan. Lewis tried to rebuild the bridge between pop and jazz not by altering his style but by choosing popular songs with which to work. "Dancing in the Street" was picked simply because it was a hit. According to bass player Cleveland Eaton, they would arrange the popular song for trio and then improvise. "We never just jammed," he said. "But every night we did it different for ten years. That's why I stayed with it so long. Every night it was a fresh tune." The single reached number 84 on the pop chart, a considerable achievement for a modern jazz trio. The album, also called *Dancing in the Street,* included other pop tunes and reached number 59 on the pop albums chart.

There was yet another phenomenon occurring as "Dancing in the Street" found its way into the pantheon of great popular music. Not only was it covered but it was imitated, and not only the music but the words. That bridge, the rhythm section, all that was special about the sound track was admired and imitated by other musicians.

LeRoi Jones, before he changed his name to Amiri Baraka, said, "Actually the more intelligent the white, the more the realization he has to steal from niggers." He was talking about music, and in music this seems true.

Touring in 1964, the Rolling Stones, especially Mick Jagger, had been deeply influenced by the black music in the United States. Apparently that strange, scrawny Jagger bird that started hopping and flapping its wings onstage was an interpretation of the broad muscular moves of James Brown. In 1965 Jagger and Keith Richards wrote "(I Can't Get No) Satisfaction" a phrase that they took from a Chuck Berry song. Both the phrase and the accompanying guitar riff supposedly came to Richards one night as he was falling asleep. The next day he not only did not like the phrase but also realized that the guitar riff sounded very much like something from the track of "Dancing in the Street." The rest of the band talked him into going ahead with the song, one of the biggest hits the Rolling Stones ever recorded.

In March 1968, about twenty-five thousand anti–Vietnam War protesters, including Mick Jagger, gathered in London's Trafalgar Square and marched toward the U.S. embassy in Grosvenor Square, calling for the victory of the North Vietnamese. The visiting German demonstrators seemed best prepared, since they were wearing helmets. At Grosvenor Square the demonstrators charged the embassy and were met by mounted police with clubs. A battle ensued. Demonstrators were clubbed to the ground and dragged away by their hair. After two hours of fighting, the demonstrators retreated. Eighty-six people were injured.

The incident, which Jagger witnessed, seemed to have been the inspiration for a song he and Richards wrote, "Street Fighting Man." Whether the song was for or against street fighting, their point of reference is America's famous "riot song," "Dancing in the Street." It wasn't Motown. There were no electric guitars, but just acoustic instruments amplified so that they sounded like a screech — actually sounded a bit like Mick Jagger's voice — and the words, for those who could make them out to the singsong tune with a hard-hit third beat, were "Summer's here, and the time is right, for fighting in the street."

The first inspiration may have been the Grosvenor Square incident — some, but not Jagger, suggested that one of the demonstration organizers, Tariq Ali, was the street fighting man — but as they were working on it, students shut down the government in France. So many bigger things were happening in the world that instead of the song being about the incident in London, it ended up being about the lack of one. In subsequent interviews, Jagger said that it was not about street fighting but the lack of it. In 1968 he told the German magazine *Der Spiegel* that he did not intend it to be about street fighting. "In America the rock 'n' roll bands have gotten very political . . . but when I come home to England, everything is completely different, so quiet and peaceful. If one lives in such an atmosphere, one has a great detachment from politics and writes completely different about them."

There was always something about Mick Jagger and the Rolling Stones that left you wondering if they were putting you on. They were always a little too earnest, a little too down and dirty. Is it counterculture or is it a spoof on counterculture? "Street Fighting Man," in which they mimic the lyrics of "Dancing in the Street," if you follow Jagger's interviews over the years, was either (a) a call for revolution, or (b) a laugh at people calling for revolution, or (c) both. It may be the reverse of "Dancing in the Street" because it came out in 1968, when everything had fiery meanings and this seemed to as well, but some thought this masked an inner complacence. In a more recent interview with a London magazine, *Student,* Jagger was asked if he was interested in politics and he said no because "I thought about that for a long time and decided I haven't got time to do that and understand other things. I mean, if you get really involved in politics, you get fucked up."

Still, British radio and record distributors did not want to handle the song. In Chicago, where that summer the Democratic Convention had turned into a police riot, Mayor Richard Daley ordered radio stations to ban the song, which greatly increased its popularity in Chicago and around America. Jagger's reaction was, "It's stupid to think that you can start a revolution with a record. I wish you could."

It was also banned in the UK. All that meant was that the BBC, which controlled the airwaves, banned it. Jagger sent the song to Tariq Ali, and asked him to publish it, which he did in his *Black Dwarf* with the headline "Fred Engels and Mick Jagger on Street Fighting."

Ali thought the song was "probably a conjunction of May '68 in France and our inability to create a similar situation in Britain." But Ali, who remembered "Dancing in the Street" from parties in his student days at Oxford, said that he "certainly didn't think of it as political in any way." Yet thirty years later, when he wrote a book about the events of 1968, he titled it *Marching in the Streets.*

Times were changing music, and it was hard to know what to do. In 1969 the Rolling Stones toured the United States again and found the country changed from how it had been in 1964. At concerts Jagger would sometimes give the peace salute and sometimes the black power fist. At a concert in Berkeley he tried giving both, and the crowd booed. Keith Richards said, "Before, America was a real fantasy land. It was still Walt Disney and hamburger dates, and when you came back in 1969 it wasn't anymore. Kids were really into what was going on in their country."

In October 1968 a group of advertising agencies and large entertainment companies offered a conference called "Selling of American Youth Market," at which for a $300 admission fee one could learn how to sell your product to young people with the use of words such as *revolution.* The age of masking was over, and so was the revolution.

# CHAPTER FIVE:
# IT DOESN'T MATTER WHAT YOU WEAR

If the summer urban disturbances were not chance riots but motivated insurrections, they were not without results. They focused attention on the conditions in ghettos of American cities. Once the Promised Land, these neighborhoods were now the symbol of the mistreatment of African Americans in American society. In a July 1967 speech, after Detroit and Newark had exploded, President Johnson said, "The only long-range solution for what has happened lies in attack — mounted at every level — upon the conditions that breed despair and violence. . . . Not because we are frightened by conflict, but because we are fired by conscience."

The Kerner Commission, which comprised Republicans and Democrats, conservatives and liberals, blacks and whites, recommended "experimental programs" to ameliorate conditions and break a cycle of "failure and frustration" in inner-city ghettos and called for "unprecedented levels of funding and performance."

The report stated, "Segregation and poverty have created in the racial ghetto a destructive environment totally unknown to most white Americans." At the height of the Vietnam War, poll findings were showing more public concern about race relations than the war. Many were feeling a sense of responsibility that the commission had clearly laid at their feet, declaring, "What white Americans have never fully understood — but what the Negro can never forget — is that white society is deeply implicated in the ghetto. White institutions created it, white institutions maintain it, and white society condones it."

Unfortunately, at the time the U.S. government was giving unprecedented funding, billions of dollars, to killing people in a small, impoverished Southeast Asian country and little was left for Johnson's "Great Society." But programs were launched to address grievances, provide opportunities, and try to end the sense of hopelessness in urban ghettos. Police departments integrated and changed both tactics and attitudes. Racism was not eliminated from the police but it at least lost its respectability and automatic acceptance within the departments.

The initial reports of the value of damaged property in Detroit, about $500 million, turned out to be an exaggeration, and the real figure was closer to $45 million. It is difficult to affix value to ghetto property, but what is clear is that the trends that accelerated following the 1967 disturbances have continued to increase into the twenty-first century. Detroit has been losing about a quarter of its population every decade. Not only have white people left — by 2010 the population was only 10.6 percent white, whereas in 1967 whites were 60 percent of the population — but companies have folded or moved. A third of Detroit's population is below the poverty level, and the average household income in this city that once had the highest-paid labor force in America is only slightly more than half of that of the rest of Michigan. To travel from Martha Reeves's family home on the Eastside to the old Hitsville studio on the Westside is to pass rows of abandoned factories that look as though they had been bombed and boarded-up houses. Families that leave Detroit often have no buyer for their property, so it is just left behind. It is a city of plywood, broken windows, and decaying walls. Detroit looks like the site of a natural disaster but there has only been an economic one.

No wonder Martha Reeves, who loved her city, hated the fact that the beginnings of its destruction in 1967 had taken place while people sang her song. Yet the downtown has sparkling high-rises, one of which Reeves lives in, and the suburbs have mansions on leafy boulevards.

Not all of the flight of people and businesses from Detroit was white. Berry Gordy never looked at his city the same way again. The little house on West Grand Boulevard had long been too small, but he had expanded by buying the surrounding houses. But in 1968 he moved operations to a cold ten-story building on downtown Woodward Avenue. Gordy said that this was not as much a response to the riots as to the growing crime rate. But this was all part of the reality that the Detroit that he grew up in was vanishing. In 1964, the year of "Dancing in the Street," Detroit had 125 homicides. In 1967, the year of the riot, the city had 281 homicides. The following year, when Motown moved, Detroit had 389 killings, more than three times the number in 1964, only four years earlier.

A final blow was a telephone call threatening to burn Motown to the ground. The new building had excellent security, which meant it was no longer a place where artists felt comfortable drifting in or out at any hour. Motown lost its family feel. Now artists had to make an appointment to see Gordy, who was to be addressed "Mr. Gordy." "Berry" or "Berry, baby" seemed to have already vanished. Once the artists were no longer part of a family, they started looking more closely at their contracts.

By 1970 Motown was the largest black-owned company in America. Despite being the majority population, there were only a handful of wealthy black people in Detroit, and Gordy was one of the richest. He lived in a mansion in the wealthy Boston-Edison section of Detroit that had cost a million dollars to build early in the twentieth century. His company was privately owned, with thousands of shares, all owned by Gordy. According to *The Story of Motown,* a 1979 study by Peter Benjaminson, he paid himself a dividend of $3,100 a share, and in this way between 1967 and 1970 Gordy was able to secure for himself $5 million of the company's money.

Much of this money was spent in California, opening an office on Sunset Boulevard, working his way into Hollywood society, and buying a Beverly Hills home from television star Tommy Smothers, for whom the 1970s were looking bleak. His close friend Smokey Robinson pleaded with Gordy not to go to California and even sent him books about the San Andreas Fault.

It was a gradual process, but by 1972 Motown was a Los Angeles company gone from the Motor City and leaving a lot of people who had thought they were stars — "divas" — behind. Mickey Stevenson was right — an important lesson in life is that "the tour does not go on forever."

The dream of black capitalism was a disappointing reality. It turned out that black artists did not get treated any better by blacks. But it is also true that through Motown Berry Gordy enormously improved the standing of black artists. They became not just black stars, but stars.

Marvin Gaye once said, "Berry thought like an oil man. Drill as many holes as you can and hope for at least one gusher. He wound up with a whole oil field." A record company is generally considered successful if 10 percent of its records become hits. Between 1960 and 1970, 67 percent of the records released by Motown made the Top 100 charts. But this meant that these records earned a great deal of money and artists started wondering where all that money had gone. Backup musicians were not even given credit on record jackets until Marvin Gaye, who had often played drums with them, listed them on the album of *What's Going On.* Percussionist Jack Ashford wrote in his autobiography, "As Motown came to dominate the pop charts and several of the acts became household names, the Funk Brothers, who pumped life into the songs, remained nameless and without recognition. We knew we were hot and we knew we were good. But the general consensus was that they would downplay our importance to avoid us from getting a representative to attempt to cut a recording deal for the Funks."

To support Ashford's claim that the Funk Brothers "pumped life" into the recordings, it is only necessary to listen to the lifeless later recordings of Diana Ross without them.

The musicians were not paid well, and many ended their lives in poverty. Eddie Willis, one of the last surviving Funk Brothers, lived in poverty in rural Mississippi. He did not seem a bitter man. He said, "Motown was the best time in my life." But he also said, "You do all this big stuff and no one knows who you are. It's ridiculous. No one knows who I am. I don't have no money." But he accepted the fact that he played under a contract that he had agreed to. "I'm not angry about the money. It just got to be bigger and bigger, and we agreed on a certain amount."

He was angry only because Gordy would not help him with the $25,000 needed to place a Funk Brothers star on the Hollywood Walk of Fame. "He let us down. . . . He won't give a hand to the musicians who put him where he is. Twenty-five thousand dollars, that's nothing for Berry. Now, that is sad."

The musicians each negotiated their own contract and, as with everything at Motown, were encouraged to compete with each other. Guitarist Joe Messina, who lived comfortably in a Detroit suburb, thanks in part to his investing money in a car-wash chain, said that he had secretly negotiated ten dollars per hour. "I was always very proud of getting that deal," he said. The standard pay was five dollars per hour. A session like "Dancing in the Street" could be an hour or two, but some sessions were nine hours. It is possible that some of the musicians who played on "Dancing in the Street" earned as little as ten or fifteen dollars. "So long sessions were in favor," said

Messina. He estimated that he earned two hundred or more a week and thought he was one of the top-paid musicians. Maybe not. There were a lot of secret deals being made. Some musicians, such as Messina and pianist Earl Van Dyke, did well while others earned below the pay scale of the musicians' union.

Songwriters did not do much better. They were all required to sign a contract with Jobete, Gordy's publishing company, which not only took a large piece of their earnings but also had a built-in mechanism to recover expenses from the record out of the writer's royalties. There were constant accusations of songs being stolen and the real writers being neither credited nor paid royalties. Clarence Paul said that this was a frequent occurrence. Ivy Jo Hunter was not credited for songwriting on the early pressings of "Dancing in the Street." Later, without any pressure from him, his name started appearing. "Someone must have put in a word for me," he said.

The artists were signed to the Gordy management company ITMI, which was supposed to look after their interests and preclude the necessity for any other representation. ITMI paid them salaries even on weeks when they produced nothing. Artists were grateful for this paycheck but then they realized that these salaries were later subtracted from their royalty earnings.

Gordy was signing high school kids who had no representation. Mary Wilson said, "Looking back, people might wonder how Motown got away with this sort of thing or why so many artists just seemed to have accepted it. In truth, few of us knew anything at all about the business, and fewer still knew to have legal counsel for any business dealings or contracts."

Don Engel, a California lawyer who both opposed and defended Gordy in various contract disputes, was testifying before the California Senate Joint Committee on the music industry, denouncing the kind of contracts Motown had signed young artists to, and he was asked if these contracts had not been negotiated. He replied, "These young kids would have paid royalties to the companies to put out their records."

The royalties they agreed to were a major issue. This was why Mary Wells had left. Motown artists earned very little in royalties for hits that earned Motown millions. In 1966 Clarence Paul, Mickey Stevenson's deputy, organized a meeting in his house for artists and producers to form a common front to demand better contracts. But they lost courage when they discovered that management was photographing their arrival from parked cars.

In 1967 Mickey Stevenson and wife, Kim Weston, left Motown. Stevenson always insists that this was simply because MGM offered him a better deal in California. But Kim Weston made it clear that she was dissatisfied with Motown's deals. Eventually she took Motown to court for a better share of the earnings on her songs, but divorced, impoverished, and in poor health, she settled for a small, fast paycheck. Said Weston, "They gave me ten thousand dollars for thirty years, and that's all I got from Motown, but I was sick, so I settled."

As the family structure broke down and artists left their "Motown bubble," they started thinking about their future and talking to artists from other companies.

The Temptations even considered going on strike. In 1967 the Holland brothers and Lamont Dozier demanded an accounting of royalties for their twenty-eight Top 20 hits. Motown's response was to sue them for $4 million, claiming they had failed to deliver on some contractual agreements. Gordy even got an injunction to stop them from working from 1969 to 1972. They wrote songs clandestinely under the name "Edythe

Wayne."

Others followed the exodus from Motown, including Barrett Strong, one of their first stars from "Money (That's What I Want)," and Brenda Holloway, the Miracles, Jimmy Ruffin, Eddie Kendricks, Gladys Knight and the Pips, the Four Tops, Maurice King, the Ashford and Simpson writing team, and Harvey Fuqua.

By 1969, Martha Reeves's relationship with Motown had grown thorny, in large part because, like other female singers, she had been shunted aside by Gordy's near obsession with Diana Ross. According to Mary Wells, Ross got into spats with all the female stars of Motown but fought the most with Martha Reeves. Wilson said, "Things happened faster for Martha and her group than they did for us, and this only fueled the rivalry between Martha and Diane. Both had drive and charisma, and neither would ever back down."

Wilson pointed out that Gordy used to refer to all the female acts as "the girls," but in the mid-1960s he started using the word to refer only to the Supremes. By 1969, Martha Reeves's standing was already in decline, but then, according to Reeves, she became one of the first to question where the money was going. "Yet after several years of million-selling records and sold-out concerts, in 1969 I realized that my personal income was but a fraction of what it should have been." She dared to question Gordy, even to argue with him and his sisters in a candid way that outraged the Gordys, and then she could feel herself being distanced from the family — worked with less, even talked to less.

Reeves often tells the story of how she learned of Motown leaving Detroit. With hurt still in her voice she said:

I was recuperating from giving birth to my son. There is no maternity leave for singers. When I was ready for my next assignment I called and was told that the company had moved to LA. It was now called Mo West — an insult to people in Detroit. They had taken the Temptations, Four Tops, Stevie Wonder, Michael Jackson, and the Jackson 5. Picked up a lot of East Coast people. Left a lot behind, including the Supremes. I was told my contract was up. I didn't know it, but it was. I had signed a ten-year contract, 1962 to '72. He didn't have to say anything to me and he didn't.

For all her criticism, Reeves seemed lost without her professional family, and struggled with performance and with substance abuse, but came through it to live a comfortable life in her home city, spending a great deal of her time touring. She and the Vandellas settled a lawsuit for their royalties in 1991. She usually speaks lovingly of Gordy and visibly glowed at a chance meeting. "He's still an all right guy," she said. "He made us famous. I didn't think I would ever be famous."

Even Diana Ross left for RCA in 1981, and Gordy sold Motown in 1988 for $61 million, but kept his cash-cow publishing company, Jobete.

Gordy could not avoid the sense that what he did, who he was, and his kind of music were out of place in more radical times. Magnificent Montague saw it when Gordy hired him to work with deejays and advise him on promotion in his Los Angeles office. Montague wrote in his autobiography:

Motown was beginning to lose its advantage; you could almost chart it from the day Dr. King was assassinated in '68. Black music quickly began to surrender its melodic core to the service of rhythm, a funkier rhythm, a fiercer rhythm, one bent on making a statement of independence.

This change contradicted the blander way Motown had been producing itself, and there was nothing Berry could do about it. He had enjoyed a window of only a few years — maybe 1963 to 1966, to be arbitrary — in which there was a rough consensus between young blacks and whites, an unverbalized understanding of what America might be, of what was right and what was wrong. It could not last.

And yet as Motown faded, "Dancing in the Street" endured. In 1971 Little Richard thought "Dancing in the Street" might be the right vehicle to revive his career. His producer, H. B. Barnum, was asked why he chose that particular song:

We just picked songs we like. I loved that song. It's a great song. The intro sets it up. You know what's coming. It's got so much energy. It's one of those songs that brings everybody together on the dance floor. It just makes everybody happy. The intro peps you up right out of the box. When you do that song, you don't have to fix it. There is nothing to change.

The same year, Laura Nyro recorded the song with Labelle, including Sarah Dash, who in 1971 thought "Dancing in the

Street" was a great way to promote the emerging wave of feminism. What Nyro and Labelle had in common was that they were forever looking for new and different ways of doing things. Patti LaBelle's group — Patti LaBelle and the Bluebelles — started as a typical R&B girl group. Then in 1971 the three stopped dressing alike and called themselves Labelle. Laura Nyro, a Bronx native born of one Sicilian and one Jewish parent, and the cherished niece of notable artists William Meyerowitz and Theresa Bernstein, was always a little different from everyone else on the music scene. A white interpreter of R&B who first came to public attention at Adler's 1967 Monterey Pop Festival, she was said to be "too intense."

The four women were planning on an album of R&B songs, mostly from Motown. Combining a white singer and a black group was still a little startling in 1971, but not as much as in 1964, when the Rolling Stones had toured the United States with Patti La-Belle and the Bluebelles and Adam Faith had sung with the Isley Brothers. Since the early days of Glenn Miller and Maurice King, blacks were slowly showing up in white bands — Billy Preston, who had played keyboard for Sam Cooke and Ray Charles and whose "natural" Afro hair eventually became far larger than his head, played with the Beatles in their famous 1969 sessions. But Nyro and LaBelle were white and black costars — equals. The album was called *Gonna Take a Miracle.* The title song, a 1965 hit for the Royalettes, was one of the few non-Motown cuts. Among the songs was Curtis Mayfield's "Monkey Time," which was Major Lance's first hit in 1963, and "Dancing in the Street." Nyro had the idea, looking for a different approach, to combine the two in one song. The cut begins with the Mayfield song, and about a minute and a half later it evolves into "Dancing in the Street." Both songs had to do with dancing and possibly more serious things. Much is made of the way this recording changes "Can't forget the Motor City" to "Don't forget the Motor City," which is often interpreted as "Remember Detroit and the 1967 uprising." The line is sung as a loud reprise for the backup, which is known in songwriting as a "drive."

In 1975, folksinger Joan Baez decided to try her hand at "Dancing in the Street." Though R&B was not her usual fare, Baez has always been courageous about trying different genres. She had built her reputation partly on the black gospel music of the civil rights movement, so she was associated with black music. Now Baez, one of the most political of singers, put "Dancing in the Street" on a program of black political music. She went on tour with James Jamerson on bass; David Briggs, who often recorded and toured with Elvis Presley, on keyboards; Danny Ferguson on electric guitar; and Jim Gordon, who had played for the Everly Brothers and the Beach Boys, on drums. The concert tour with this distinguished band began with the freedom song "Ain't Gonna Let Nobody Turn Me Around" and went on to more of the usual Baez repertoire, such as "Boulder to Birmingham," "Swing Low, Sweet Chariot," and the gospel song "Oh, Happy Day." She would then sing the Bob Dylan song "Forever Young," and then wind up the evening with that great closer "Dancing in the Street." But even with James Jamerson himself setting the groove, Baez's brave attempt to growl and affect other African American blues vocal styles came off as hopelessly white, and the finale failed to be rousing.

This was near the end of James Jamerson's life. Jamerson, one of the few musicians to follow Gordy to California, felt alone and lost there. Guitarist Eddie Willis, the last

Funk Brother to see Jamerson, had stopped by with bongo player Eddie Brown. Jamerson wept to see two from the old band. Always suffering from alcoholism, he deteriorated further in LA and died of cirrhosis of the liver in 1983. His famous Fender bass had been stolen from his home days before his death.

By the mid-1970s it seemed everyone was doing "Dancing in the Street," from reggae to psychedelic. The Royals, a Jamaican group that came up in the 1960s with the Bob Marley–led reggae craze, recorded a not-at-all reggae version of "Dancing in the Street," although it is striking how much the hard downbeat of Motown resembles the slower drop beat of reggae.

In 1976 Michael Bolton recorded "Dancing in the Street" for his second RCA album of R&B music. Bolton achieved stardom in the 1980s with his hard rock band Blackjack and in the 1990s with softer ballads, but he started his career as a white R&B singer named Michael Bolotin from New Haven, Connecticut. He began as a teenager in New Haven and in 1976 was still only twenty-three years old. Few remember that his early R&B was performed with top jazz musicians including the great bassist Wilbur

Bascomb, who played with notables from Bo Diddley to James Brown. "No one outside of my family noticed," Bolton quipped about his early R&B career. Looking back as a mature, experienced performer and songwriter, he says about his somewhat rash decision to cover what was already recognized as one of the all-time greatest popular music recordings, "I was too young, too naïve to be intimidated. I was too unaware of what to be intimidated by.

"In 1976 we were simply looking for songs that would feel good and I would sound good." Bolton had the kind of strong tenor that this song could showcase, as it did for Reeves's strong soprano. " 'Dancing in the Street' feels good and upbeat and Martha nailed it. I wanted to do the same thing — an upbeat celebration . . . you love something someone else has done, love the way it makes you feel, and then ask how does it feel for your voice? When you are looking for songs that will make the body of work feel good, those factors become overriding.

"Martha's track was a great track but the singer has to tell the story — breathe life into the song. I didn't know that back then. I just thought, 'I got to do that.' I didn't know enough to be intimidated and I'm glad." He was glad because he liked his recording. But looking back he said, "I like mine but . . . it's nowhere near the class of Martha's record, with her vocal delivery and that staggering band."

It was not until 1986, when he was recording a cover of Otis Redding's great "(Sittin' On) The Dock of the Bay," that he began reflecting on this idea of covering great songs. His team had reassured him that he was "a white Otis Redding," which may be the ultimate reverse crossover compliment, but then, "Someone asked how are people going to feel about something embraced reverentially?" This was an intimidating notion. But he did record the song and had a hit. He then had another hit with his recording of the Hoagy Carmichael song "Georgia on My Mind," which no one could possibly sing better than did Ray Charles in 1960. In 1991 Bolton dared to cover Percy Sledge's "When a Man Loves a Woman," a 1966 number 1 hit and recording legend. Sledge's bass player, Calvin Lewis, and his organist, Andrew Wright, had given him the tune with no lyrics or title. Sledge, reeling from his girlfriend's decision to leave him for a modeling career, stepped into the studio and improvised the words, setting them to the song's rhythm. Bolton won a Grammy award for his cover.

It seemed that if you could capture the spirit of the song and make it work for your voice, covering a classic could be a hit. But neither Bolton nor most of the others who tried were able to accomplish this with "Dancing in the Street." Artists hear the Reeves recording, love it, and want to do it, too, but it is not easy to "nail it" the way Martha did.

In 1977, the Grateful Dead, who had previously performed several versions of the song, recorded a psychedelic cover that has a long drum and organ introduction and drifts for eight minutes, which is five minutes and twenty-five seconds longer than the original Motown recording. In 1979, the gravelly voiced balladeer Neil Diamond, whose music was a long way from R&B, did his own "Dancing in the Street." Diamond was pushing forty, attracting an older crowd, and though unarguably unhip, well on his way to ending the twentieth century as the third top-selling artist of the century on *Billboard* charts, behind the equally unhip Barbra Streisand and Elton John. The top sellers are seldom hip because neither is most of the public. Diamond begins "Dancing in the Street" by shouting out to the audience "Are you ready to let it happen tonight?" and a female crowd, who may or may not have decided what "it" referred to, shouts back, whereupon Diamond tries for a soulful sound with grunts that sound like something accompanying karate chops, and then sings with neither the driving rhythm nor the sense of melody of the original.

More artists covered the song in the 1980s, including Tim Curry, Van Halen, and Kingfish, on their 1985 *Alive in Eighty Five* album, which featured a number of other R&B classics. But for all the copies, variations, and homages, only Van Halen made the charts with the song, although never rising above number 38. Only the original Martha and the Vandellas had made it to the Top 10. But then, in 1985, there was a fund-raiser for starving Ethiopia, Live Aid.

Bob Geldof, the Irish singer who created Live Aid, the star-studded fund-raising concert, wanted the two superstars Mick Jagger and David Bowie to record a duet to be played at the concert, which took place in overlapping time slots in London and Philadelphia. Bowie was in London, working on his *Absolute Beginners* film, and Jagger was in New York. Jagger, still an R&B enthusiast, chose "Dancing in the Street." The plan was for Bowie and Jagger to sing the duet by satellite. The concert specialized in such transatlantic gimmickry. Phil

Collins appeared at both venues, hopping a Concord supersonic jet in between. Think of it, two of the biggest stars in pop music singing a transatlantic duet via satellite. But the flair for show business was not matched by technological acumen. It turned out that between London and New York there is a one-second delay in satellite transmissions. For a brief time they contemplated having one of them placed on a space shuttle. Though this seems ridiculous now, at the time NASA was looking for ways to send non-astronauts on space shuttle rides. Bob Geldof actually claimed that he called NASA to ask if they had "any rockets going up. We'd like one to put Mick Jagger on."

In the end, Jagger flew to London — just on an airplane — and the song was cut very quickly in a break from Bowie's album session. According to Jagger, they "banged it out in two takes." According to some accounts, it was only one take.

The day before, Bowie had called video director David Mallet, who made most of Bowie's videos. "In those days," said Mallet, "there was no such thing as a record without a video." Bowie told Mallet that he was recording "Dancing in the Street" that next day and wanted to shoot a video that night. Mallet said, "I rang all the really good crews and they were there at seven at night." He and his team of sixty donated services free to the charity, shooting at the London Docklands. "It was a wasteland of smelly old warehouses," said Mallet. The site was later rebuilt for the 2012 Olympics.

Jagger and Bowie showed up in the costumes they had chosen, Bowie in an oversized yellow raincoat and leopardish jumpsuit and Jagger in yellow sneakers and a flouncy electric-green blouse. They began the video by shouting out places around the world such as Japan and South America in order to internationalize the song, and then sang in duet with a backup from the day's session that attempted, not entirely successfully, to stay close to the original Paul Riser arrangement. Filming at night, they staved off daybreak by lining up their cars and flashing headlights until they were done.

Mallet said that in those days "a lot of videos were just go and do it," and this one certainly was. It is hard to understand what is going on in this video of these two men dancing and hopping around each other. Bowie had been losing his following, and the previous year had been his worst commercially since he started in the 1960s. At the time, the Rolling Stones were in disarray, so Jagger, too, was struggling not to be on his way down. The two appear to be jockeying for position. If so, then Jagger clearly comes out as the more aggressive one. The video in which the two flounce around each other and sometimes sing with only centimeters between their mouths also encouraged speculation that has continued to this day that the two were lovers.

None of this had anything to do with Mallet's vision of the video he directed. "My only thought was I was trying to get a really great performance. What was really important was to see them together in performance. Two really big stars, and people wanted to see them together. Choreographed on the spot. We can go down this alley. We can use this warehouse."

The two performed the song together live only once at another charity, in London on June 20, 1986, at the Prince's Trust, Prince Charles's charity to help youth, this time dressed for the royals in suits. As the years have passed, Mallet has grown increasingly pleased with both his video and the recording, which he judges to be "the best cover ever made of 'Dancing in the Street.' " Some agree, though many musicians and music critics are highly critical of it. British music critic Barney Hoskyns, writing in the *Independent* in 2002, said, "The nadir for any true Bowie fan was the grotesque Live Aid duet with Mick Jagger on 'Dancing in the Street.' "

But the public liked it. The record rose to number 1 on the UK chart and number 7 in the United States, making it the second most successful recording ever done of the song. It was Bowie's last number 1 UK hit, which saddens some Bowie fans, since to many, "Absolute Beginners" was better work. All proceeds from the Jagger-Bowie recording, millions of dollars, were donated to feeding the hungry people of Africa, giving yet another meaning to "Dancing in the Street."

It would be difficult to say exactly what the Jagger-Bowie cover means to the millions of British fans who continue to love it, but it seems to be more about celebration than rebellion. In 2011 PRS for Music, a wing of the British Performing Rights Society, which manages royalties for songwriters, conducted a poll of three thousand people across the UK, asking them what music they would play if they held a street party to celebrate the wedding of Prince William and Kate Middleton. The overwhelming favorite choice was the Jagger-Bowie "Dancing in the Street," now a song for celebrating royalty.

The song continues. In 1993 the Red Army Ensemble, the celebrated deep-voiced official chorus and band of the army of the dissolved Soviet Union, recorded "Dancing in the Street" with the Leningrad Cowboys, a Finnish rock group in exaggerated pompadours who delighted in outrageous covers of pop classics. Kim Weston finally recorded a reputable version in 1997. Carole King, Mary J. Blige, and Fergie performed it in Japan in 2007. They used the song to energize the crowd, asking them if they were ready for dancing. It was an effective setup for the finale, King's hit "(You Make Me Feel Like) A Natural Woman." Chaka Khan, "the Queen of Funk" in the 1970s, with the funk band Rufus, in the late 1990s turned to R&B classics and sang "Dancing in the Street." Even Barry McGuire of "Eve of Destruction" fame was singing it in Europe in 2011.

There have been more than thirty-five covers recorded of the song, with more recordings expected.

Asked about the proliferation of covers of "her" song, Martha Reeves said grandly, "It is the highest form of flattery." But does she really enjoy this type of flattery? When asked which versions she liked best, she said, "I don't think I have any of their CDs."

Nothing is more revealing of the cultural standing of "Dancing in the Street" than its cinematographic history.

Logically, *Cooley High* would be the best chance for a historic and meaningful film role for "Dancing in the Street." First, because it was released in 1975, while the 1960s were still a recent memory, and second, because it was about black people with a screenplay by a black writer, Eric Monte, who specialized in scripts about African Americans. The film is a slice of life about black kids in a vocational high school in Chicago in 1964. This is the kind of realism that holds that dialogue is uneventful and real plotlines are tediously meandering. Anything more scripted would be false. The film also suffers from a lot of Michael Schultz's self-consciously artsy directing. But it shows some of the lesser-known realities of music in northern black ghettos in 1964, such as kids harmonizing on the street, which is at the heart of the Motown story, and it shows a rent party, which is also at the heart of Motown. The characters sometimes seem like stereotypes, and among those stereotypes is the sound track. Black people, it seems, listen nonstop to Motown even though many of these songs had not yet come out in the school year of 1964. The songs fit into the plotline through literal readings of the lyrics, which of course is the white, not the black reading. So "Dancing in the Street" is played at a dance. A few kids are trying to distract the kid at the door so that they can get into the rent party without paying. Inside they are dancing to "Dancing in the Street," which actually won't be released until July, when the school year is over. Here it is a party song, an invitation to dance; the music says that there is a great party inside and they have to be there.

The 1983 film *The Big Chill,* written and directed by Lawrence Kasdan, was a depressing expression of 1980s depression. Musically and politically, the 1980s began with a strong sense that "It's over." In 1980, Mick Jagger in an interview with *Rolling Stone* said, "Basically rock 'n' roll isn't protest. It never was. It's not political. It promotes interfamilial tension — or it used to. Now it can't even do that, because fathers don't ever get outraged with the music. So rock 'n' roll's gone, that's all gone."

In 1980, Ronald Reagan, an ex-actor who

as governor of California in the 1960s had been a great proponent of violence against demonstrators, launched his presidential campaign in Philadelphia, Mississippi, the symbol of violent racism. He had long been viewed as a second Barry Goldwater, a frightening candidate so extreme and so incapable that he was not likely ever to get elected. But he did. That 27 million who had voted for Goldwater in 1964, the losing end of a landslide, was a base that could be built on. And soon after taking office, Reagan began dismantling the social programs for urban ghettos that had been created following the summer uprisings of the 1960s. Soon public schools were being stripped of their funding, and music and art programs were first to go, so that today high school students in Detroit and elsewhere do not graduate with the music skills of a James Jamerson or a Martha Reeves. The result can be heard in twenty-first-century R&B, which has none of the musical sophistication of Motown tracks.

And so *The Big Chill* is the story of seven depressed and aging leftovers from the 1960s. This is a movie about people who seem empty and unhappy about it, which they probably should be. They keep saying that back when they were in college they used to be radicals and have beliefs. This is hard to believe, but they do keep telling us. All that's left is that they still get stoned on marijuana and they still play their old R&B records. The music is also all that remains of black people, another bygone frivolity of their youth. They make a passing mention of Black Panthers Huey (Newton) and Bobby (Seale) — another thing they remember from their past. The music may once have had meaning for them but is now just nostalgia. They clear the dishes to Marvin Gaye and get stoned to Smokey Robinson and the Miracles and bob their heads to "Dancing in the Street." This movie could have been titled *The Death of R&B*.

Jabari Asim is the editor in chief of the NAACP magazine *The Crisis,* founded by W. E. B. Du Bois. Asim, a black man barely old enough to remember the 1960s — born in 1962 — was saddened by *The Big Chill* because he still found the old Motown songs full of meaning, not nostalgia. In 2008, when Barack Obama was elected the first black president, Asim wrote an editorial titled "The Age of Purpose" in which he paraphrased "Dancing in the Street" — he described the response to the election as "dancing in the streets of New York, Washington, DC, Chicago." Asim said in 2011,

"It was a conscious reference to 'Dancing in the Street' — an inherited idea because I have read so much about that song being a call to action. I am forty-nine but it has always had that reference in the cultural conversation. That song has always been mentioned in connection with urban rebellion. You could trace a line from that to overt Motown music in the '70s. Norman Whitfield. Edwin Starr's 'War' to Stevie Wonder 'You Haven't Done Nothin'.' In the community I grew up in the '70s, R&B, especially Stevie Wonder, was an articulator of concerns and sentiments in the Afro American community, a real conduit of African American communication, political or otherwise. When I saw *The Big Chill,* I first started thinking about how the meaning of R&B was changing. Motown was the track but white people singing along and I thought the meaning of the songs was different, altered somehow."

But it also is possible that once again the black and white points of view had diverged, and *The Big Chill* was the white point of view. It is also possible that the fictitious characters in the film may have never grasped another meaning to these songs. Or the fault may lie with the filmmakers.

In 1966 Amiri Baraka wrote:

But R&B now, with the same help from white America in its exploitation of energy for profit, the same as if it was a goldmine, strings that music out along a similar weakening line. Beginning with their own vacuous understanding of what Black music is, or how it acts upon you, they believe, from the Beatles on down, that it is about white life.

It is surprising which movies show a deeper understanding of "Dancing in the Street." In the 1993 *Sister Act 2,* a meaningless sequel to the equally meaningless 1992 comedy *Sister Act* — comedies with no pretentions toward ideas or reflection — Whoopi Goldberg plays a Las Vegas singer disguised as a nun who wants to raise $2,000 so that a Catholic school can send its glee club to the state finals. She goes out on the street in their San Francisco neighborhood and rallies the community to support them by singing "Dancing in the Street," a close imitation of Martha but not the track. She is "Calling out" and the community responds with contributions. The movie may have hit on a truth about this song's longevity. Whatever your agenda — organizing a party, a revolution, or a glee club — this song will rally people to the cause. Whoopi the nun is in reality doing what H. Rap Brown did twenty-five years earlier for a different cause.

Even more surprising is the 2001 Disney animated cartoon *Recess: School's Out,* based on a Disney television series. When the last day of school ends and summer vacation begins, "Dancing in the Street" is heard. "Summer's here and the time is right . . ." The kids celebrate. One teacher says, "Look at those hooligans" to another teacher, who responds, "Actually I think it's a wonderful expression of freedom and joy."

One of the consequences of entering into classic song literature is that snippets of both the music and the lyrics have turned up in other songs. The first famous instance of this was the Rolling Stones' "Street Fighting Man." The next most famous instance is Bruce Springsteen's 1978 "Racing in the Street." The song is considered one of Springsteen's best, and as with "Dancing in the Street," fans love to develop interpretations of its meaning. Though on the surface, it is about racing cars in New Jersey, and Springsteen insists that it recalls such racing near his home in Asbury Park, just as Reeves insists that her song is about street parties in Detroit, surely there are other meanings. It seems to be about freedom, about male freedom but also sometimes the status of women. The title's similarity to the Motown song is not a coincidence. Springsteen is a fan of the Motown song. In 1999 he opened a concert in Detroit by singing "Dancing in the Street," though he never recorded it. And "Racing in the Street" does contain the line "summer's here and the time is right." But Springsteen, when he talks about his song, is more apt to talk about "Street Fighting Man" than the Motown original.

Jon Landau, Springsteen's manager, who was intimately involved in the development of "Racing in the Street," insists that there was no real thinking about the Motown song. According to Landau, "The song is part of the literature, and obviously Bruce referenced it. The lyrical nod is obvious, but I'm just suggesting it not be overemphasized because the music, the arrangement, what it is saying, and how it is being said are all unrelated to 'Dancing in the Street.' "

It is in the nature of literature that it becomes part of the cultural language in the same way that when Lyndon Johnson called 1964 "the summer of our discontent" he was not intending to bring Shakespeare into the discussion. Springsteen and numerous others, such as Pete Seeger and Joni Mitchell, have used phrases from "Dancing in the Street" without really intending to use the song. Seeger, in his nineties, started singing a song he wrote, "Take It from Dr. King," about lessons from the civil rights movement, in which he uses the phrase "dancing in the streets." And the Los Angles hip-hop group People Under the Stairs, in their 2009 recording "Down in LA," uses a clip of Martha Reeves as background, with just the phrase "as long as you are there" played repeatedly.

The standing of the 1964 song keeps growing. In 2005 the Martha and the Vandellas recording was entered into the National Recording Registry, the Library of Congress's collection of recordings that "are culturally, historically, or aesthetically important, and/or inform or reflect life in the United States." In 2011, at a celebration of Motown at the White House, President Barack Obama called "Dancing in the Street" "the sound track of the civil rights era."

The song turned up in singing competitions for the reality television series *American Idol*. In 2011 Naima Adedapo, twenty-six, made it to the final ten with "Dancing in the Street." With a low, strong voice she did a veritable homage to Martha Reeves but with African dancing included, which it is hard to imagine Martha doing. Adedapo said she chose the song because even though Reeves had said it was just "about having a good time, it was also an anthem for the civil rights movement."

The various interpretations of the song are still alive. A 2005 collection of anarchist writing was titled *Dancin' in the Street,* and the book was dedicated to "Martha and the Vandellas, who suggested what we might do once the doors were opened."

In 2001, after an airplane attack on the World Trade Center and the Pentagon spread panic in the United States, Clear Channel Communications, the largest radio station owner in the country, issued a list of more than seventy songs that they advised the radio stations to avoid playing. "Dancing in the Street" was on the list.

Many in the music industry have reflected on the extraordinary durability of "Dancing in the Street" and other Motown songs. Jon Landau said:

One of the distinctive features of Motown, along with a few other records such as the Beatles, is that their music sounds incredibly contemporary today. You listen to "Dancing in the Street" today and there is a modernism there, a contemporary feel. Stax were great. When you compare, Motown was the most forward looking. "Dancing in the Street" when it comes on right from the first second it is so in your face in a very good way. There is such clarity to the sound. On Motown records it's obvious that all the producers and artists went for very clear diction. You get every word. Martha Reeves is clear as a bell. People did check it out on car radio, but the reality is that the clearest and brightest recording is what will sound the best on anything. They were among the first where the bass on these records was much more legible but also at the upper register the strings and horns. You could read the whole register.

The song lives because it keeps meaning different things to different people in different circumstances and with different experiences. When Peter Yarrow of Peter, Paul, and Mary was asked what he thought of "Dancing in the Street," he said:

It had such a marvelous groove. I loved Motown music. I love the spirit of Motown.

The spirit was that it was a home where music developed. It was played with such joy and you could hear that they liked and admired each other. It felt like they really cared about each other. We had that, too. It's more than just playing together.

For any meaning, the song offers an energy and drive that gets people on their feet. On November 7, 2012, Michael Bolton had been watching election returns on television in his home in Westport, Connecticut. Barack Obama had just been reelected president and a crowd had gathered at Chicago's McCormick Place waiting for the president to arrive. Watching this on television Bolton recognized a familiar tune in the background. They were playing Martha Reeves's recording of "Dancing in the Street." Bolton thought, "This is what you want to do. Write songs that are going to outlast you. It's a form of celebration. There are a lot of up-tempo hits but that one keeps coming up. It's such an important theme in my life. Already five generations have embraced it, this one in particular being played in celebration after the election. In my work, which I think of every day of my life, I am constantly aware that there is a body of work that is continually embraced.

Not everyone has a song that is going to live on like that. I remember how the song made me feel when I first heard it. That was not so much different than hearing it now. The enduring power is how it makes you feel. Uplifted." No doubt that is why Obama's Republican opponent, Mitt Romney, had also used the recording in his campaign.

As for the meaning of the song, that is always in the mind of the listener. Bolton said that he did not think about what songs mean. "I am not saying I know the ultimate intention of the lyricists. You as a composer can assert. You can intend to win over a certain segment of population and later let them find out what it means. I just love the way it makes me feel."

In the twenty-first century it is still meaningful to twenty-year-olds, but it does not mean the things that it did in the 1960s. In America, we often act as if the old work is finished, that racism has been vanquished, and that integration has at last been achieved, especially since a black man was elected president. But most social research shows a different story: in the fall of 2012, the Associated Press released a survey claiming that 51 percent of Americans still felt comfortable openly expressing racist attitudes toward African Americans.

That is one reason why it is important to remember history and to remember the historic role of this "crossover" music, to recall it as Obama did that night in the White House. Martin Luther King called it "a cultural bridge" that brought blacks and whites together. In August 1967, during that summer of riots, he addressed black deejays at the National Association of Television and Radio Announcers in Atlanta and talked about this music, saying, "School integration is much easier now that they share a common music, a common language, and enjoy the same dances. . . . It is quite amazing to me to hear the joyful rhythms, which I found time to enjoy as a youth here in Atlanta years ago, coming back across the Atlantic with an English accent." He told the black deejays that promoted the music, "You have taken the power that Old Sam had buried deep in his soul and through our amazing technology performed a cultural conquest that surpasses even Alexander the Great and the culture of classical Greece."

Bolton said, "A lot of barriers were removed because of what came out of Hitsville U.S.A. That is historically more important, a more profound statement — music that created unity and made us all feel so good and made white America more appreciative of black America. Here is a revolution that happens from an evolution of mankind. Music has been a great uniter."

That is what Martha Reeves and almost everyone who performed at Motown had said they were doing. Reeves kept performing and always singing that song. In 2005 she started a new career after being elected to the Detroit City Council. She would show up for city council meetings as she had for Motown in her chauffeur-driven Cadillac — an early 1980s model from back when they were still really long — and designer clothes. Politicians found her overdressed and too showy to be taken seriously but she said, "The women in the city government were fat and badly dressed."

In 2009, to her great happiness, she failed to get reelected and returned to a full concert schedule. "I never get tired of singing 'Dancing in the Street,' " she said. "Every time you sing it, it is different. Different musicians, different crowd, a different happy. It makes me happy to sing it. My greatest joy is to walk out of a dark wing into the lights. Everything else is all right."

Part of the strength of the original recording, as Berry Gordy observed when he first heard it, is that it hooks the listener so incredibly quickly. As Michael Bolton put it, "You get eight bars of Martha and you're feeling good." Many listeners would say even less than eight bars.

She traveled the world singing some of the old songs and some new material, but at a certain point right at the end of every concert, two trumpets would blare out, "TaDa dela Da da." The audience would always rise to their feet and scream, sometimes clapping hands. They knew what was coming.

"Calling out around the world . . ."

# ACKNOWLEDGMENTS:
## AS LONG AS YOU ARE THERE

First and foremost a huge thank-you to Ace Lichtenstein for his kindness, generosity, and invaluable assistance. I also want to thank my friend Clifford Carter, the great keyboardist, for his advice and assistance, and the great drummer Steve Jordan for his help. A special thanks to the wondrous cellist Jessie Reagan Mann, who has taught me so much about music. A warm thank-you to Martha Reeves, who shared her time and stories, showed me her town, and introduced me to some of her old friends. And a grateful appreciation for all the musicians who spent time helping me understand.

Thanks to the people at that exciting house, Riverhead: Laura Perciasepe for a million things, Rebecca Saletan for all her advice, editing, and polishing, and especially Geoffrey Kloske for his support, advice, editing, and flawless and thrilling publishing. And as always, thanks to my agent and dear friend, Charlotte Sheedy.

I especially want to thank my unstoppable wife, Marian Mass, for all her research, enthusiastic beyond my control, and my daughter, Talia, who also lovingly contributed a great deal. Somehow this book became a family project and I am grateful to my smart and loving family.

# APPENDIX ONE:
## TIMELINE OF
## THE SUMMER OF 1964

**APRIL 22** The New York World's Fair opens and young black militants shut down their cars on the Long Island Expressway to create a "stall-in" to block the fair.

**APRIL 26** SNCC activists form the Mississippi Freedom Democratic Party as an alternative to the state Democratic Party, which excludes blacks.

**FEBRUARY TO JUNE** Four of the six songs to occupy the number 1 slot on the charts during this period were by the Beatles. Only Elvis Presley surpassed this, in 1956.

**JUNE 1** The Rolling Stones leave for their first U.S. tour.

**JUNE 11** St. Augustine, Florida, police arrest civil rights demonstrators, including

Martin Luther King Jr.

**JUNE 14** Hundreds of volunteers report to Oxford, Ohio, to receive training to register voters in Mississippi.

**JUNE 17** Motown releases "Where Did Our Love Go" by the Supremes, and it rises to number 1 on the summer charts.

**JUNE 17** The Ku Klux Klan burns down the Mount Zion Church in Longdale, Mississippi. It was to be one of twenty black churches to be burned this summer. The FBI starts to investigate under the code name MIBURN, for "Mississippi burning."

**JUNE 19** At 7:49 p.m., the Civil Rights Bill passes the Senate by a vote of 73 to 27.

**JUNE 19** In South Africa, Nelson Mandela is sentenced to life imprisonment.

**JUNE 21** The first two hundred SNCC volunteers leave Ohio for Mississippi.

**JUNE 21** Three young men working with the Mississippi summer project — James Chaney, Michael Schwerner, and Andrew Goodman — are reported missing.

**JUNE 22** The FBI begins to investigate the three missing in Mississippi.

**JULY 2** The Civil Rights Act is signed by President Lyndon B. Johnson.

**JULY 13 TO 16** The National Republican Convention at the Cow Palace in San Francisco writes a conservative platform, marginalizes the liberal wing of the party, and nominates Barry Goldwater for president.

**JULY 16** The first major uprising of the summer erupts in Harlem and the Bedford-Stuyvesant section of Brooklyn after a white police officer kills a black teenager. The disturbance lasts more than five days.

**JULY 31 Motown releases "Dancing in the Street" by Martha and the Vandellas on the Gordy label.**

**AUGUST 2** The destroyer U.S.S. *Maddox* engages with three North Vietnamese torpedo boats in the Gulf of Tonkin.

**AUGUST 4** A second naval engagement that may have been a misreading of radar is reported from the Gulf of Tonkin.

**AUGUST 4** The bodies of Chaney, Schwerner, and Goodman are found in an earthen dam.

**AUGUST 7** Congress votes President Johnson the right to go to war with North Vietnam without a further declaration of war.

**AUGUST 11** Race riots erupt in Elizabeth and Paterson, New Jersey.

**AUGUST 19** The Beatles arrive and play to 17,130 people at the Cow Palace in San Francisco.

**AUGUST 22** "Dancing in the Street" enters the Top 100 chart at number 68.

**AUGUST 24 TO 27** The National Democratic Party Convention in Atlantic City, New Jersey, nominates Johnson but alienates the left wing of the civil rights movement by not seating the Mississippi Freedom Party.

**AUGUST 29** Race riot in Philadelphia.

**SEPTEMBER 20** After twenty-five stops and thirty-one performances, the Beatles end their tour at New York's Paramount Theatre. In all, they have performed live for 425,950 people in North America.

**SEPTEMBER** 24 The Warren Commission presents its report to President Johnson, saying that Lee Harvey Oswald acted alone in Kennedy's assassination. Three days later, the findings are made public, but the report does little to calm public suspicion.

**SEPTEMBER** 29 Veterans of the Mississippi Freedom Summer refuse to have their activities curtailed on the UC Berkeley campus, leading to the first of many student campus demonstrations.

# APPENDIX TWO:
# THE DISCOGRAPHY
# OF THE SONG

| RELEASED | GROUP |
| --- | --- |
| JULY 31, 1964 | Martha and the Vandellas |
| JANUARY 25, 1965 | Cilla Black |
| FEBRUARY 15, 1965 | Brenda Lee |
| MARCH 5, 1965 | The Kinks |
| 1965 | The Everly Brothers |
| 1965 | Petula Clark |
| 1965 | The Rokes |
| DECEMBER 1965 | The Walker Brothers |
| 1966 | Red Squares |
| AUGUST 1966 | The Mamas and the Papas |
| 1967 | Ramsey Lewis |
| 1971 | Little Richard |
| NOVEMBER 17, 1971 | Laura Nyro and Labelle |
| 1976 | Michael Bolotin |
| 1976 | The Royals |

| | |
|---|---|
| 1976 | Donald Byrd |
| JULY 27, 1977 | The Grateful Dead |
| 1979 | Teri DeSario and K.C. |
| 1979 | Nohelani Cypriano |
| DECEMBER 1979 | Neil Diamond |
| 1981 | Tim Curry |
| 1982 | Van Halen |
| 1982 | The Who |
| AUGUST 12, 1985 | Mick Jagger and David Bowie |
| 1985 | Kingfish |
| 1993 | Leningrad Cowboys and the Alexandrov Red Army Ensemble |
| 1996 | Günther Neefs |
| 1997 | Kim Weston |
| 1999 | The BB Band |
| 2000 | Jimmy Barnes |
| 2001 | Atomic Kitten |
| 2002 | The Power Station |
| 2003 | Dynamo's Rhythm Aces |
| 2004 | Sugar Beats |
| 2004 | The Charades |
| JANUARY 27, 2005 | René Froger & Maud |
| OCTOBER 14, 2006 | Human Nature |
| MARCH 21, 2007 | The Condors, featuring Miu Sakamoto |

| 2009 | Asian Sensation |
| DECEMBER 2, 2010 | Sandrine |

*Around the World — Foreign-Language Covers*

1965   "Dans tous les pays" by Richard Anthony (French)

1980   "Hakaniemeen tanssinmaan" by Eeroja Jussi (Finnish)

1989   "Dansen op het strand" by Reginald & BRT Big Band (Danish)

1990   "Makuuvaunussa" by Clifters (Finnish)

# BIBLIOGRAPHY

## Books

Abbott, Kingsley, ed. *Calling Out Around the World: A Motown Reader.* London: Helter Skelter Publishing, 2001.

Ashford, Jack, with Charlene Ashford. *Motown: The View from the Bottom.* New Romney, England: Bank House Books, 2003.

Baldwin, James. *Early Novels and Stories.* Washington, DC: Library of America, 1998.

————. *Nobody Knows My Name: More Notes of a Native Son.* New York: Dial Press, 1961.

Beschloss, Michael R. *Taking Charge: The Johnson White House Tapes, 1963–1964.* New York: Simon & Schuster, 1997.

Branch, Taylor. *Parting the Waters: America in the King Years 1954–63.* New York: Simon & Schuster, 1988.

―――――. *Pillar of Fire: America in the King Years 1963–65.* New York: Simon & Schuster Paperbacks, 1998.

―――――. *At Canaan's Edge: America in the King Years 1965–68.* New York: Simon & Schuster, 2006.

Brown, H. Rap. *Die Nigger Die!.* Chicago: Lawrence Hill Books, 2002.

Buckley, David. *Strange Fascination: David Bowie: The Definitive Story.* Revised and updated. London: Virgin Publishing, 1999.

Carmichael, Stokely, with Ekwueme Michael Thelwell. *Ready for Revolution: The Life and Struggles of Stokely Carmichael [Kwame Ture].* New York: Scribner, 2003.

Carson, Clayborne, David J. Garrow, Gerald Gill, Vincent Harding, Darlene Clark Hine, eds. *The Eyes on the Prize Civil Rights Reader: Documents, Speeches, and Firsthand Accounts from the Black Freedom Struggle, 1954–1990.* New York: Viking, 1991.

Cateforis, Theo, ed. *The Rock History Reader.* New York: Routledge, 2007.

Charters, Ann. *The Portable Sixties Reader.* New York: Penguin Classics, 2003.

Cohen, Rachel. *A Chance Meeting: Intertwined Lives of American Writers and Art-*

*ists.* London: Jonathan Cape, 2004.

Collins, Lisa Gail, and Margo Natalie Crawford, eds. *New Thoughts on the Black Arts Movement.* New Brunswick, NJ: Rutgers University Press, 2006.

Collins, Ronald K. L., and Sam Chaltain. *We Must Not Be Afraid to Be Free: Stories of Free Expression in America.* New York: Oxford University Press, 2011.

Cruse, Harold. *The Crisis of the Negro Intellectual: From Its Origins to the Present.* New York: William Morrow, 1967.

Dalton, David, ed. *Rolling Stones: An Unauthorized Biography in Words, Photographs, and Music.* New York: Amsco Music Publishing, 1972.

Dannen, Fredric. *Hit Men.* New York: Vintage Books, 1991.

D'Emilio, John. *Lost Prophet: The Life and Times of Bayard Rustin.* New York: Free Press, 2003.

Doggett, Peter. *There's a Riot Going On: Revolutionaries, Rock Stars, and the Rise and Fall of '60s Counter-Culture.* Melbourne: Canongate, 2007.

Dr. Licks. *Standing in the Shadows of Motown: The Life and Music of Legendary Bassist James Jamerson.* Wynnewood, PA: Hal Leonard Publishing, 1989.

Early, Gerald. *One Nation Under a Groove: Motown and American Culture.* Hopewell, NJ: Ecco Press, 1995.

Ehrenreich, Barbara. *Dancing in the Streets: A History of Collective Joy.* New York: Metropolitan Books, 2006.

Ellison, Ralph. *Shadow & Act.* New York: Random House, 1964.

Farber, David. *The Sixties: From Memory to History.* Chapel Hill: University of North Carolina Press, 1994.

Gavrilovich, Peter, and Bill McGraw, eds. *The Detroit Almanac: 300 Years of Life in the Motor City.* Detroit: Detroit Free Press, 2000.

George, Nelson. *Where Did Our Love Go? The Rise & Fall of the Motown Sound.* Sydney: Omnibus Press, 1985.

———. *The Death of Rhythm & Blues.* New York: Pantheon Books, 1988.

Goldstein, Gordon M. *Lessons in Disaster: McGeorge Bundy and the Path to War in Vietnam.* New York: Times Books, 2008.

Gordy, Berry Jr. *To Be Loved: The Music, the Magic, the Memories of Motown.* New York: Warner Books, 1994.

Gordy, Berry Sr. *Movin' Up: Pop Gordy Tells His Story.* New York: Harper & Row, 1979.

Halberstam, David. *The Fifties.* New York:

Villard Books, 1993.

Harris, William J., ed. *The LeRoi Jones/Amiri Baraka Reader.* New York: Thunder's Mouth Press, 1991.

Hayden, Tom. *The Long Sixties: From 1960 to Barack Obama.* Boulder, CO: Paradigm Publishers, 2009.

————. *Rebel: A Personal History of the 1960s.* Los Angeles: Red Hen Press, 2003.

————. *Rebellion in Newark.* New York: Vintage Books, 1967.

Hirshey, Gerry. *Nowhere to Run: The Story of Soul Music.* New York: Times Books, 1984.

Horne, Gerald. *The Watts Uprising and the 1960s.* New York: Da Capo Press, 1997.

Jones, LeRoi (Amiri Baraka). *Blues People: Negro Music in White America.* New York: William Morrow, 1963.

————. *Black Music.* New York: William Morrow, 1967.

————. *Digging: The Afro-American Soul of American Classical Music.* Berkeley: University of California Press, 2009.

Kane, Larry. *Ticket To Ride: Inside the Beatles' 1964 and 1965 Tours That Changed The World.* Philadelphia: Running Press, 2003.

Kempton, Arthur. *Boogaloo: The Quintes-*

sence of American Popular Music. New
York: Pantheon Books, 2003.

Kerner Report: The 1968 Report of the National Advisory Commission on Civil Disorders. New York: Pantheon Books, 1988.

Kurlansky, Mark. 1968: The Year That
Rocked the World. New York: Ballantine
Books, 2004.

———. Nonviolence: Twenty-Five Lessons
from the History of a Dangerous Idea. New
York: Modern Library, 2006.

Lewis, John, with Michael D'Orso. Walking
with the Wind: A Memoir of the Movement.
New York: Harcourt Brace, 1998.

Lipsitz, George. Time Passages: Collective
Memory and American Popular Culture.
Minneapolis: University of Minnesota
Press, 1990.

Lynskey, Dorian. 33 Revolutions per Minute:
A History of Protest Songs, from Billie
Holiday to Green Day. New York: Ecco
Press, 2011.

Maclin, Frances. I Remember Motown: When
We Were Just Family. Tulsa, OK: Yorkshire
Publishing Group, 2010.

Martin, Bradford D. The Theater Is in the
Street: Politics and Public Performance in
Sixties America. Amherst and Boston:
University of Massachusetts Press, 2004.

Martin, Linda, and Kerry Segrave. *Anti-Rock: The Opposition to Rock 'n' Roll.* New York: Da Capo Press, 1993.

Montague, Magnificent, with Bob Baker. *Burn, Baby! Burn!: The Autobiography of Magnificent Montague.* Urbana: University of Illinois Press, 2003.

Neal, Mark Anthony. *What the Music Said: Black Popular Music and Black Public Culture.* New York and London: Routledge, 1999.

——. *Songs in the Key of Black Life: A Rhythm and Blues Nation.* New York and London: Routledge, 2003.

Payne, Charles M. *I've Got the Light of Freedom: The Organizing Tradition and The Mississippi Freedom Struggle.* Berkeley: University of California Press, 1996.

Perry, Eugene H. *A Socrates for All Seasons: Alexander Meiklejohn and Deliberative Democracy.* Bloomington, IN: iUniverse Publishing, 2011.

Posner, Gerald. *Motown: Music, Money, Sex, and Power.* New York: Random House, 2002.

Ransby, Barbara. *Ella Baker and the Black Freedom Movement: A Radical Democratic Vision.* Chapel Hill: University of North Carolina Press, 2003.

Reeves, Martha, and Mark Bego. *Dancing in the Street: Confessions of a Motown Diva.* New York: Hyperion, 1994.

*Reporting Civil Rights: Part Two: American Journalism 1963 to 1973.* Washington, DC: Library of America, 2003.

Ritz, David. *Divided Soul: The Life of Marvin Gaye.* New York: McGraw-Hill, 1985.

Rosemont, Franklin, and Charles Radcliffe, eds. *Dancin' in the Streets! Anarchists, IWWs, Surrealists, Situationists & Provos in the 1960s as recorded in the Pages of The Rebel Worker and Heatwave.* Chicago: Charles H. Kerr, 2005.

Sloan, Alfred P., Jr. *My Years with General Motors.* New York: Doubleday, 1963.

Smith, Suzanne E. *Dancing in the Street: Motown and the Cultural Politics of Detroit.* Cambridge, MA: Harvard University Press, 1999.

Sullivan, Denise. *Keep Pushing: Black Power Music from Blues to Hip Hop.* Chicago: Lawrence Hill Books, 2011.

Van Deburg, William L. *New Day in Babylon: The Black Power Movement and American Culture, 1965–1975.* Chicago: University of Chicago Press, 1992.

Ward, Brian. *Just My Soul Responding: Rhythm and Blues, Black Consciousness,* and *Race Relations.* Berkeley and Los Angeles: University of California Press, 1998.

Watson, Bruce. *Freedom Summer: The Savage Summer That Made Mississippi Burn and Made America a Democracy.* New York: Penguin Books, 2010.

Weissman, Dick. *Talkin' 'Bout a Revolution: Music and Social Change in America.* New York: Backbeat Books, 2010.

Werner, Craig. *A Change Is Gonna Come: Music, Race & the Soul of America.* Revised and updated. Ann Arbor: University of Michigan Press, 2006.

White, Theodore H. *The Making of the President 1964: A Narrative History of American Politics in Action.* New York: Atheneum, 1965.

Wilson, Mary, with Patricia Romanowski and Ahrgus Julliard. *Dreamgirl: My Life as a Supreme.* New York: St. Martin's Press, 1986.

Wright, Nathan, Jr. *Ready to Riot.* New York: Holt, Rinehart and Winston, 1968.

Zinn, Howard. *SNCC: The New Abolitionists.* Boston: Beacon Press, 1964.

## Articles
## Chronology of Unsigned Articles

"Who the Biggest Hoodlums Are." *Newsweek*, April 23, 1956, p. 31.

"Freed Is Indicted over Rock 'n' Roll." *New York Times*, May 9, 1958.

"Rock 'n' Roll Rolls On 'n' On." *Life*, December 22, 1958.

"Clay Takes a Jab at Civil Rights Bill." *New York Times*, May 20, 1964.

"Changes in Mass Are Made Public." *New York Times*, May 22, 1964.

"Negroes Are Found to Be Uninterested in Mixed Marriage." *New York Times*, May 25, 1964.

"Equal Job Laws Exist in 26 States." *New York Times*, June 7, 1964.

"Civil Rights Bill Passed, 73–27." *New York Times*, June 20, 1964.

"Picture Phones Go into Service." *New York Times*, June 25, 1964.

"Kennedy Labels Oswald a Misfit." *New York Times*, June 30, 1964.

"The Harlem Riots." *Life*, July 31, 1964.

"Message Time." *Time*, September 17, 1965.

"The Biggest Car." *Time*, April 1, 1966.

"Is Beatlemania Dead?" *Time*, September 2, 1966.

## Signed Articles

Alterman, Loraine. "Meet the Graduates of the Motown Sound." *New York Times,* July 28, 1974.

Altham, Keith. "The Rolling Stones: The Banned Stones Cover." *NME [New Musical Express],* 1968.

Auchmutey, Jim. "Al-Amin: A Life Layered with Irony." *Atlanta Journal-Constitution,* March 18, 2001.

Bedingfield, Robert E. "G.M. Auto Sales Are Highest Ever." *New York Times,* May 23, 1964.

Benjamin, Philip. "Kirk Tells 6,273 Graduates at Columbia That the American Dream Is Over." *New York Times,* June 3, 1964.

Bigart, Homer. "Eggs Are Thrown at Barnett Here." *New York Times,* May 22, 1964.

Frankel, Max. "U.S. Reaffirms Its Objective in Southeast Asia." *New York Times,* June 7, 1964.

Franklin, Ben A. "Troops May Stay in Cambridge, Md." *New York Times,* June 7, 1964.

Gansberg, Martin. "Mayors Warned on Racial Issue." *New York Times,* May 25, 1964.

Gould, Jack. "Elvis Presley: Lack of Responsibility Is Shown by TV in Exploiting Teen-Agers." *New York Times,* September 13, 1956.

Greene, Andy. "Mick Jagger: Stone Alone." *Rolling Stone,* October 4, 2007.

Havemann, Ernest. "The Emptiness of Too Much Leisure." *Life,* February 14, 1964.

Hechinger, Fred M. "Class of '64." *New York Times,* June 7, 1964.

Hoskyns, Barney. "David Bowie: Ziggy Stardust, Now a Man of Wealth and Taste." *Independent,* June 15, 2002.

Kihss, Peter. "Goldwater Warns Graduates over 'Illusion of Coexistence.' " *New York Times,* June 8, 1964.

Killens, John Oliver. "Explanation of the 'Black Psyche.' " *New York Times Magazine,* June 7, 1964.

Landau, Jon. "A Whiter Shade of Black." *Crawdaddy* 11, September–October 1967.

Lingeman, Richard R. "The Big, Happy, Beating Heart of the Detroit Sound." *New York Times,* November 27, 1966.

MacDonald, Ian. "Laura Nyro: The Five-Year, Five-Album Span of High-Pressure Creativity." *NME,* June 29, 1974.

McKinley Jr., James C. "At the Protests, the Message Lacks a Melody." *New York*

*Times,* October 18, 2011.

Parke, Richard H. "Small Cars Prove Poor Seconds in Crashes with Bigger Models." *New York Times,* June 2, 1964.

Samuels, Gertrude. "Why They Rock 'n' Roll — And Should They?" *New York Times Magazine,* January 12, 1958.

Snellings, Rolland. "Keep On Pushin': Rhythm & Blues as a Weapon." *Liberator,* October 1965.

Thigpen, David. "Her Second Act." *Time,* November 26, 2006.

Vitullo-Martin, Julia. "The Day the Music Died." *Wall Street Journal,* July 20, 2007.

Watts, Daniel H. "Black Power." *Liberator,* September 1966.

Wenner, Jann S. "Jagger Remembers." *Rolling Stone,* December 14, 1995.